THE VIOLENCE OF VICTIMHOOD

THE
VIOLENCE
OF
VICTIMHOOD

DIANE ENNS

THE PENNSYLVANIA STATE UNIVERSITY PRESS
UNIVERSITY PARK, PENNSYLVANIA

Library of Congress Cataloging-in-Publication Data

Enns, Diane.
The violence of victimhood / Diane Enns.
p.   cm.
Includes bibliographical references and index.
Summary: "Analyzes current understandings of victimhood in discussions
of child soldiers, identity politics, violent conflict, and global responses to
atrocity"—Provided by publisher.
ISBN 978-0-271-05243-4 (pbk. : alk. paper)
1. Victims of violent crimes.
2. Violence.
I. Title.

HV6250.25.E56 2012
362.88—dc23
2011035540

Whoever fights monsters should see to it that
in the process he does not become a monster.
And when you look long into an abyss, the
abyss also looks into you.

—NIETZSCHE

CONTENTS

ACKNOWLEDGMENTS

Most of the ideas in this book were elaborated in classrooms to students quite unaware of their assistance in the process of writing a book. My first words of appreciation are reserved for these students at McMaster University—too many to name—who entered into discussions with me about child soldiers, the moral ambiguity of violence, the condition of victimhood, or the crisis in Israel and Palestine, and who shared personal experiences with me that confirmed this or that idea and inspired others. A special thank-you goes to the students of my first and formative course on global feminism in 2004, who resisted me every step of the way and gave me the worst evaluations I have ever received as a teacher. I am grateful to them for providing the impetus to tackle many of the nagging questions of this book.

During the course of my research I was fortunate to meet a number of researchers and practitioners in the field of peacebuilding who gave generously of their time and expertise to discuss victimhood with me. I am immensely grateful to the researchers and staff at Berghof Conflict Research (formerly the Berghof Centre for Constructive Conflict Management) in Berlin for welcoming me as a guest researcher in the summers of 2006 and 2007 and in the fall of 2010. I owe particular thanks to David Bloomfield, the director of Berghof during my first two visits, who spent many hours telling me stories about his work in conflict zones and expressed enthusiastic support for this project from our very first correspondence. David's resourcefulness, inspiration, and encouragement were essential for the creation of this work. I am also grateful to Beatrix Austin, Véronique Dudouet, Astrid Fischer, Martina Fischer, Daniela Körppen, Barbara Unger, and Oliver Wils for animated conversations in the garden or over lunch at the Freie Universität *Mensa*, and to Claus-Dieter Wild for assistance (and a never-ending supply of chocolates) in the excellent Berghof library. At the end of the project, Ljubinka Petrović-Ziemer described for me the "normal" of daily life after war with her story of the Bosnian woman who wondered whether to report the bones she kept finding in the forests, unsure if they were human or animal. I thank all of these kindhearted folks for continuing to provide valuable information and contacts for my research, and for reminding me that working toward peace is a process that must begin over and over again—a life's ambition.

I would like to thank Ivana Franović, Adnan Hasanbegović, Helena Rills, and Tamara Šmidling for introducing me to the extraordinary work of the Centre for Nonviolent Action in Bosnia and Herzegovina, Serbia and Croatia. I admire the work they do to help rebuild community life in the face of the most daunting obstacles. Don Browne, Alistair Little, and Wilhelm Verwoerd deserve appreciation for introducing me to all the difficult moral issues faced by ex-combatants, in their workshop "Rehumanizing the Enemy" at the Glencree Centre for Reconciliation in Ireland. During an all too brief visit to Sarajevo, I had the good fortune to meet Goran Božičević, whose passionate advocacy for civil society politics inspired some optimism when formulating my conclusion. While these encounters were all extremely brief compared to the weeks and months spent poring over literature, the words and emotional responses of individuals directly affected by violence and its chaotic aftermath will always stay with me.

Five outstanding research assistants traveled with me through parts of this project. Melissa Eberly, Alexia Hannis, Branka Marijan, John McCurdy, and Alanda Thériault were diligent and conscientious researchers, thoughtful with contentious material, and mindful of deadlines. I am grateful not only for their hard work but for getting excited about the project as they went about their (sometimes mundane) tasks. I owe special thanks to Branka Marijan for introducing me to "the Bosnian way."

At McMaster University I'm truly fortunate to have amiable colleagues and staff members in the Department of Philosophy, the Peace Studies Program, and the Institute on Globalization and the Human Condition, who make for a supportive working environment. I would especially like to thank Kim Squissato and Daphne Kilgour, whose cheerful efficiency and patience with my inability to submit an error-free travel expense report make my working life much more pleasant.

Some of the material in these chapters was presented at conferences or by invitation. I wish to thank my colleagues in the Department of Philosophy and at the Institute on Globalization and the Human Condition; the Department of Philosophy at Wilfrid Laurier University; the Humanities Research Group and Department of Philosophy at the University of Windsor; and the Canadian Society for Women in Philosophy for inviting me to discuss my work and for asking thoughtful questions. The Humanities Research Group at the University of Windsor, my home away from home for some time during the writing of this book, generously provided office space for me as a visiting scholar. I thank Stephen Pender for facilitating this arrangement.

There are a few individuals I would like to thank for their enthusiastic support throughout the arduous and all-absorbing process of writing a book. Alexia Hannis spent countless hours reflecting with me on the monumental challenges that the condition of victimhood presents and patiently helped me work through—or accept—the most irresolvable tensions. Her insights into human behavior and her impeccable instincts when it comes to expression have helped to make this a better book. Antonio Calcagno commented on earlier drafts of a number of chapters and combed through the completed manuscript, provoking me to rethink a number of issues with his usual philosophical acumen and deep appreciation for the human condition—in all its tragic and splendid elements. He encouraged me from the earliest moments of my interest in the subject of victimhood. I am most grateful to Michael K. Potter for reading several drafts of this work in its awkward fledgling stages and helping to give it form and definition, with his admirable passion for precision. Our running dialogue about the controversial issues I grappled with during the writing stage was indispensable for the development of my ideas, as was his unflagging moral support when staring down the toughest questions. I am indebted to him for the title of my sixth chapter, "Mercy for the Merciless." Karen Enns and Daniel Fast deserve my utmost appreciation for indulging me, as always, in my penchant for dark subjects, and providing comic relief at all the right moments.

Finally, I would like to thank Todd May for urging me to send my book prospectus to Sandy Thatcher at Penn State University Press (who unfortunately left the Press before receiving my manuscript). Kendra Boileau, Stephanie Lang, and Laura Reed-Morrisson at the Press, and Suzanne Wolk of Grindstone Editorial Services, have impressed me with their efficiency, patience, and consideration. Two anonymous reviewers gave valuable criticisms that assisted me in the fine-tuning process. I would also like to thank the Social Sciences and Humanities Research Council of Canada and the Arts Research Board at McMaster University for financial support.

Parts of chapter 3 have appeared in "At the Limit: Violence, Belonging, and Self-Determination," in *Violence, Victims, Justifications: Philosophical*

Approaches, ed. Felix Ó Murchadha (London: Peter Lang, 2006). I'm grateful to Peter Lang for permission to reprint.

This book is dedicated to my parents, Peter Enns and Amalie Enns, whom I can never thank enough for their gifts of life, love, and conversation, and for giving me all that time in the strawberry patches and cherry orchards to think and daydream.

INTRODUCTION

We know that victims of violence are capable of violence themselves. Our media bombard us with daily examples, from the pedophile who was once the victim of sexual abuse to the bullied youth who goes on a killing spree. What we don't know is how to deal with the messy moral and political quandaries caused by the violent actions of victims. When the line between guilt and innocence wavers, when we are not sure who is responsible for what, and when we are overwhelmed by compassion or pity for the victim who victimizes, we can become unsettled by the ambiguity of events and our resulting ambivalence. To avoid the discomfort and the dogged work of moral judgment and political action that the situation demands, we might respond that everyone is a victim—that *no one is responsible*—and that any one of us would have acted the same way under such circumstances. We may then wash our hands of the mess and leave it to the law.

The hard questions of this book arise out of such ambivalence. Many have commented on an increasing concern—even obsession—with victims in contemporary Western society, or perhaps globally.[1] It could be traced to Freud's writings, to the postwar years in Europe, when the returning soldier's trauma came to light, to the Nazi Holocaust and the establishment of the Jewish victim as the standard for victimhood, and to feminism's interventions in the legal system's response to rape. Tracing this history would constitute a study in its own right. I am more interested in exploring its effects in a number of divergent realms.

Expressions of the ambivalence and moral anxiety aroused by the victim who turns to violence are not difficult to find. In a political philosophy course I taught to undergraduates at a Canadian university in 2008, such ambivalence quickly became apparent when we read Ishmael Beah's *A Long Way Gone: Memoirs of a Boy Soldier*. This autobiographical account relates the harrowing tale of Beah's life as a child soldier in Sierra Leone's brutal civil war, leading up to the dramatic events that preceded his rehabilitation and new life in the

United States. Abducted at the age of twelve and forced to kill under the influence of drugs and ideology, Beah's predicament provides an excruciating moral and political paradox for anyone concerned with the condition and status of the victim of violence in these times. In a final assignment, I invited my students to reflect on Beah's status as a "victim-turned-perpetrator," asking them to discuss the ambiguity of his condition and how we should respond to it. Only two out of many more than one hundred students considered—reluctantly and apologetically—Beah's responsibility for acts of murder and torture. Overwhelmingly, despite three months of discussions considering the moral and political challenges of dealing with victims who turn to violence, the students were unable or unwilling to negotiate competing claims for a compassionate, merciful response and the demand for moral judgment and accountability in the case of Ishmael Beah. He was quite rightly acknowledged as a victim who was forced to kill by circumstances, but this acknowledgment created a blind spot when it came to his victims. In theory the students could grant Beah's status as both victim and perpetrator, but in practice it seemed impossible for them to respond to him *as a victim* while simultaneously requiring that he be accountable *as a perpetrator* in order to respond to the suffering of *his* victims.

Beyond my classroom, we don't have to look far to find the telltale effects of our ambivalence toward the condition and status of victimhood. Taking the cultural pulse on the question of victimhood is not difficult, starting with the Oprah Winfrey show, which Eva Illouz calls "a popular cultural form that makes sense of suffering at a time when psychic pain has become a permanent feature of our politics."[2] Oprah's guests, as well as her audience, often identify as—or with—victims whose suffering invites the emotional catharsis of the talking cure. Contemporary films corroborate the Oprah effect. In Paul Haggis's film *Crash* (2004), which depicts the state of racism in Los Angeles, we are invited to empathize with every perpetrator of a racist or sexist act of violence. The viewer is tempted to absolve even the obnoxious white police officer who molests a black woman while on duty, when we discover his poignant tenderness toward an ailing father, and his final act of bravado—pulling the same woman he previously molested out of a burning car at the scene of a near-fatal accident. The recent vampire film by Swedish director Tomas Alfredson, *Let the Right One In* (2008), elicits compassion for a vampire who must kill to sustain herself. Indeed, her victims solicit less pity than does the vampire. Who is the victim? The vampire or the individual whose blood keeps her alive? This may not be new—Mary Shelley's *Frankenstein* gave us insight into the monster's own heartache—but the extent to which this ambivalence is exerting itself in the realm of politics and ethics, encouraging moral relativism and a reticence to judge, *is* something new, and troubling.

Consider Slavoj Žižek's concern over the "humanization" of soldiers, a current cultural phenomenon he believes is apparent in films but also in the reality of daily life in Israel. *The Hurt Locker*, for example, is a recent film depicting the ordeal of soldiers who risk death while dismantling terrorist bombs meant for civilians. "Can there be anything more sympathetic to our liberal sensibilities?" Žižek asks. For these squads appear to be just like the U.S. Army—a humanitarian force in the war against terror, patiently dismantling the weapons of terrorism for the sake of civilian safety. This effect is replicated in films like *Lebanon* and *Waltz with Bashir*, which narrate events from the perspective of Israeli soldiers, highlighting "the perpetrator's traumatic experience." Žižek concludes, "Such a 'humanization' thus serves to obfuscate the key point: the need for a ruthless analysis of what we are doing in our political-military activity and what is at stake. Our political-military struggles are not an opaque history that brutally disrupts our intimate personal lives—they are something in which we fully participate."[3]

In each of these examples, a certain "regard" for the perpetrator waylays judgment, whether compassion, pity, empathy, tolerance, or even veneration. We are invited into the emotional or psychic existence of the perpetrator—to identify with her suffering—and no longer feel that it is our place to judge the rightness or wrongness of her actions; we substitute pity for "ruthless analysis," or a false empathy for accepting our own responsibility. It would be simplistic to criticize this ambivalence as unequivocally misguided or dangerous, as such portrayals of perpetrators as victims have also made us keenly and rightly aware of the human vulnerability and fragility of the perpetrator. Or at least of some perpetrators. There are the terrorists, whom we perceive to be monstrous in their wrongdoing, and then there are the normal people we all know, who commit wrong because somewhere along the way they were misinformed, badly raised, or victimized by abusive and neglectful adults. We could add the soldier, who may occupy a category of his or her own—those who are forced to do the dirty work for the rest of us, their deeds forgotten in our gratefulness for their sacrifice and our pity for their struggles. That these films reveal this vulnerability and make us doubt our perhaps typical responses to perpetrators is to their credit, but it places us smack in the middle of a difficult quandary: how do we make moral judgments against those whose circumstances solicit overwhelming compassion? Once we see the soft, frail underbelly of the perpetrators—killers, genocidaires, racists, misogynists, rapists, warmongers, even a lonely young vampire—how do we demand their accountability? I will argue that it is precisely our familiarity with others' vulnerability that allows us to make judgments—merciful judgments that require the ruthless analysis of which Žižek speaks, but also respect for another's agency and compassion for her predicament.

Cultural commentators have dealt with the dangers of noting this fragility impatiently and contentiously—but not without humor—in recent years. Charles Sykes argued in the early 1990s that America has become "a nation of victims." From the cyclist who claims to be victimized by "motorism" to the feminist who argues she is victimized by Western ideals of beauty, "this squalling howl of grievance," Sykes suggests, has "become a national chorus." The consequences are significant: we don't need to accept responsibility for our actions because there is always someone else to blame; we actively compete for victimhood status; we experience "compassion fatigue" and learn to ignore the appeals of "real" victims whose voices are drowned out by the ever growing list of "certifiable" victims; we become hypersensitive to actions deemed discriminatory and use resentment as a weapon of social advantage. These are the problematic results of "victimism," a discourse that Sykes argues is reshaping America's employment practices, criminal justice system, and education policies. He is particularly wary of the manifestations of victimism in academia, where political correctness is constantly raising the stakes. From handbooks filled with words and phrases that should be shunned in order to avoid giving offense (Sykes mentions "disabled," "he," and "black mood"), to the grumbling of students who are forced to read the work of "dead white males" with whom they do not identify, the intellectual landscape of academia has been transformed. "American life is increasingly characterized by the plaintive insistence, *I am a victim*," Sykes concludes. It is a remarkable egalitarian victimization that expresses itself in the mantra "*I am not responsible; it's not my fault*."[4]

Sykes's argument is meant to inflame, but he has a point, and it is significant that he made it some time ago. The message seems to have fallen on deaf ears. The examples he uses are often superficial and extreme, leaving him open to criticism from scholars such as Alyson Cole, who dismisses him as one more right-wing proponent of "anti-victimism"—defined as a campaign especially targeting feminists and antiracists that associates victimization with "weakness, passivity, dependency, and effeminacy." While it seems as though contemporary American society is increasingly concerned with and responsive to suffering, from new laws and public funding to the therapy industry and the victim's rights movement, Cole insists that current political discourse is in fact dominated by claims that are not sympathetic to victims but against them. Indeed, she goes so far as to say that victimhood is "vilified," especially by those, like Sykes, who turn "victim" into an epithet, dismissing, ridiculing, condemning, shaming those who claim victim status.[5]

Cole does not limit her critique to the politically conservative, however. She claims that those on the left who wish to dissociate themselves from victim politics also contribute to an anti-victimist discourse that ends up blaming the victim. This is especially obvious, according to Cole, in the current "anti-feminist backlash," particularly visible in the "crusade" against identity politics.[6] As she sees it, this crusade mistakenly criticizes "almost any form of collectivism" as inherently victimist, since it encourages dependency on a group and nurtures an ideological basis for emancipatory action. Cole refers to Wendy Brown as a representative of the Left who has contributed to the anti-victimist distaste for identity politics. Her conservative counterpart is Shelby Steele, well known for his description of the melancholic black man who cannot "disengage from the past of slavery and discrimination" and refuses to assume responsibility for his own condition.[7]

Sykes argues that we have arrived at this point because naming and identifying victims has taken the place of public discourse and conscience. In other words, it has become a substitute for politics and good moral judgment. In the academy, especially, we are failing to judge, and to perform the political acts that judgments should inform, in the name of tolerance or cultural sensitivity. This criticism flies in the face of concepts and practices we have come to embrace, particularly in the academic discourses of emancipation: empowerment, recognition, responsibility for the "other." But it is time we ask: empowerment and recognition for the victim at what cost? The "immense powers" ascribed to victims cannot remain unexamined; we are reaping what we sowed when we decided that the rights of victims and the desire to empower them should take precedence over all other moral and political considerations. Our response to suffering may not cure it.

This project was initially conceived on a double plane, taking issue with certain emancipatory discourses prevalent in the Western academy that venerate the status of "otherness" while simultaneously becoming interested in the victim of political conflict and the aftermath of war, colonization, occupation, or genocide. Despite some opposition, I hold to the idea that this starting point is significant not only for developing my particular argument but for the larger picture as well. A product of a generation of students who absorbed, without much debate, the seductive discourse of otherness, I became more and more disillusioned by the politics this discourse engendered, particularly through my experience teaching courses in women's studies programs (more on this in chapter 1). I maintain that the identity politics we find today on North American campuses, and in society in general, is different only in its scale and effects from the politics that plays out in political arenas elsewhere. This does not rule out other vast differences that contribute to political conflict, like economic disparity, corrupt governments, and, increasingly, environmental destruction and scarcity of resources, but these factors are beyond the scope of my concerns here.

It is urgent that we consider the limits of the discourse of the other and its assumed association with victimhood, for the discrete borders of these terms break down when we consider the violence of the Palestinian suicide bomber, or of the Hutu killing his or her Tutsi neighbor. I will argue that the victimized other has acquired a status beyond critique, that it has become a metaphor for "the good." This is a function of guilt on the part of those who feel responsible for the wounds of yesterday's victims, and of revenge on the part of those who vow never again to be victimized, rendering justice a matter of either self-recrimination or revenge.

I am interested in identifying these limits, but we must go beyond a simple deconstruction of victimhood. While a critique of identity politics and its production of the binary logic of victimhood is still relevant, indeed urgent, it is not my only concern here. The work of Jacques Derrida and his contemporaries—proponents of a phenomenological and poststructuralist approach to philosophy—appeals to me for its attention to unsettling essentialist claims. I have argued in previous work for the usefulness, even the necessity, of this kind of destabilizing work for politics—of attending to difference, incommensurability, ambiguity, paradox, aporia, and indeterminacy.[8] Derrida and many of his interlocutors—Hélène Cixous, Gilles Deleuze, and Michel Foucault, among others—have provided what is probably the best critique of the dangers of identity politics. But what has come to be known as the "ethicopolitical" is unsatisfying on another level. There is strong resistance to making moral claims of any kind in the interests of preserving particularity, historical context, and contingency. Despite Derrida's stance against capital punishment, for example, his conditional/unconditional formula—the calculable/incalculable, determinate/indeterminate—leaves ambiguous one side of the dialectic: calculative decisions are necessary in matters of morals, law, and politics, but they can be dangerous or damaging without the incalculable, the unconditional, which is alleged to give rise to these decisions.[9] This point is purposely left obscure, as anything "calculable" is considered a plan, normative programming, or technology, all of which are condemned as problematic because they cannot account for difference. There is no middle ground here—a serious irony, given that Derrida's work is generally preoccupied with middle grounds; one either accepts the terms deconstruction sets out (that politics is undecidable) or falls in with the misguided folks who promote a normative approach.[10]

Moral judgment has become an unpopular concept and practice since the rise of a certain ideology concerning cultural difference. Todd May argues that the French thinkers associated with the poststructuralist tradition have been reluctant to engage in moral discourse. Morality has become the undisputed jurisdiction of the political Right, associated with family values and prominent in conservative discourse. On the left, morality itself is believed to contain a certain conservative element, May suggests, one that denies difference. Thus, for example, the Left must defend multiculturalism on the grounds that humans possess no common values. "The universalist claims put forward by morality, it is said, fail to recognize diversity that characterizes different people's moral lives. The argument runs roughly like this: since there are no universal moral values, no set of values can claim ultimate superiority over any other; therefore, people should be exposed to a diversity of moral views."[11] Foucault provides a good example of this avoidance of moral discourse. He makes a case against "universal necessities in human existence" and against "speaking for others" (a sacrosanct policy in feminist discourse).[12] No matter that Foucault certainly speaks *for* the insane, the imprisoned, and sexed subjects throughout his work (Herculine Barbin and Pierre Rivière especially). Emmanuel Levinas's work is said to provide no moral theory but to promote an "ethical relation to the other" as first philosophy. Morals are passé, replaced by responsibility. As I argue later, however, this is a responsibility *for the other* without judgment, an abstract ethical relation that leaves no room for grappling with moral dilemmas or for the agency and responsibility of the victimized other.

It is curious, then, that these philosophers speak in the name of a politics that is purported to be ethical, and yet we are left with theories—beautiful and seductive, perhaps—that are of limited use when it comes to political practice and moral judgment. Their work has had a tremendous impact on the ethicopolitical, a term that captures what is central to both ethics and politics: the demand for deliberation and urgent action in answer to the question "what should I do?"[13] In privileging responsibility, however, they ignore moral judgment, not morality itself. Ethics becomes about one's relation to the other and one's infinite responsibility to that other; questions about right or wrong actions are avoided. As in discussions of "the political" (rather than "politics"), "the ethical" is abstracted from any reality that might require a moral act. Hence the conclusion of the first chapter of this book: that Levinas leads us to a benevolent but empty regard for an abstract other.

My initial enthusiasm about the usefulness of the poststructuralist tradition for political action has waned as I have become more exposed to the actual details of political work, to the energy and persistence of political actors, and to the perplexed expressions of those practitioners with whom I attempt to discuss the political claims of poststructuralism. I am not referring to the perplexity of the uneducated in the face of difficult intellectual ideas but to the skepticism of the political practitioner in the face of the often presumptuous, untested hypotheses of the armchair philosopher. Our interest and intervention in political events cannot remain solely on the plane of textual critique.[14]

While this book does not engage with the work of these thinkers in a sustained manner, I take their work and the tradition of which they are a part as my point of departure. Since my initial attraction to Derrida's insistence on the undecidability of politics, preceded by Maurice Merleau-Ponty, who rigorously defends the contingency of politics, and Simone de Beauvoir, whose marvelous description of the ambiguity of ethics is as relevant today as ever, I have wrestled with how to negotiate what is for many the greatest challenge in the politics of the poststructuralist tradition: how to reconcile contingency with the desire for practical solutions. Derrida demonstrates, perhaps better than most, the impossibility of this reconciliation, and therefore often leaves his readers in the frustrated state of wanting more—more reassurance, security, universality, and normativity. It isn't reassurance or security I seek, however, but relevance and utility, a pragmatic approach to moral and political dilemmas that needs no "unconditional" reference point.[15]

If our current political practice, arising out of these discourses on difference and otherness, is based on identity claims, and on justice as vengeance, it is urgent that we develop alternative political paradigms. Despite my reservations about the usefulness of poststructuralist political thought, it has provided us with a rich terrain for discussing the meaning of politics. "The political" may be an abstraction from political events and "politics" as we know it—governing institutions, deliberative democracy, the structures that enable public life—but it has also made us think deeply about what it means to speak of political thought and action. These thinkers have given flesh to any dry understanding of politics in its institutional and organizational forms. Politics is agonistic, contingent, full of conflict but also of solidarity, respect, and friendship, the very stuff of life among human beings who must get along together despite our many differences and ways of understanding the world.

We find in Hannah Arendt the same warning against following prescribed norms or rules without the turn toward an "unconditional" that Derrida and Levinas insist must break in on the conditional if it is to have any meaning at all. There is no "outside," no "beyond" or transcendent element in Arendt's historical analysis, no anxiety about "sameness," and yet she is of the same generation of scholars, born in proximity to totalitarianism. While Arendt remains skeptical about the effects of political solidarity, her emphasis on action, agency, and responsibility always occurs in the context of a pluralistic community of thinking individuals. And her analyses are always pragmatic.

Arendt's view of politics has informed this project deeply. In *The Human Condition* she observes that "action is the political activity par excellence." It is natality, then, and not mortality that is central to politics; each new act is a new beginning, unpredictable, unforeseeable. This means that we can expect the unexpected from one another; we can "perform what is infinitely improbable."[16] It is a daunting freedom, but one we would never want to do without, for otherwise we would be destined to repeat our errors. Such a politics requires imagination and vision—old paradigms must be rethought— as well as collective moral judgment and action against injustice. I assume *politics* to mean the activities and relations in which humans engage in order to live (and, ideally, flourish) among one another. I am more interested in what occurs at the level of community life, however, than in affairs of state or global governance. Politics is perhaps most of the time the clash between these two levels.[17] It is my contention that we too often neglect this sphere of activity and relations, believing ourselves isolated, powerless individuals. In this respect, Arendt can inspire.

Most of the discussions in this book concern victims of political violence who have been harmed personally by acts of war, genocide, rape, ethnic discrimination, occupation, the murder of loved ones, or economic devastation. What constitutes "harm," of course, is open to interpretation, as is suffering. The violent event that cripples one victim for life may not cripple another, as personal resources vary among individuals and alter perceptions of suffering. Victims may refuse the condition of victimhood. Cultural differences, politics, and law can all influence the meaning of victimhood. For the purposes of this book, I define a victim as one who has been intentionally harmed by another, either physically or psychologically, whether directly or indirectly through the suffering of a loved one. All of the examples I discuss involve victims who have experienced significant harm, that is, the infliction of unnecessary suffering without their consent.

Exposing and analyzing the violence of the victim, rather than of the perpetrator, is immediately subject to the criticism that one is playing into the hands of the enemy. If we focus on the violence of women against men, we are accused of failing to address the much graver problem of male violence against women. If we address what is referred to as "reverse discrimination," we are criticized for not first dealing with the more pernicious phenomenon of discrimination, whether it be misogyny, white racism, or Western imperialism. Arendt was vilified for pointing out that Jewish leaders in Europe cooperated with the Nazis during the era of Nazi socialism. Although her comments were only a brief part of her coverage of the trial of Adolf Eichmann, the Nazi war criminal convicted of war crimes against humanity, she was criticized and ostracized by the Jewish community for betraying her own people. But these criticisms only reinforce the pure innocence of the victim and the pure guilt of the perpetrator. Much of the time, the distinction is not so unambiguous. We certainly need to address state-sponsored and other forms of violence that clearly have power and resources at their disposal. I leave that work to others, with the caveat that victims often become the worst perpetrators of all. It is at our peril that we fail to understand, prevent, or mitigate the violence of victimhood.

Deconstructing the binary victim/perpetrator opposition is hardly sufficient for analyzing the current discourses on victimhood and their political effects, not to mention for understanding political conflicts that are in some way premised on an acceptance of this opposition. We must avoid at all costs a critical analysis of victimhood that leaves us floundering in the kind of moral relativism that claims we are all victims to some extent or other, all wounded and in need of redemptive outlets like resentment. Even if this were true in some fundamental sense, we are victims to different degrees. Some victims need our attention more urgently than others. Some victims need to have their psychological needs addressed before any consideration of punishment or demand for accountability. In other words, we must add to the critique of the victim/perpetrator dualism the concept and practice of merciful judgment.

I have divided this book into seven chapters, all of which build on a number of central arguments but address different issues. This work is unconstrained by disciplinary boundaries, which some readers will find liberating and others unsatisfying. Nor do I impose order along a theory and practice divide, choosing instead to shift back and forth between ideas and the events that shape them.

In chapter 1 I explore an ideology prominent in the "emancipatory" discourses of the North American academy. Scholarly interest in "the other" on the part of critical theorists, feminists, and antiracist scholars concerned with the legacy of colonialism, imperialism, and patriarchy has had an enormous impact on how we view the condition and status of the victim. The "post" discourses—postmodernism, poststructuralism, postcolonialism—are in large part responsible for rightly drawing attention to "the wretched of the earth" as well as problematically venerating "the other," a veneration that ultimately robs the subaltern (the native, woman, "those who have no part")[13] of moral agency and responsibility. While there are a number of important intellectual and political sources of this veneration, I trace it to a tradition in what has come to be known broadly as continental philosophy, which has greatly influenced and been influenced by contemporary feminist scholarship. This veneration of the other has resulted from readings—or misreadings—of the work of Emmanuel Levinas and Frantz Fanon, among others, rendering the other a pure victim, beyond moral and epistemic reproach—a *good other.* Its undesirable effects include the abdication of politics for an impotent ethics; a reticence to make moral judgments in the name of sensitivity to cultures other than one's own, both cultures rendered essentialist and immutable in their incommensurability; and an impoverished sense of justice—motivated by guilt or *ressentiment,* synonymous with retribution.

We are left with a bleak picture of political practice as *policing* and a moral judgment premised only on accepted ideological principles.[19] A community of victims stand in judgment over those deemed responsible for their subordination. Justice becomes a matter of balancing the scales of suffering by making the perpetrator suffer as the victim has. Responsibility belongs solely to the perpetrator group. Yet no one has been able to establish why the view "from the margins" equips the victimized with a superior moral sensibility and power of judgment that others ostensibly lack on the grounds of their privilege.

In chapter 1, then, we witness the antagonistic dynamic between essentialized categories of privileged and oppressed—characterized by an incommensurable, nonreciprocal, morally unequal relationship—that theorists of difference promote. Ironically, it is a mirror image of the antagonism, essentialism, and moral reproach inherent in the circumstances that reduced an individual or group to inferior status to begin with. This irony is the point of departure in chapter 2, which elaborates a theme prevalent in Mahmood Mamdani's analysis of the Rwandan genocide. Rather than privilege the view from the margins, Mamdani warns of the dangers of assuming the "worldview" of the victim, constructed as it is on the very hierarchical system politicized by the perpetrator. While a similar binary logic of victim versus perpetrator is evident in the identity politics of the West, the stakes are much higher in the context of violent conflict purported to be "ethnopolitical." In the case of an intractable conflict like the ongoing crisis in Israel and Palestine—characterized by a severely asymmetrical power imbalance but also by the utmost conviction on both sides of a superior claim to victimhood and thus to truth, history, land, and a future state—the stakes are higher yet.

The focus of this second chapter is the troubling extent to which we often justify the violence of the victimized as a legitimate course of action, whether in the name of empowerment, self-determination, or—most often today—security. This is evident in analyses of Palestinian suicide bombing that justify killing on the basis of despair and misery, as well as in the American and Israeli governments' reliance on a paradigm of security to legitimize a brutal military occupation. Here we witness the moral capital of the victim writ large, each side of the struggle firm in its conviction that it fights a just war. The Palestinians fight to end an occupation of more than sixty years, with its systematized, normalized inequality and disenfranchisement, impassioned by the collective memory of expulsion. The Israelis fight a war against terror and anti-Semitism, impassioned by the collective memory of genocide and persecution. The asymmetry of political power and economic well-being is often ignored by supporters of the Israeli government and used to add moral currency to the Palestinians' position by those who act in solidarity with them.

Relying on the work of Frantz Fanon and Hannah Arendt to understand the nature of political violence, particularly in its emancipatory form, I conclude in this chapter that the violence of the victim is not a justifiable response to victimhood, nor is it as inevitable as we are led to believe. The unrelenting nature of violence and counterviolence, and the willful blindness to the binary logic of victim versus perpetrator, means that dissenting voices and the actions of those who *do not comply* are usually ignored. As in chapter 1, the view of politics here is bleak; "never again" is the mantra of a politics of death and destruction propelled by fear—or rather of a failure of politics, and a corresponding failure to take responsibility and exercise moral agency. The solutions can be found, I argue, in the work of countless individuals and groups who are not permitted the political tools necessary to make the leaps required for a viable future for all Palestinians and Israelis. Since it is the ideological framing of the conflict that blinds us to these solutions, it is our responsibility, as bystanders, to engage in conceptual reframing, not to impose peace plans or political solutions ourselves but to stop preventing Israelis and Palestinians from creating them.

The third chapter elaborates the subjective or psychic effects of victimization. I seek to provide a phenomenology of victimhood based on the narratives and analyses of Jean Améry, Susan Brison, Frantz Fanon, and others who have explored the condition of victimhood and the process of recuperating a sense of self after a traumatic experience. I discuss these writers in the context of a contemporary discourse on trauma in the fields of psychology, psychoanalysis, feminism, anticolonialism, and military psychiatry. An overview of the "birth of trauma" demonstrates that we have moved from recognizing injury to naturalizing it, and to a universalization of pain and suffering that trivializes the meaning of trauma, rendering indistinguishable the experiences of those who survive genocide, rape, or sexual harassment. Historicizing the experience of victimhood makes it impossible to essentialize the condition of the victim—that victims respond in diverse ways to acts of violence and violation should not be neglected—but I point to a number of features that broadly constitute what it means to be victimized.

Despite the focus in chapter 3 on the psychic pain and suffering victims experience—the alienated consciousness, dehumanization, self-enslavement, "amputation," or shattered self—I argue that our empathic regard must not preclude judgment or the acknowledgment of responsibility for wrongdoing when we consider the violence that victims themselves perpetuate. While Fanon stresses the agency of the colonized subject in the work of reversing the alienation he suffers, Améry dwells in a kind of melancholia. valorizing what Nietzsche calls *ressentiment*—resentment against those who tortured him in a Nazi camp and against the German people who enabled the Nazi regime to carry out genocide.

How do we arrest the evolution of grief into grievance before further violence occurs in the name of victimhood? Brison provides an answer, demonstrating that victims can eventually forget their victimization, to some extent, through the long and painful process of narration. Raped and nearly beaten to death, Brison describes the pain of displacement and exile from her own body as well as from the human community, but she recognizes that although the self can be destroyed by others, it is also created and sustained by them. The devastating loss of security her attacker caused is mitigated over time by her acceptance that absolute control over one's life is never possible—we cannot escape our vulnerability—and by narrating the event into her past. The contrast between the reflections of Améry and Brison, however, points to the power of unconscious desires and motivations that render survival an individual matter. We are not all equal in our capacity to struggle and overcome.

The first three chapters throw into question the association of the victim with pure innocence and political incapacity or passivity, in effect accomplishing a deconstruction of the victim. They also demonstrate that this critical labor is not enough. We must do more than point out that victims and perpetrators are complex, the lines dividing them often blurry, or we are left with a perfect alibi for inaction. In chapter 4 I turn to Hannah Arendt for guidance in thinking through the provocative issue of responsibility and judgment with respect to the victim. Arendt was vilified and ostracized by her own friends, and by the Jewish community in general, for ostensibly "blaming the victim" in her controversial coverage of the Adolf Eichmann trial in 1961. But her emphasis on collective historical responsibility, as well as individual moral responsibility for the future, victims notwithstanding, neither blames victims for their own misfortunes nor detracts from the necessary judgment against the worst atrocities humans can commit. Rather, I argue, it enables us to conceive of a political future in which the seemingly inevitable transformation of victim into victimizer might be suspended.

With Arendt's help, we discover that moral judgments help us to create a world in which we want to live. Morality is not about following a moral code but about choosing with whom we want to live in proximity, and what kind of life we will share in our communities. We judge our own behavior in order to live with ourselves; we judge others in order to live among our fellow human beings and cultivate community in relative safety and trust. Accounting for our actions, acknowledging our freedom to make decisions and to act, and taking responsibility for this freedom are all inextricably linked to judgment. It is this careful discernment, derived as much from thinking, in concert with others, as from respect for others, that distinguishes judgment from the veneration described in the first chapter.

Chapter 5 plunges us into what I consider the toughest moral problem of this study: responding to the child soldier who is forced to kill or be killed.

The suffering experienced by the tens of thousands of children in the world who currently live and kill within armed military groups cannot help but evoke an intense emotional response. We consider children, more than any other group in society, purely innocent. This is evident in the public response to several popular autobiographical accounts of "rehabilitated" child soldiers. And yet these children are capable of horrific acts of violence, prized by warlords for their fearlessness, conditioned to brutality. Here we reach the limits of personal responsibility, for some victims *are* purely innocent, although they must bear the burden of responsibility for their own responses to victimhood and for their own survival.

We must acknowledge, respect, and encourage children's moral agency, like that of their adult counterparts, if we are to understand how war and violence seduces—and "narcotizes"—its participants, effectively immunizing them from accountability. Without this understanding, not only will international attempts to prevent child soldiering be ineffective but we will perpetuate the very victim/perpetrator binary logic that invited and forced children to kill in the first place. If we do not acknowledge that children and young adults often *wish* to fight, in the name of revenge, empowerment, or sheer survival, then we forfeit the possibility of formulating preventive strategies. But the tragedy of the child soldier also demonstrates the need for mercy and the limits of the law in its demand for responsibility, accountability, and punishment. It exposes a small blind spot in Arendt's work on judgment, demanding a more prominent place for empathy and compassion than her stress on thinking and willing allows.

The excruciating predicament of the child soldier thus exacerbates a tension, exposed in the preceding chapters, between compassion and judgment. In chapter 6 I address this tension as it appears in a burgeoning "global justice industry" that is increasingly juridical and punitive in its approach to dealing with past atrocities and assumes that justice means retribution—an ideal of balance and reciprocity. The predominant paradigm of this industry is "transitional justice," a global approach that many have criticized for its emphasis on criminal prosecution and a strictly legal understanding of justice that often comes at the price of peace. This paradigm has led to the expenditure of vast amounts of energy and resources—including millions of dollars—in the work of distinguishing victims from perpetrators in order to punish the latter and empower the former, especially through the International Criminal Court.[20]

Our response to atrocity cannot be limited to justice mechanisms. Death is irreversible; after genocide and war, the scales of justice cannot be balanced.

Measures that are believed to foster reconciliation are offered as an alternative to the institutional, juridical approach to dealing with the past, motivated by forgiveness or a desire to judge wrongdoers with mercy. Notwithstanding the potential for political manipulation, forgiveness and mercy are useful in fleshing out the role of compassion in responding to victims. I argue in chapter 6 that the useful element of forgiveness is the will to forget, to the extent that we can release one another from the full consequences, sometimes tragic, of our actions for the sake of a more peaceful future. This approach is relevant also to a merciful judgment that acknowledges the wrongness of actions but also the circumstances in which they are carried out.

Compassion can appear to contradict the demands for moral judgment. Readers of Ishmael Beah's autobiographical narrative are swept up in the force of their compassion for Beah, the boy forced to kill, and often spare little compassion for his victims, who remain nameless and faceless. Likewise, a sympathetic response to the despairing Palestinian refugee who straps a bomb to her chest and kills the innocent may blind one to the anguish of her injured victims and the dead victims' loved ones. This is not compassion, I argue, but a pitiful regard that paralyzes thinking, excuses our unwillingness to judge, and robs the victim of agency. It is a regard that ignores the circumstances of the actor and sees all victims as equally responsible or equally innocent. Compassion in our response to the agents of atrocity must respect *their* agency. This is mercy as Martha Nussbaum defines it (relying on Seneca): mercy is not acquittal but a "gentle" judgment that yields before the difficulty of life.

In the final chapter I consider what it means to lay down one's arms, articulating what a moral and political life that departs from security logic might look like. Responses to atrocity often miss the opportunity to develop civil society's potential to engage in nonviolent politics, preoccupied as they are with legal judgment and social repair. Current political theorizing exhibits a similar tendency, failing to point out the potential of a political vision centered on principles of nonviolence and a culture of peace rather than a culture governed by the logic of militarization and security. Vulnerability is the human condition, but a politics that attempts to eliminate it only builds walls and weapon stocks, not community life.

1

THE GOOD OTHER

In October 2004, I was accused of racism. A student at the university where I teach charged me with promoting "racist and ethnocentric ideologies and practices" that were "poisonous" to our institution. This accusation followed a guest lecture I had delivered for an introductory women's studies class in which this student was a teaching assistant. The official charge she brought to our Human Rights and Equity Services Office was "racial discrimination and harassment." Several months later a second student, from a senior undergraduate seminar I was teaching called Global Feminism, brought forward a similar charge—of "discrimination based on race, color and ethnic background"—for not granting authority to the voices of women of color in my classroom and for teaching practices she deemed "offensive," "condescending," and "unnecessarily stubborn." These incidents, while painful, were instructive. They provided me with a powerful incentive to investigate what it means to be a victim and why victims are currently invested with a moral authority that many feel unable or unwilling to challenge.

The subject matter of my guest lecture and a good part of my seminar was the contradiction inherent in identity—namely, that it appears to be both necessary and dangerous in politics. Necessary when discrimination is meted out on the basis of belonging to this or that category, dangerous for its reification of that very category and because it risks replicating the initial discrimination. I reflected on the actions sometimes carried out in the name of identity, from brutal raping and killing in Darfur to the more benign exclusionary practices perpetuated by identity politics in the North American academy. I took issue with the simplistic oppositions promoted by such a politics, between "privileged" and "other," white women and women of color, or First World and Third World women, distinctions all too comfortably settled and morally differentiated in the minds of many women's studies students. In the hope of unsettling these categories, I turned to some of the most important critics of identity politics and the "veneration of the other" it has inspired—Gayatri Spivak, Sara Suleri, and Trinh T. Minh-ha, among others—to address the irony with which feminism is confronted when we consider that the "other" is also capable of violence (and not only in Darfur or Palestine).

While I was sufficiently familiar with the feminist positions that would prompt many to balk at my critique, I was completely unprepared for the vitriolic responses of the two students who accused me of racism, and for the stunning silence and assumption of my guilt on the part of colleagues from whom I expected some sympathy and support. The first student in particular misconstrued my lecture completely—twisting my claims into racist declarations, faulting me for sentiments and assumptions I neither held nor expressed. The situation was exacerbated when the acting director of the program that year, after hearing the student's complaint, canceled the second guest lecture I was to give without so much as a glance at my lecture notes. The hurt I had supposedly caused this student was one of two exclusive considerations. The most important fact was that her skin was black and mine white—the only reason given for the fact that the chances of clearing my name were slim if the matter went to a university hearing. Months later, during an enforced "mediation" session between my first accuser and me in the presence of my faculty dean, it was again the only reason given for why this student experienced my teaching as racist. Nothing else could be established (aside from the charge that I was stubborn, which I freely admitted). It seems that this student heard what she expected to hear from a white professor she deemed indisputably privileged and therefore morally reprehensible.

I spent the better part of that year caught between my own feelings of indignation and certainty that I had done no wrong, and the doubt and self-recrimination that several decades of feminism in the academy and "other talk" had imprinted on my consciousness. In women's studies departments today, if you are white and were born in the West, you may be considered morally crippled and asked to wear the acknowledgment of guilt like a sign on your forehead, a guilt that can prevent reasoned judgment of any communication or relationship between "privileged" and "other." This painful event made several things very clear to me. First and foremost, it illuminated the deleterious effects of a scholarly and political focus on the "other" in academic emancipatory discourses such as feminism and antiracism, and in multiculturalist discourse more generally, but also in political, philosophical, and cultural theory. Second, it led me to question why such an investigation is often stymied before it begins. I argue in this chapter that the "other" has come to signify the pure innocence of a victim relieved of the burden of historical responsibility on the grounds of injury. We can observe this phenomenon in the context of the kinds of emancipatory discourses, favored in the academy, that purport to address and relieve systemic oppression, but also on a more general sociocultural level. Bereft of responsibility, the "other" has become "the good other," a victim with moral currency and epistemic authority that if thrown into question leave the critic open to the charge of generating "poisonous" ideas. How did we get to this point? "How did we become cops anyway?"[1]

The Legacy of the Other

One of the most prominent preoccupations of late twentieth-century critical thought has been "the other." From the most abstract to the most empirical formulations, the ubiquitous use of this concept has rendered it rather trite. Unfortunately, owing to the moral authority claimed by or granted to those who speak in its name, any critique of this overuse is effectively silenced by the accusation that the critic is playing into the hands of the "oppressor." This partially explains the tenacity of the term, the lack of serious inquiry into its legacy, and the risks such an inquiry entails. We could trace these effects to several European and North American intellectual traditions, and to the events in the twentieth century that had an important role in forming them.

We could probably thank Hegel for bringing the concept of the other to our philosophical and, later, political attention. This is ironic, given that the French thinkers who became most interested in the concept enjoyed spurning Hegel. If the other is constitutive of self-consciousness for Hegel, it is an other unequal and antagonistic to the self, subsumed back into a unity or totality. In fact, the self must supersede the other in order to become certain of itself as an essential being, and in doing so it supersedes its own self, for this other is itself.[2] Hegel famously describes this development of consciousness in terms of the master/slave relationship: each struggles for recognition by the other, yet only one can hold the position of essential being.

Jean-Paul Sartre accepted this antagonistic model but gave flesh to an otherwise abstract discussion. He named Hegel's master and slave: the French settler was the master, and the colonized Algerian native, his slave.

In this naming Sartre was indebted to Frantz Fanon, the psychiatrist treating Algeria's colonized subjects who wrote several of the most important anticolonial revolutionary texts of the twentieth century, intimately describing the psychopathological condition of the colonized. The antagonism of the self/other relation in Sartrean existentialism turned out to be a critical formulation for understanding colonial and patriarchal relations, evident in the work of other revolutionaries of the time, including Albert Memmi and Léopold Senghor, the Pan-African and Black Panther movements, and the leaders of the 1960s women's liberation movement. These revolutionary actors and the writers and philosophers who inspired them had an impact on the climate of protest at universities and on the increasing focus of critical theory, in humanities and social sciences departments, on the terms of oppression: otherness, marginality, difference, and subalternity.[3]

We could trace an interesting trajectory, then, from the philosophical concern with an abstract self in relation to an equally abstract other, to the political use of an unequal and antagonistic self/other relationship to define the dynamic between oppressor and oppressed. The political upheavals of the twentieth century inspired ideas and gave rise to interpretations of these ideas that would otherwise have seemed inappropriate or off the mark. The meaning of otherness was significantly shaped by the intellectual ferment in Europe after World War II, for example, spurred by anxiety over fascist and genocidal politics. We could also allude to the discourses of an anticolonialist movement that in turn fueled feminist and civil rights movements. But how the other relates to the self is always in question, as is how the philosophical or abstract other relates to the other made flesh. Hegel's belief that the self sees itself in the other was later considered an erroneous reduction of alterity to "sameness." It could not account for difference, which created an enormous blind spot, obliterating the subjectivity of women, the colonized, and anyone else who laid claim to the consciousness of the enslaved.

This is why Emmanuel Levinas insisted on describing the other as "otherwise than being," which means not simply one entity distinct from another but something "wholly other," outside the realm of being altogether. Levinas, who wrote in the aftermath of the Nazi Holocaust and like many of his European contemporaries remained preoccupied with an ethics of "never again," was one of the most important—if also the most obscure and abstract—theorists of "otherness." While, to a large extent, Levinas's obscurity has meant that his readers are restricted to a narrow intellectual community, the influence of his ideas (which are frequently stretched beyond recognition) is profound. We could argue, in fact, that we are witnessing the effects of a largely unexamined synthesis between philosophical ideas about alterity that originated primarily with Levinas and the emancipatory discourses that blossomed in the academy from the 1960s onward. It was the other—the "absolutely other," the "otherwise than being," which could not even be represented in the language of ontology—that urged us to acknowledge, and embrace, a radical form of difference as incommensurability and incomprehensibility between oneself and another.

There is a historical context to this privileging of difference over sameness. As Todd May argues in *Reconsidering Difference*, the work of French poststructuralist thinkers in particular is "haunted by the specter of what we might call (and what [Jean-Luc] Nancy and Levinas have called) 'totalitarianism.'" This is a broad construal of totalitarianism, one that May defines as "the attempt to capture all of reality within a narrow conceptual framework" and that is deeply tied to foundationalism. Most important, the problem, as May puts it, is not merely that totalitarianism is false but that it is "insidious"; it is considered evil in that it marginalizes or eliminates that which is different. May sums up this approach from the point of view of one who believes that sameness is indeed insidious:

> Thinking of community in terms of a common substance that we all must participate in marginalizes those who are different from the participants in that common substance; thinking of language in terms of presence masks the difference that subtends it; thinking of ethics in terms of the likenesses or analogies of others to oneself refuses the insight that what is ethically relevant is often the difference of others from oneself; thinking of ontology in terms of identity precludes consideration of ontological possibilities that are irreducible to any identity. In all these cases, the different—although in each case it is a different "different"—is lost, distorted, repressed, or reduced.[4]

Consider, for example, the group of French philosophers generally referred to as "poststructuralists" or "postmodernists." Their anxiety over the totalitarian movements of their time is profound. Hélène Cixous, Gilles Deleuze, Jacques Derrida, Michel Foucault, Félix Guattari, Luce Irigaray, Emmanuel Levinas, and Jean-Luc Nancy, among others, were instrumental in the attempt to articulate and valorize a concept of difference that would avoid what they considered the "logic of the same." For Irigaray, it is sexual difference that interrupts this logic, for woman is never one in herself but always two. Deleuze and Guattari avoided sameness with their formulation of the concept of the "rhizome." The rhizome is without origin, without unity; unlike a tap root, it is a network of multiple branching roots and shoots. In his preface to their *Anti-Oedipus*, Foucault writes that we need to guard against the fascism in us all, and free political action "from all unitary and totalizing paranoia."[5]

One effect of this trend is that difference has become the mark of the "other"—not a universal or generalized other, as many of these thinkers intended, but an "oppressed other." It is only the other as victimized through systemic oppression of one kind or another who embodies all the morally superior qualities of the other inscribed as different. The subject of privilege, whether it is the privilege of skin color, economic well-being, or genitalia, appears to have no claim to difference. As Irigaray puts it in her discussion of sexual difference, women have a multiplicitous sexuality—they have erogenous zones everywhere, it seems—while men are boringly focused on the sexual pleasure of one organ.[6] Ironically, as we will see, the difference of the other is also reduced to sameness: both other and self become monolithic, essentialist identities when the terms of alterity are politicized.

It appears that one legacy of theorizing otherness is an unwillingness to challenge the concept of the other. Totalitarianism is not synonymous with totality. We live under a different shadow of terror now, perhaps more adequately characterized by fragmentation and differentiation than by unity and gathering. The political uses of difference and incommensurability—from one's Muslim, Arab, Tutsi, or Palestinian neighbor—are bringing with them death and destruction. The moralism of a commitment to absolute incommensurability between subjects must be reevaluated in light of the often deleterious consequences to which such thinking has led.[7]

The Other Woman

This particular type of moralism is quite prominent in academic feminist discourse in the West. The emancipatory movements that have occupied institutional space in the academy have found the poststructuralist train of thought highly appealing. While Derrida, Levinas, and others were extremely wary of any simple displacement of an essentialist self by an essentialist other, this is precisely what has happened, and for obvious reasons. An identification with the other, now the primary ethical concern, would reverse the order of domination. Unfortunately, Sartre's antagonistic model of self-other relations—there can only be one essential subject struggling for supremacy—is all too evident in this turning of the tables.

Feminism in the North American academy adopted the language of otherness and its affiliates: marginality, alterity, difference. As Sartre named the slave as colonized subject, Simone de Beauvoir took the philosophically abstract other we find in Levinas and named it female. In one of the most famous passages of *The Second Sex*, she writes: "And [woman] is nothing other than what man decides; she is thus called 'the sex,' meaning that the male sees her essentially as a sexed being; for him she is sex, so she is it in the absolute. She is determined and differentiated in relation to man, while he is not in relation to her; she is the inessential in front of the essential. He is the subject; he is the Absolute. She is the Other."[8] Beauvoir goes on to explain that the category of the other is primordial, the partner of the ancient duality self/other. No group ever sets itself up as the One without at once setting up an Other in opposition: native and stranger, Jew and anti-Semite, Negro and white, aborigine and colonist, proletariat and privileged classes. In a footnote Beauvoir quotes a passage in Levinas's *Le temps et l'autre* in which he suggests that the feminine represents the other in its absolute sense. Sex is not a specific difference, nor is it a difference that ends in a duality of two complementary terms that would imply a preexisting whole. Rather, Levinas says, "Otherness reaches its full flowering in the feminine, a term of the same rank as consciousness but of opposite meaning." Beauvoir complains at the end of the note that Levinas has deliberately taken "a man's point of view" in this passage, disregarding the reciprocity of subject and object and asserting masculine privilege rather than maintaining objectivity.[9]

This operation was repeated indefinitely in the body of feminist scholarship that burgeoned after Beauvoir's introduction to North America. For a woman to criticize a male philosopher for taking "a man's point of view" was not considered an abuse of the very "objectivity" that Beauvoir demanded of Levinas, despite the fact that this would certainly be taking a "woman's point of view." The clue as to why no one minded lies in her following claim: the terms of "masculine privilege" are always morally distinct from the terms of feminine oppression. In a nutshell, the victim of patriarchy is considered incapable of performing the same morally suspect operation as the perpetrator.

Had she lived to see it, Beauvoir might have been surprised by the way these ideas took hold in academic emancipatory discourses, establishing an uncritically embraced foundation for studies in feminism, colonialism, and racism. The "other" as feminine has come to signify pure innocence, a victim bereft of historical responsibility and, at the extreme, paralyzed by the trauma of oppression. Despite the frequent attempt to focus on women's resistance to patriarchal forms of power, the relentless competition for "othered" status belies such efforts. That the other is capable of any degree of violence is almost never considered—an omission justified by the much more urgent need to investigate the greater violence of patriarchal power.[10]

The valorization of difference in this tradition has had a powerful impact on the analysis of oppression and the other as subject of that oppression, leading to a pronounced veneration of the other. The moral authority granted to those with unambiguous claims to this category is rarely thrown into question. This is particularly evident in feminist discussions concerning the legacies of imperialist racism.

In *The Dark Side of the Nation*, Himani Bannerji writes:

> The possibilities for constructing a radically different Canada emerge only from those who have been "othered" as the insider-outsiders of the nation. It is their standpoints which, oppositionally politicized, can take us beyond the confines of gender and race and enable us to challenge class through a critical and liberating vision. In their lives, politics, and work, the "others" hold the possibility of being able to expose the hollowness of the liberal state and to provide us with an understanding of both the refined and crude constructions of "white power" behind "Canada's" national imaginary. They serve to remind us of the Canada that could exist.[11]

This is the passage I criticized in the guest lecture for which I was accused of racism. I asked the students to think about the assumptions Bannerji was making in this passage about the category—"white Canada"—she had constructed, and whether this was at all problematic. I asked whether there were not many white Canadians also interested in making our country a better place, free of inequality and discrimination. Bannerji appears to assume in this collection of essays that only people of color are interested in class and gender analyses, that whites are merely self-interested, privileged, and therefore incapable of political action. But why celebrate those who have been "othered" here? Why can a new Canada emerge *only* out of the work of those who have been "othered?" What criteria are we given for understanding and assessing "othering"? Bannerji is guilty of performing the very operation she critiques: that "Europeanness as 'whiteness' thus translates into 'Canada,'" as she puts it, is indeed lamentable, but why is the solution to "translate into Canada" the person of color—unquestionably defined as other? Why homogenize the category of white Canada? In other words, why attribute the ambiguity of the position of being both inside and outside—an identity marked by difference—only to the woman of color, and fail to acknowledge the ambiguity of the identity of those with white skin? For these questions I was accused of silencing the voice of a woman of color.[12] It was immaterial that Bannerji is a prolific and well-known professor and the author of numerous books and essays as well as fiction and poetry. One hopes that she would welcome the kind of critical engagement with her work that is allegedly expected and encouraged in the academy.

Bannerji is certainly not the only scholar granted the epistemic privilege and moral superiority of the "other." Chandra Mohanty's *Feminism Without Borders: Decolonizing Theory, Practicing Solidarity* (2003) is an extremely popular text in women's studies classes now that academic feminism prides itself on being inclusive of the concerns of women of color. In the attempt to redress the wrongs of early second-wave feminist Eurocentric and class-based exclusivity, Mohanty levels her critique at "white, liberal, middle-class feminism"—the description Western feminism is often given. Despite lip service to a feminism that recognizes borders only in order to transcend them, Mohanty's critique of Western feminism relies on a rather rigid understanding of the border between the "Third World" woman and the "First World" woman. With the caveat that Western feminism is not monolithic, she proceeds to outline what she calls its "coherence of affects," primarily a monolithic view of Third World women as essentially oppressed, ignorant, poor, uneducated, traditional, domestic, and victimized. In contrast, she writes, we find an implicit self-representation of Western women as educated, modern, in control of their own bodies and sexualities and free to make their own decisions. While these essentialized representations certainly pose questions that feminism must address, Mohanty neither acknowledges her own contribution to a monolithic understanding of Western feminism nor considers the possibility that Third World women themselves could exhibit such tendencies regarding either their own self-identification or their representations of First World women.[13]

A more serious cause for concern, however, is the implicit value judgment in Mohanty's distinctions between "white, western, middle-class liberal feminism" and the feminist politics of women of color in the United States. The former is faulted for a singular focus on gender as a basis for sexual rights, while the latter is applauded for a focus on gender in relation to race or class as part of a broader liberation struggle. Such a distinction polarizes white women and women of color, along with their concerns, and it suggests that a "good" feminist is one who is oppressed. Mohanty is by no means the first, or the last, to make this argument. Her distinction is similar to Bannerji's implied moral distinctions between whites and the "othered." And bell hooks makes a comparable case when she writes that black women are in an "unusual" position in American society, for they are "collectively at the bottom of the occupational ladder" and have an "overall social status" that is "lower than that of any other group." Occupying this position, she argues, "we bear the brunt of sexist, racist, and classist oppression. At the same time we are the group that has not been socialized to assume the role of exploiter/oppressor in that we are allowed no institutionalized 'other' that we can exploit or oppress."[14] Ironically, this is the same argument once made by the feminists Mohanty defines as "white, western, middle-class, and liberal" as they struggled to define themselves as other in relation to men. The victim of patriarchy or racism is not considered capable of the kind of injury to which she is subject—not, that is, until her own victims come forward.

Class and race issues are not exclusively the concern of women of color, nor are all women of color concerned about class and race issues. We don't have to look far to find poor white feminists, or economically and socially privileged women of color who engage in the exploitation of others. This seems an obvious point, yet it sets off alarms of protest when raised. It is as though *all* women from a Third World country, or *all* women of color in the privileged West, must occupy the category of oppressed other in order for there to be any other at all. We are invariably led down a path of pointless moralism and competition for victimhood. Mohanty is making a moral judgment against a feminism that does not arise from the periphery. This is not a political claim—the question is not whether political practice is more or less effective depending on one's position on the center/periphery spectrum—but a moral claim that *to be right*, to be a "good feminist," one *must* think and struggle from the margins. Who defines these margins is a question that feminists do not want to ask. That Mohanty wishes to locate herself on the "correct" side of the divide is apparent when she declares that although she is a part of the privileged social minority, living and teaching in the United States, her "political choices, struggles, and vision for change" place her with the social majority, the "Two-Thirds" world of have-nots.[15]

We need to consider why it appears necessary to make these claims to begin with. At stake for these authors is an unsullied claim to victimhood and the moral authority such a status confers. The common feminist response to my criticism of this phenomenon, one that was made repeatedly in my class on global feminism, is the protest that our primary focus should be the struggle against oppression, and that to point out the potential for power imbalances and abuses among the victims ends up depriving the victim of the limited power granted to her. The very suggestion that the victim could also be a perpetrator leaves one open to the accusation that one is blaming the victim. Calling attention to the agency of the victim is considered wrong, a betrayal of the victim's status as a victim. This argument fails to acknowledge that the self/other opposition or victim/perpetrator logic can be reproduced, with all of its potentially damaging effects, from within the worldview of both the oppressed and the oppressor.

It is curious that an exceptionally cogent critique of this feminist position appeared some time ago, from the very thinkers whom we are accused of silencing if we dare to pose their questions. Gayatri Chakravorty Spivak, criticizing the homogenization of the margins and the quest for authenticity, jokes in an interview about a bad habit indulged by her American colleagues out of sensitivity for her ethnic specificity: "I talk a lot, right? And when I get very excited I interrupt people; and I am making a joke, but in fact it is never perceived as a joke unless I tell them. I will quite often say, 'You know, in my culture it shows interest and respect if someone interrupts': and immediately there are these very pious faces, and people allow me to interrupt."[16]

Spivak, perhaps better than anyone else, relentlessly critiques the homogenization to which such "respect" leads. In the search for an authentic other, theoretical problems become associated only with the person who knows: "The person who knows has all of the problems of selfhood. The person who is *known*, somehow seems not to have a problematic self."[17] Sara Suleri concurs, claiming that while feminist discourse is disturbed by questions of identity formation, "it is still prepared to grant an uneasy selfhood to a voice that is best described as the property of 'postcolonial Woman.'" This coupling of the terms "postcolonial," stripped of its historical specificity, and "woman," Suleri concludes, encourages "the simplicities that underlie unthinking celebrations of oppression, elevating the racially female voice into a metaphor for 'the good.'" What results is an "embarrassed privilege granted to racially encoded feminism."[18]

The popularity of Mohanty's work in feminist classrooms corroborates Suleri's conclusions. In my global feminism classroom I encountered tremendous resistance to any kind of critical engagement with Mohanty. Despite the fact that her critique originates in diasporic Third World women's scholarship, students vehemently dismissed the suggestion that there might be something very wrong with this reification and veneration of the other. Why *not* privilege the woman of color now, when historically she has been underprivileged, the students protested. The student who accused me of racist teaching practices argued in her report to the Human Rights and Equity Services Office that I should have interpreted Spivak's joke as demonstrating "a newfound willingness in the academic community to respect what they believed to be a person's culture." My agreement with Spivak on the dangerous effects of this reification, not to mention my enjoyment of her humor, was considered proof of racist assumptions that silenced nonwhite women. Evidently, challenging the unspoken assumption that oppression grants privileged access to truth and therefore to moral authority is considered racist. My classroom interactions ironically confirmed Suleri's argument: the voice of the woman of color has become a metaphor for "the good." The other is always a good other.

Guilt and *Ressentiment*

We need to think carefully about what is at stake here. Why is this perspective appealing, and what are its effects? At first glance, the argument appears simple: white, privileged women, in their theoretical and practical interventions, must take into account the experiences and conceptual work of women who are less fortunate and less powerful, have fewer resources, and are therefore more subject to systemic oppression. The lesson of feminism's mistakes in the civil rights era is that this "mainstream" group must not speak for other women. But such a view must be interrogated. Its effects, as I have argued, include a veneration of the other, moral currency for the victim, and an insidious competition for victimhood. We will see in later chapters that these effects are also common in situations of conflict where the stakes are much higher.

We witness here a twofold appeal: otherness discourse in feminism appeals both to the guilt of the privileged and to the resentment, or *ressentiment*, of the other. Suleri's allusion to "embarrassed privilege" exposes the operation of guilt in the misunderstanding that often divides Western feminists from women in the developing world, or white women from women of color. The guilt of those who feel themselves deeply implicated in and responsible for imperialism merely reinforces an imperialist benevolence, polarizes us unambiguously by locking us into the categories of victim and perpetrator, and blinds us to the power and agency of the other. Many fail to see that it is embarrassing and insulting for those identified as victimized others *not* to be subjected to the same critical intervention and held to the same demands of moral and political responsibility. Though we are by no means equal in power and ability, wealth and advantage, we are all collectively responsible for the world we inhabit in common. The condition of victimhood does not absolve one of moral responsibility. I will return to this point repeatedly throughout this book.

Mohanty's perspective ignores the possibility that one can become attached to one's subordinated status, which introduces the concept of *ressentiment*, the focus of much recent interest in the injury caused by racism and colonization. Nietzsche describes *ressentiment* as the overwhelming sentiment of "slave morality," the revolt that begins when *ressentiment* itself becomes creative and gives birth to values.[19] The sufferer in this schema seeks out a cause for his suffering—"a *guilty* agent who is susceptible to suffering"—someone on whom he can vent his affects and so procure the anesthesia necessary to ease the pain of injury. The motivation behind *ressentiment*, according to Nietzsche, is the desire "to *deaden*, by means of a more violent emotion of any kind, a tormenting, secret pain that is becoming unendurable, and to drive it out of consciousness at least for the moment: for that one requires an affect, as savage an affect as possible, and, in order to excite that, any pretext at all."[20] In its contemporary manifestation, Wendy Brown argues that *ressentiment* acts as the "righteous critique of power from the perspective of the injured," which "delimits a specific site of blame for suffering by constituting sovereign subjects and events as responsible for the 'injury' of social subordination." Identities are fixed in an economy of perpetrator and victim in which revenge, rather than power or emancipation, is sought for the injured, making the perpetrator hurt as the sufferer does.[21]

Such a concept is useful for understanding why an ethics of absolute responsibility to the other appeals to the victimized. Brown remarks that, for Nietzsche, the source of the triumph of a morality rooted in *ressentiment* is the denial that it has any access to power or contains a will to power. Politicized identities arise as both product of and reaction to this condition; the reaction is a substitute for action—an "imaginary revenge," Nietzsche calls it. Suffering then becomes a social virtue at the same time that the sufferer attempts to displace his suffering onto another. The identity created by *ressentiment*, Brown explains, becomes invested in its own subjection not only through its discovery of someone to blame, and a new recognition and revaluation of that subjection, but also through the satisfaction of revenge.[22]

The outcome of feminism's attraction to theories of difference and otherness is thus deeply contentious. First, we witness the further reification of the very oppositions in question and a simple reversal of the focus from the same to the other. This observation is not new and has been made by many critics of feminism, but it seems to have made no serious impact on mainstream feminist scholarship or teaching practices in women's studies programs. Second, in the eagerness to rectify the mistakes of "white, middle-class, liberal, western" feminism, the other has been uncritically exalted, which has led in turn to simplistic designations of marginal, "othered" status and, ultimately, a competition for victimhood. Ultimately, this approach has led to a new moral code in which ethics is equated with the responsibility of the privileged Western woman, while moral immunity is granted to the victimized other. Ranjana Khanna describes this operation aptly when she writes that in the field of transnational feminism, the reification of the other has produced "separate ethical universes" in which the privileged experience paralyzing guilt and the neocolonized, crippling resentment. The only "overarching imperative" is that one does not comment on another's ethical context. An ethical response turns out to be a nonresponse.[23] Let us turn now to an exploration of this third outcome.

Ethics as Responsibility

When it comes to moral considerations, the hallmark of other talk is nonreciprocity or incommensurability. The shift in terms—from morals to ethics, from morality as doing the right thing to "the ethical relation to the other"—signals a sea change in how we approach moral discourse and behavior. In the new formula, I am responsible for the other, but the other is not responsible for me. It appears that we have come to accept the association of ethics with responsibility to the other to such an extent that questioning the terms of this acceptance seems not merely radical or politically audacious but immoral—enough to justify a charge of racism. The result, again, is a dangerous moralism that posits the other as blameless, unequivocally good, absolved of reciprocal responsibility because of her own victimhood. Nonothers alone—those who cannot claim the status of otherness—are held accountable and often seem anxious to bear the burden of responsibility for the world in the name of moral restitution. Responsibility comes before freedom here: we are absolutely responsible without choice, whether we rise to the occasion or not. As Kelly Oliver suggests, we are called to a "truly hyperbolic ethics," a responsibility so absolute that it is constitutive of subjectivity.[24] The other, in this equation, is rarely scrutinized, let alone defined.

"The ethical relation to the other" is a phrase coined by Levinas, who structures this relation on an absolute responsibility that we never choose and will never adequately meet; it is a responsibility that the hungry and destitute who surround us nevertheless demand. The vast commentary on Levinas's work on ethics has been one of the contributing factors to the broader academic and cultural preoccupation with the status of the other and the perceived necessity of our responsibility for it. The enthusiasm this interest has generated may not, as Rudi Visker puts it, be due to the "originality and sheer intellectual brilliance" of Levinas's work, but rather to something in his position "that deeply resonates with the spirit of our times and our preoccupation with the fate of 'the Other.'" I want to echo Visker's questions here: "Why do we state with such passion that we are responsible for, and that we always fall short of ourselves in approaching the Other?"[25] Why this propensity to declare and disparage our own injustice? The wide appeal of Levinas's ideas (often misread) must mean something. What possible comfort could such an ethical attitude afford us?[26]

One of the distinguishing features of "the spirit of our times" that Levinas has tapped into is the collective guilt on the part of the privileged vis-à-vis the oppressed other, as we have noted in feminist discourse. Levinas's invocation of responsibility, persecution, and passivity appeals both to those who feel the burden of this responsibility to the other—who identify with the center rather than the periphery, the self or same rather than the other—and to those who identify themselves as other. The former are motivated by guilt—suffering *does* perhaps bestow the magical power of atonement, despite what Levinas tells us—and the latter by wounded indignation, *ressentiment*, and possibly the desire for revenge.

We do not encounter in Levinas the idea that the *I* designates only a privileged *I*, while the other names a strictly *oppressed* other. His emphasis on the substitution of myself for the destitute, hungry, and naked other, however, lends itself well to this interpretation. Consider the terms of Levinas's essay "Substitution," a remarkable elaboration of a completely nonreciprocal responsibility. Here he describes the relation of one ego to another as one of proximity, designating not spatial closeness but immediacy. The geographically distant foreigner is as proximate, in this sense, as my next-door neighbor. I don't have to know this stranger, yet I am still responsible for her. This proximity is never close enough, and it forgets reciprocity, as a love that doesn't expect to be shared. So stark is this nonreciprocity that the other substitutes itself for the ego. The ego is usurped by the other; its ascendancy is overturned by the other. This asymmetrical displacement of one for the other is described in the strongest terms in "Substitution," as obsession, as persecution, as suffering, and as passivity beyond passivity, terms that bespeak the intolerable weight of my responsibility for an other who is not expected to be responsible for me.

We are thus persecuted by another, according to Levinas, and taken hostage by the other's accusation "though [we] have not done anything." This is the very basis of solidarity. What can this be, he asks, but a substitution of me for the other?[27] It means that I have the other inside my skin, like the pregnant woman who Levinas claims loses all substantiality and identity in her suffering for the other. In her absolute passivity, she listens anxiously to the other but lacks free choice. She is evicted from her own being—her body is devoted to the other before being devoted to itself—becoming an authentic figure of responsibility, of the substitution of "the-one-for-the-other" par excellence.

We can see the appeal that this rather masochistic notion of substitution would have for the guilt-ridden feminist, but its appeal to anticolonial thinkers is also apparent. The politicization of the category of the other—the appropriation of an abstract other as an oppressed other—is unambiguous in the work of Enrique Dussel, for example. The question "to be or not to be," a query that barks up the wrong tree, according to Levinas,[28] becomes "to be or not to be *other*" in Dussel's hands, betraying a significant if intentional forgetfulness of the *otherwise than being* that Levinas took great pains to distinguish from simply nonbeing, or being's "other." For Dussel, it is the impoverished Latin American other who is capable of escaping what he believes are the totalitarian gestures of an imperialist European philosophical tradition. "Our thinking *sets out from* non-being, nothingness, *otherness*, exteriority, the mystery of no-sense," he writes.[29] He claims that his project of liberation philosophy maintains respect for this other *as other*, as exteriority, yet it is quickly apparent that Dussel's ethics is premised on the question of *who* can claim the status of otherness. There is no exteriority in this alterity but rather, as Ofelia Schutte argues, a new absolute constructed in the name of the poor, the exploited, and the oppressed.[30]

A more recent example can be found in Kelly Oliver's discussion of the psychic effects of oppression. Like Dussel, but in the context of psychoanalytic theory, Oliver argues that we need to start from the subjectivities of those "othered" owing to the suffering of the abject, excluded, and oppressed.[31] If we fail to consider social position, she notes, we render all subjects alike and subsume all differences, which is the predicament presented by the normative subject of psychoanalysis. Psychoanalytic theory must instead revolve around those who are "othered" by the Freudian normative subject. Surprisingly (or perhaps not), Oliver does not acknowledge that starting from the subjectivity of the other is merely another form of normativizing. While Oliver wants to rewrite the historical relation, generally antagonistic, between self and other, or self and the social, like Bannerji, she fails to recognize that her own categories of "normative" and "othered" only reinforce this antagonistic divide.

This is magnified when Oliver blames popular notions of the individual for fixing the subject as self-contained and oppositional with respect to others. That the subject is in control of itself and of others and the world is an illusion, which, she claims, leads to a sense of entitlement and privilege, of mastery over, rather than fear of, what one cannot control, and ultimately to "self-righteous killing in the name of justice, democracy, and freedom."[32] This is an obvious reference to the U.S. government, associating a generic Western subject with guilt and an unspecified other with blamelessness.[33] The opposition here is between a guilty "we" and a good "other," a guilty we that Oliver invokes with her call for a "hyperbolic" ethics that goes beyond even Levinas's elaboration of an ethics that demands our accountability even for deeds we do not commit ourselves. "We are responsible for the effects of our affects on others," Oliver insists. "We are responsible for what we do not and cannot ever completely know about ourselves." It seems that we are also responsible for what we do not know of the other, for Oliver adds that we can never know or understand others, either.[34] It is entirely unclear how this undermines, rather than reinforces, the tradition of antagonism between self and other that Oliver rejects. And where does this hyperbolic responsibility come from? Finally, we might want to ask, who is this "we"?

Levinas's warning that although it is I who must suffer in the place of the other, "it is not a question of humiliating oneself, as if suffering were in itself, in its empirical essence, a magical power of atonement," generally falls on deaf ears.[35] There is no great leap required to move from an asymmetrical relation in which the other takes precedence and commands me, to an other that functions as a paragon of innocence and blamelessness: a good other. Levinas's I/other relation has been transformed, over several decades of attention to the center/margin dichotomy, into an imperialist I and an oppressed other. The stringent nonreciprocity of the relation between these is taken quite seriously, if not dogmatically. If it is I who must take the place of the other, must suffer in her stead, then my task is not to chastise or punish the other for not bearing the weight of her responsibility to *me*. "It is Me who is a substitution and sacrifice and not another," writes Levinas.[36] While I am to give the other the bread from my own mouth, there is no reciprocal demand for the bread from the other's mouth. She appears to be immune to the injunction. There is no consideration of what may happen to the ethical relation when the oppressed, victimized other literally *demands* the bread from my mouth. The obsession with one's own responsibility that Levinas meticulously describes has thus turned erroneously into an obsession with the privileged I's responsibility for the oppressed other.[37]

Oliver argues inexplicably that the fact that "we do not know or understand others" enables communication, communion, love, and forgiveness, and "provides the impulse for interpretation" through which our lives become "meaning full."[38] To the contrary, I maintain, promoting an absolute ethical responsibility that is infinitely beyond my capacity to fulfill, a responsibility to an oppressed other whom I can never know or understand, is not a useful approach but leads to a comfortable piety, an excuse for not responding. Since we cannot understand the other, we are in no position to judge and have nothing to offer. Where is ethical responsibility to be found when we show such alleged sensitivity to the other that we absolve ourselves from making judgments and engaging in critique? When the "we" implied in the discussion is always an abstract community of privilege, guilty by virtue of location, and when the other who demands the responsibility for this "we" is an equally abstract figure of helplessness, then *who* is responsible? How is this "we" being faithful to the call to responsibility if we claim, as my students have, that we can't make ethical judgments about violence in Israel and Palestine because we are not there and can't comprehend their situation—or that we are not entitled to criticize the intellectual work of a woman of color because our critique "silences" her? If we are required only to maintain an attitude of sensitivity or tolerance while relaxing in the night of our own nonknowledge—of other cultures and experiences, other ways of thinking—it is difficult to comprehend how this constitutes responsibility of any kind.

Ultimately, we must ask whether this approach to ethics—characterized as an ethical relation to the other—assists us in changing our lives, motivating us to act compassionately and justly, or whether it fails to compel us to respond in any meaningful way to moral crises, which, we could argue, are always political as well. More specifically, we need to inquire into the kinds of political practices that follow an ethics of responsibility that not only refuses to acknowledge the victimized other's agency (and thus responsibility) but maintains that even pointing this out is a travesty of my own responsibility and ethical commitment to others. We have not given any honest thought to *why* the view from the margins would lead to better ethical relations or better political visions for the future. Nor have we seriously considered *why* the victimized would be better equipped to deal with the fraught nature of ethical and political dilemmas. It seems obvious that the opposite possibility might be true: that the victim's relative powerlessness, lack of resources, and experience of injury, even trauma, might compromise any ethical or political vision for the future.

I am proposing that we investigate whether understanding ethics as absolute responsibility has abandoned politics. We desperately need political solutions to current inequalities and injustices, and we need to formulate these solutions collectively. In order to do this, we must be critical of the "separate ethical universes" we have created in the name of incommensurability, and sometimes in the name of guilt and *ressentiment*. How to acknowledge and account for the injury of the victimized other and simultaneously escape the binary logic of victim and perpetrator is perhaps one of the most important ethical challenges we face today. In order to think further an ethics that does not forgo political strategy in the name of an ethics that privileges a victimized other, we must acknowledge the other's responsibility for her own others, including me. The pregnant woman may be occupied by another life, but she must recognize the power of that life to destroy her own.

Accused

As many have discovered, criticizing the practices and effects of emancipatory or empowering discourses, even from within them, can lead to excommunication. If we explore the problems inherent in the discourse of victimhood, for example, we may be accused of blaming the victim; if we presume to criticize the ubiquitous but ill-defined "other," we may be charged with indifference, or worse, toward those who are oppressed.

I have related my experience of being accused of racism in order to set up the problem that drives this book. The moral authority of the victim and the moral failure of the privileged are in dispute here, not the facts of privilege and oppression. In the months that followed the accusation, I struggled to understand this event and the responses to it from a faculty and student community informed by feminist ideals. I spent the next six months wondering if I would have to face a university hearing, unable to trust that any of my new colleagues would support me—for who would dare to question the experience of a black student in such a matter? Those whom I did trust with my story spoke to me gently about the challenges of teaching in a multicultural environment, referring me to campus services that could train me to be more sensitive to issues of race in the classroom. Even several years later, long after one of the students dropped her accusation and expressed regret over the incident to one of my colleagues, I remained surprised that no one in this apparently close-knit feminist community ever commented on the injustice of the charge against me. Indignation and empathy were reserved for the female faculty member who was subjected to sexual harassment by a student via e-mail—a safer ground for solidarity.

What I felt, immediately and for many months afterward, was a profound sense of injustice but at the same time persistent self-doubt. This led to a certain defensiveness when explaining the incident to others who were not immediately sympathetic. The less understanding I perceived in my listener, the more defensive I would become. At the same time, attempting to look at myself from my accuser's perspective, I asked myself whether she could have been right, whether I had indeed committed an act of racism. I wanted to say that I was unjustly accused of racism, but what I had learned from decades of scholarly emphases on difference and marginality made these words difficult to say. Feminism had taught me that the experience of victimhood is sacrosanct, beyond critique or judgment. Vindicating myself entailed making a judgment against a black woman who experienced racism in my classroom, something we are not prepared to do.

This confusion brought home to me how far we have come in bestowing on the "other" the status of innocent victim, a status that in this case was superficially equated with skin color. The question whether this young, assertive black woman bore any responsibility for the events that transpired was never raised. Her motivation, perception, and interpretation were considered guileless, and only because of the facts of her skin and mine, mere accidents of birth. Hers rendered this student an innocent victim; mine, a perpetrator of racism.

2

WHEN VICTIMS BECOME KILLERS

So, if we want to remain alive, we will have to kill and kill and kill.
All day, every day. If we don't kill, we will cease to exist.

Victory for us is to see you suffer.

Humans are capable of carrying out extraordinarily evil deeds while feeling righteous.[1] Perpetrators of violent actions may fervently believe that they are committing an act of self-defense. Killers may see themselves as victims balancing the scales of justice. Constructing a narrative that justifies one's actions seems a requirement in order to injure or kill another without compunction; otherwise, many perpetrators could not live with themselves.

The title of this chapter is borrowed from Mahmood Mamdani's remarkable analysis of the 1994 genocide in Rwanda, *When Victims Become Killers: Colonialism, Nativism, and the Genocide in Rwanda*. Mamdani describes the genocide as the native's violent response to the settler—to use Franz Fanon's terms—the violent impulse of those who considered themselves sons and daughters of the soil, their mission one of "clearing the soil of a threatening *alien* presence."[2] Mamdani makes an analogy that is useful for my purposes here. He warns of the dangers of becoming locked into the world of the rat and the cat, that is, the political world of the Hutu and the Tutsi, or the native and the settler. It is a world in which identities are generated endlessly in binary pairs. The rat believes his worst enemy is the cat—not the lion, the tiger, or the elephant—while the cat thinks there is nothing more delicious than the rat. In a world where cats are few and rats are many, the cats come up with a clever way of stabilizing their rule: they make distinctions based on ethnic and racial origins that become normalized into a political order. Rats are tagged through "a discourse on origins, indigenous and nonindigenous, ethnic and racial." It is quite possible that in a world in which rats have managed to triumph over cats, rats may continue living in a world defined by cats, that is, by identities generated in the era when cats ruled.[3]

My objective in this chapter is to look carefully at the logic of Mamdani's analogy in the context of the ongoing crisis in Israel and Palestine. When victims of a political regime bent on eliminating a people become killers themselves, he argues—crying out to their oppressor, "never again!"—they confirm rather than transform the binary worldview that rendered them less than human, able to kill with impunity. They remain locked in the worldview of the victim, no less dangerous than that of the perpetrator, for it is a worldview bound by the same terms. Without acknowledging the limits of this binary perspective, without questioning the historical context of its instigation and reification, a victim's identity "is likely to generate no more than an aspiration for trading places," and "every pursuit of justice will tend toward revenge, and every reconciliation toward an embrace of institutional evil."[4] While the historical and political circumstances that led to the genocide in Rwanda are very different from those that gave rise to the current situation in Israel and Palestine, Mamdani's analysis of the logic of victimhood helps us to understand a largely misunderstood dynamic of the conflict, one that contributes considerably to its impasse.

I began writing this chapter at the start of Israel's massive military assault on Gaza in December 2008. Three weeks later, Israel and Hamas declared a ceasefire. The details are by now familiar and the severity of the violence frozen into statistics: the operation included air strikes and a ground offensive, killed between 1,387 and 1,417 Palestinians—roughly a third of them children—injured more than five thousand, and uprooted thousands of Gazan civilians from their homes, many of which were reduced to rubble. Hamas rockets and mortars killed four Israelis, three of them civilians; five Israeli soldiers died during the fighting in Gaza, and four more were killed by friendly fire. Gaza's infrastructure—such as it was for this virtual open-air prison of 1.3 million people, 80 percent of whom subsist on less than $2 a day—was destroyed, to the tune of $3 billion in damages.[5]

It is difficult to fathom the stunningly disproportionate terms on which the "war" was fought. The crushing force of military muscle against an imprisoned population without means of escape except through death, the dismembered and dying children deprived of medical care, the venom and lack of compunction expressed in daily blogs responding to the assault in such media outlets as *Ha'aretz*—these facts would appear to demand immediate moral condemnation of state brutality. And yet the Canadian government felt confident enough to be the only nation (of forty-seven member nations) to oppose a UN Human Rights Council motion calling for an investigation into Israel's "grave" human rights violations and the ensuing humanitarian crisis.[6] Canada's representative explained that the language of the motion was "unnecessary, unhelpful and inflammatory" and did not make clear that Hamas rockets "triggered the crisis."[7] Thirteen other nations, mostly European, abstained. Intelligent, politically astute scholars on campuses across North America stayed mute and believed they had good reasons for their silence. Campus events attempting to respond to the conflict struggled to stave off the seemingly inevitable eruptions of blame and exoneration, accompanied by sporting event–style cheers. In this, they mostly failed.

In Israel and Palestine we are witnessing the pernicious effects of the worldview of the victim, mirrored on both sides of the conflict. What is played out on the land to which Jews and Arabs lay claim is the victim's struggle to exercise all the vengeance it can, in the name of morally legitimate self-defense—"*victory for us is to see you suffer.*" We witness here the same dynamic and effects described in the previous chapter, only in this case the stakes are drastically higher. The moral power of the victim results in death, destruction, and the silencing of dissent. There is no parity in this case, however, in anything but the logic of blame and revenge and the unwavering belief in the virtue of one's own position. Power over life and death are not on par. How do we take this incontrovertible fact into account when considering matters of judgment and responsibility? I would submit that the demand for "balance" amounts to a refusal to accept responsibility, to judge, and to act. As observers of conflict, we can and must make moral judgments of individual acts on both (or all) sides of a political conflict, even while declaring that one side is more responsible for the crisis than another. How we achieve this without dissolving all discussion into a game of blame and vindication requires a vigilant focus on one's own responsibility, acting as if the other will do the same.

These issues have plagued me in recent years, as discussions of the Israeli-Palestinian conflict have degenerated into a terrible deadlock, causing many to disengage from any discussion of the crisis altogether. To those who have asked why I would want to write on this issue, when so many others have done so (seemingly in vain), and when we write from a safe distance, untouched by bombs, bulldozers, or stones, I respond that the deadlock speaks precisely to the global significance of the crisis, and hence to our responsibility to engage with the questions it raises.

As Étienne Balibar suggests, Palestine is "a universal cause," a "concentrated and reduced but also intensified image of the kind of problem that has to be solved in a post-colonial era, if we are not to have prominent wars and latent or rampant processes of extermination everywhere in the world. In a sense, they are testing for us the possibility of inventing post-national politics, and in the most difficult of conditions since it is not a dialogue among equals." "Something has to be invented," Balibar argues, which is why Palestine is so important: a postnational politics or, I would venture awkwardly, a *post-identity-politics* politics that will interrupt the "irreversible process" of colonization on which Israel embarked in 1948 and from which it cannot or will not now extricate itself.[8] Such a politics must succeed in overcoming the deadlock caused by death-defying claims to victimhood.

At this excruciating time, when a solution appears unattainable, when the Israeli government and many of its citizens are fed up with years of inter-mittent rocket fire and feel justified in the state's terrible demonstration of military might,[9] and when Palestinians are suffering from the occupation, their own violent internal politics, the world's indifference, and the bru-tal reprisals for their own retributive acts of terror, it is necessary for us to think further about the conceptual framing of the conflict. The deadlock has much to do with the moral power of the victim granted in the wake of our unwillingness, as bystanders, to judge wrongdoing.

Critique of Counterviolence

Several years ago, in an undergraduate philosophy course I taught on violence and self-determination, I introduced the students to readings that I hoped would help them understand the phenomenon of suicide bombing as it is practiced by Palestinians. I shared the worries of Ghassan Hage, who warned, after Israel's reinvasion of the West Bank in March 2002, of a clear political risk in trying to explain suicide bombings. Hage claims that there is a "con-demnation imperative" in the Western public sphere that censors any attempt to explain why suicide bombers act as they do, rendering it a challenge to "leav[e] condemnation aside in order to concentrate on explanation, without this being seen as a form of 'justification.'"[10]

What surprised me was that there was in fact little resistance in the class to understanding the motivation of suicide bombers. I had hoped that they would suspend their moral condemnation long enough to understand why a young man or woman would decide to take up arms in this horrific act of murder and self-destruction. But most of the students who spoke in class appeared not to be disturbed at all by the justification of violence as a political response to violence, accepting that violent retribution could set the scales of justice right again. As the chorus of "what else can they do?" reached the front of the classroom, I found myself backpedaling, worried that the texts they read had justified for them this egregious form of violence simply and neatly, before any hard questions could be asked. For these students, condemning the violence of the victimized group—in this case, the suicide bombers— seemed immediately to affirm the legitimacy of Israeli state violence. I thus discovered a profound investment in upholding the victim group's immunity to moral judgment—an investment difficult to criticize without appearing to contribute to the group's victimization. Furthermore, I discovered that this dynamic in my classroom betrayed my own ambivalence regarding the violence of the victimized. In my desire to understand suicide bombing, and in my compassion for the plight of the Palestinians, who continue to appear superfluous in the eyes of the world, I also resisted expressing an explicit moral condemnation of suicide bombing. It seems that we can only accept one perpetrator and one victim in any account of conflict. The violent response of the victim to victimization is particularly difficult to condemn.

What moral distinction is thus accepted in the very term "counterviolence," and what are its effects? To answer these questions, we could return to one of the most extensive descriptions of the condition of the colonized, a condition that fosters the desire for vengeance. Frantz Fanon's *The Wretched of the Earth* is a pivotal text on colonialism and decolonization, responsible for influencing a number of twentieth-century social movements and transforming our perceptions of the victims of oppression. Fanon poignantly and forcefully describes the relation between the native Algerian and the French settler, and the violence that produces and sustains it. While he argues that the native is brought into being by the settler and acknowledges the ambiguity of such an identity, Fanon insists that the native's self-determination requires that he reclaim this very identity and, through violence, replace one species of men with another. The native thus embarks on the path from victim to perpetrator, from the colonized, native Algerian who freezes under the dehumanizing gaze of the French settler, to the decolonized man who grasps history through a murderous desire to annihilate the settler, albeit with a violence implanted by the colonizer. Here we see already that the victim is considered innocent to begin with, the potential for violence not simply a human attribute that can be provoked but a seed sown by the colonizer.

Fanon's claim that decolonization is "always a violent event" has been read variously as a justification of violence in the name of liberation or as descriptive rather than prescriptive, contingent rather than universal.[11] While he may have been the first critic of decolonizing violence, Fanon's visceral and moving description of the native's experience of oppression and desire for freedom has often foreclosed any critique of the violence of the victim. What is both remarkable and disturbing about Fanon's account is that we are permitted a glimpse into the violent dreams of the victims of colonization. Without mincing words, he exposes his reader to an unabashed desire for the death of one's oppressor, yet he solicits our compassion toward the fundamental humanity of the suffering native. We come to *understand* the impulse to violence; it appears a natural and necessary means to dignity and self-determination for a disenfranchised, dehumanized population.

The violence of the colonized therefore presents us with a kind of moral ambiguity that the settler's violence does not. For Fanon, the settler is responsible for the Manichean world the native must burst apart; the native's very humanity is at stake. From this perspective, that the native Algerians risked their lives was the proof of their humanity, their killing of French settlers a terrible outcome, but the lesser of two evils. Here we find a compelling presentation of the logic repeated in every violent struggle for liberation: "counterviolence" is the violence of self-defense—the violence of victimhood—and must therefore be considered in a different moral light. It is justifiable because necessary. It is the final recourse of a desperate people who have exhausted all avenues in the attempt to reclaim the humanity that was stripped from them.

Unfortunately, in addition to Fanon's tremendous insight into the plight of the colonized, his legacy includes a notion of justice as vengeance, and the displacement of politics by violence. *The Wretched of the Earth* has been read as a revolutionary manifesto, and cautionary criticism of nationalist fervor in Fanon's work has been sadly neglected. The polemical tone of Jean-Paul Sartre's preface to the book clearly demonstrates a Manichean logic that works on the guilt of the European reader. Sartre warns his French audience that the violence of the native will return to them: "we [Europeans] will only be fueling in their bodies a volcanic fury whose power matches the pressure applied to them. They only understand the language of violence, you were saying? Of course; at first the only violence they understand is the colonist's, and then their own, reflecting back at us like our reflection bouncing back at us from a mirror."[12] Sartre asks why the European cannot recognize his own cruelty, now turned against him, and remains vehemently unapologetic about the reciprocation of this cruelty. If anything, we detect here a smug moralism—the guilt-ridden liberal European advocating on behalf of the oppressed. The innocence of the native seems unquestionable, as though the very potential for violence arrived only with the settler, rendering actual violence, the native's counterviolence, unavoidable. Evidently, the agency and responsibility that Sartre demands of the European isn't required of the Algerian.

In the scholarly response to Fanon's commentary on counterviolence, Hannah Arendt's critique stands out for its decided rejection of the use of violence to advance the cause of freedom and social justice. Writing in the midst of the American civil rights movement and student protests around the world, Arendt complains of the "glorification" of violence in Fanon and Sartre, which she holds partly responsible for the turn to violence in some of the protests of the 1960s. If it were true, as Sartre claims, that "violence, like Achilles' spear, can heal the wounds it has inflicted,"[13] then revenge would cure most of our ills, Arendt comments wryly. Sartre's declaration is an abstract myth, she notes, as mythical as Fanon's worst rhetorical excesses. Who has ever doubted that the violated dream of violence, Arendt asks, or that the oppressed dream of taking the oppressor's place? As Marx ventured, dreams never come true. The "mad fury" that Sartre warned his European audience about could turn everyone's dreams into nightmares.[14]

Unfortunately, the romanticization of revolutionary violence by those on the political left has carried on unabated, encouraged by a philosophical preoccupation with a violence ever more abstractly and nebulously defined. The poststructuralist tradition carries out a deconstructive operation that demonstrates beautifully the contradictions inherent in violence but leaves us with no mandate or method for judging violent acts. Thus we learn that violence occurs in the very operation of language as a kind of colonizing force, that law itself is violent when it declares that those who do not uphold it are violent, that since every state is founded in violence, the distinction between legitimate and illegitimate violence crumbles, and that violence may be found even at the heart of a blind political preference for peace.[15] We end up mired in the bog of Slavoj Žižek's bizarre logic when he argues that "the same act can count as violent or non-violent, depending on its context; sometimes a polite smile can be more violent than a brutal outburst." Violence, according to Žižek, means a "radical upheaval" of basic social relations. "Crazy and taste-less as it may sound," he concludes, "the problem with historical monsters who slaughtered millions was that they were not violent enough. Sometimes doing nothing is the most violent thing to do."[16] Perhaps this is why Che Guevara T-shirts are everywhere worn in good conscience.

If violence is inescapable, as many would have it, then the only recourse is to choose the lesser violence.[17] Balibar is right to suggest that if this is the case, then the field of politics has progressively permeated the field of violence, to the extent that extreme violence has become built into the very heart of emancipatory politics.[18] Choosing the lesser violence, as Arendt reminds us, is still choosing violence.[19]

Last Recourse

The acceptance of counterviolence as morally distinct from "originary" violence and therefore as defensible is embedded in narratives that describe Palestinian suicide bombing as the political resistance of a people struggling to be free. Significantly, resistance is always depicted as a last resort—*we had no choice*. It is a romanticized view of victims' violence that betrays a binary logic of innocent victim versus guilty perpetrator, defending the victim as bereft of historical responsibility and *entitled* to carry out acts of brutality. Substitute Israeli state violence for Palestinian violence in this equation and the resulting logic is the same. If our moral judgments depend on whether violence is originary or retributive, the distinction becomes paramount, which explains the current impasse in discussions of the conflict in Israel/Palestine; each side must vie for the position of innocent victim. "Beware a people that boasts its own virtue."[20]

As we will see, in this particular context, self-defense as a justification for violent retribution will never open avenues to a resolution. Every perpetrator could have been a victim at one time, and before that a perpetrator, and so forth. How far back do we search in history for the "original" act of violence? We could return to 1967, when Israel fought and won the Six-Day War. We could go further back, to 1948, when the state of Israel was declared and some eight hundred thousand Palestinians were displaced. We could return to the period of Irgun terrorism in the 1930s, to the Palestinian massacre of Jews at Hebron in 1929, to a time when the land belonged to Jews, or earlier, when it belonged to the peoples of Canaan, ad infinitum. A critical analysis of this desperate search for vindication is necessary if we are at all concerned about the human rights violations of a global politics premised on the priority of security at all costs. If any act of violence can be excused by the perpetrator as a response to an earlier violation, then violence ceases to be a moral issue at all.

Since the beginning of the second intifada, a discussion of Palestinian suicide bombing has developed among leftist scholars and commentators that resonates with Fanon's analysis of revolutionary violence. The occupied Palestinian stands in for the Algerian native, his or her existence constituted by the Israeli occupier as less than human, rendering violent resistance inevitable in the attempt to regain dignity and human worth. From this perspective, the suffering Palestinian has no other recourse. Destroying one's body and murdering innocent bystanders in order to exact revenge on the occupiers is thus considered a legitimate response to despair. It is an act of self-defense, of political resistance in the name of self-determination and the struggle for human rights. Such an act of violence can be interpreted as the recuperation of meaning for a people who found it increasingly impossible to create such meaning—a redemptive act, in other words, one that restores to life the significance it lacks.

It is a seductive argument, particularly in a Western world that has become more attuned to the suffering of victims. We read about the appalling conditions of life in Palestinian refugee camps, breeding grounds for young men and women willing to sacrifice their lives for a better future. The refugee camp has come to symbolize the expulsion of the Palestinians, the place where, according to Faisal Darraj, conditions are "so wretched that rebelling, and taking up arms, eventually becomes *the only understandable response*" (emphasis added).[21] The "social unavailability" of the opportunity to make something of one's life in the camps means that throwing stones, facing the tanks, risking death, and wishing for martyrdom all become meaningful events that create the strong sense of individual or collective identity that Palestinians are normally denied. After fifteen-year-old Mohammed Dauoud was killed while throwing stones at a main clash point in Al-Bireh during the early days of the second intifada, his sister Soha said in an interview with Wendy Pearlman, "How can you express yourself other than going to the checkpoint and throwing a stone?... You feel like you have to do something, even if you know that the stone won't even reach them—even if you know that, in the end, it's useless."[22]

The violent response of the Palestinians is considered a direct consequence of the inhumanity of their occupiers. Eyad El-Sarraj, a frequently quoted psychiatrist and human rights activist from the Gaza Strip, draws attention to the fact that suicide bombers are the children of the first intifada, more than half of whom witnessed the killing or humiliation of their fathers at the hands of Israeli soldiers. El-Sarraj concludes that witnessing this helplessness, and the inability of fathers to protect their children, has a devastating psychological impact: "Children who have seen so much inhumanity... inevitably come out with inhuman responses. That's really how to understand the suicide bombings."[23]

I do not want to make light of the despair and trauma that the Israeli occupation has caused, or of its debilitating and enduring effects, but we should be asking why so many have come to accept that such despair *necessarily* leads to violence, justifies retaliatory killing, and grants moral immunity to the victim-turned-perpetrator. How far are we willing to go in our sympathetic understanding of "emancipatory" violence? For the British philosopher Ted Honderich, Palestinian suicide bombing is both a sign of desperation *and* an act of terror—but a legitimate one. If the highest moral principle is, as he believes, to take "rational steps to get people out of lives of wretchedness and deprivation," then Palestinians have "a moral right to their terrorism." The critical question for Honderich is whether a particular practice of terrorism can be proved to be an act of violence *for* humanity. He calls this kind of violence "terrorism for humanity," defining it as "terrorism with the aim of the principle of humanity," which means getting people out of "lives of wretchedness and other deprivation."[24]

Honderich concludes that since Palestinians have been denied freedom, power, and respect in their homeland since the start of a new Zionism in 1967, and given that terrorism is an "established necessity" due to the absence of any alternatives, Palestinian terrorism is a paradigmatic case of "terrorism for humanity." In fact, he writes, terrorism "is their only effective and economical means of self-defense, of liberating themselves, of resisting degradation."[25] The suicide bomber who kills an Israeli child, therefore, in Honderich's words, "was morally permitted if not obliged to do what she did."[26]

Honderich's claims reveal the morally repugnant ends to which an emphasis on the pure innocence of victimhood—and the moral immunity this status implies—leads. In its insistence that there is no alternative to violent retribution, the argument lacks political vision; it fails to imagine a future beyond a global human community in which the only certainty is that violence is an inevitable and necessary response to violence. It exchanges politics for violence, as Ghassan Hage implies when he argues that such a perspective "risks normalizing the situation rather than perceiving it as the product of an inviable political framework... It is only because of the failure of the political that such a state of nature becomes the cultural norm and violence emerges as a matter-of-fact possibility."[27] This failure is spectacularly evident in the consequences of suicide bombing for Palestinians, although this point is often ignored by the Left. As Balibar reminds us, the violent retribution of suicide bombing not only creates Israeli victims; it is "deeply self-destructive" and "catastrophic for the struggle of Palestinian people."[28] An act of violence—even if it meets Honderich's criteria for "terrorism for humanity"—will simply create more victims, who will in turn be "obliged" to kill in the name of humanity. It is a self-defeating argument.

Thus we have an argument from the political Left that, in defining Palestinian suicide bombing as a political act of resistance for a people that has no other recourse, ultimately imprisons Palestinians in their own agent-less victimhood. We set the bar very low in terms of intelligent political solutions when we argue that there is nothing Palestinians can do but blow themselves up in order to kill innocent civilians. Furthermore, it absolves the bystander of responsibility.[29] This perspective confirms rather than transforms the Manichean world of the victim and perpetrator, merely turning the tables. To argue that desperate people have no other choice but to commit acts of terror would be to claim that there has never been as desperate a people as the Palestinians. How can we know when we have reached the "last recourse?" If human history has not given us many examples of liberation struggles that succeeded without violence, it has certainly given us numerous examples of violent struggles that failed miserably.

Apology for Terror

The "last recourse" argument inevitably leads to an apology for terror. It is, sadly, characteristic of the Left's response to violent acts carried out in the name of emancipation, and is the logical consequence of justifying violence on the basis of the moral status of victimhood. For example, Simon Cottee points to the leftist logic underlying commentaries on the terrorist attacks in the United States on September 11, 2001: "Yes, what happened was awful, but it was hardly very surprising." From the perspective of the far Left, according to Cottee, the root cause of terrorism lies in "the humiliations and injustices visited upon the Arab and Muslim world by the West, particularly the United States." Terror is a response—the wrong response, of course—but a response nonetheless, and the only way to circumvent terror is to put an end to the evils that nurture it. This would mean, for example, that withdrawing financial and military aid from Israel would appease the jihadist terrorists. Cottee cites a number of examples: Gore Vidal writes of the provocations that "drove" the 9/11 terrorists to such terrible acts. Tariq Ali warns that the war against terror will only "push" young Muslims into violence. Douglas Kellner points to the failures of the U.S. government's foreign policy and intelligence systems but does not, Cottee observes, even mention the actual perpetrators of the 9/11 attacks.[30]

The result of this apologetic discourse, according to Cottee, is a refusal on the part of the Left to assign moral blame to those who seek revenge against the criminality of the West. The more appropriate object of moral condemnation is the West—here we find the real culprits, while those who take revenge are merely caught in a set of historical circumstances over which they have no control. Cottee concludes that two denials occur simultaneously here: responsibility is denied, and the "real victim" is denied. The perpetrator (in this case the terrorist) assumes the position of an avenger, and the victim (the United States) is transformed into a wrongdoer. "At no point in this discourse," he remarks, "is it entertained that young Muslim fanatics are morally autonomous human agents, responsible for the consequences that follow from their independently chosen actions. Nor is it made explicit—still less demonstrated—how the West, particularly in the form of George W. Bush and Tony Blair, is morally responsible for the murderous actions of the fanatics themselves."[31]

Of interest in Cottee's analysis is the fact that horrible deeds can be justified on the basis of tolerance or political interests when they are carried out by individuals or groups perceived to be victims with a claim to absolute innocence. But Cottee himself slips into the binary logic of the victim/perpetrator. In defending the United States against its leftist critics, he appears to maintain its complete innocence, using the logic of Norman Geras: that someone else contributes causally to a crime does not mean that he is as morally responsible as the direct agents are, if what he has contributed causally is not wrong in itself. This argument would require believing that the U.S. foreign policies that preceded the war on terror were not wrong.

This is the road that Arendt warned against during the violent turbulence of the anticolonial and civil rights struggles of the 1960s and 1970s. We have reified the categories of victim and perpetrator to such an extent that innocence and culpability are viewed as clean, discrete, and incommensurable categories, and responsibility is reduced to a question of blame. We demand that the victim be absolutely innocent and the perpetrator absolutely guilty in order to justify violence in the name of victimhood and to claim the moral power of the victim. This is by no means an innocent or innocuous power. If we remain caught in this dynamic, the conflict between Jewish Israelis and Palestinian Arabs will never end. Alternatively, we could acknowledge that there are different degrees of responsibility and accountability. Rather than look to the past to justify actions in the present, we need to assess the current situation. Who is responsible for what? Who has the resources and capacity to change the circumstances? Who has the fortitude and foresight to be the first to lay down their arms?

While Cottee provides an important critique, he continues to play according to the rules of the blame game. He exposes the same kind of apology proffered by the feminists and multiculturalists discussed in chapter 1: we are bad imperialists, responsible for oppressive colonization, and we understand why the subjects of our imperialist gestures would dislike us. Consequently, we must accommodate them, not judge them. But even if this argument were sound, it is completely powerless to transform the circumstances of conflict. The rather masochistic attitude arising from Western academic discourses— we started it; go ahead and hit us back—has no politically transformative effects. It is another manifestation of the belief that the other—even the terrorist other—is a good other. We must ask how this acceptance of violent counterinsurgency, and the essentialized categories of us and them on which it relies, makes "us"—the bystanders—complicit in the worst forms of terror.

Palestinians must bear the responsibility for their actions, as we have witnessed the terrible consequences of Hamas's tactics for its own people, and for innocent Israeli citizens. But their capacity to alter their situation is severely restricted. Prisoners of an occupation that is suffocating the possibility of collective political action, and captives of extremist factions among their own population, their options are limited. This is not an apology for terror. On the contrary, if we are to have productive discussions concerning the conflict in Israel and Palestine, those who are working toward equality and freedom for Palestinians (and therefore for all Israelis as well) must resist the temptation to excuse the death and destruction caused by suicide bombings and rockets.

The defensive position leads nowhere. Beyond the reasons already provided, it is a position that the Israeli government and those who agree with its policies have mastered to far better effect.

The reader at this point may either cheer at my criticism of Palestinian terrorism or condemn me for supporting the Israeli occupation and destruction of Palestinian lives. If the intent is to criticize state as well as insurgent violence, then the critic has no "side" with which to claim solidarity; one is anti-Israeli (or anti-Semitic) according to one camp and anti-Palestinian (or anti-Arab) according to the other. There is no exit from this seamless operation except to resist the defensive impulse and carry on in uncharted territory. But judgment must be a part of this discussion. It is essential that we criticize all excuses for violence yet acknowledge that the burden of responsibility for change must be disproportionately borne by the Israeli government and its people, for the simple reason that they disproportionately hold the power to dictate the terms of Palestinian-Israeli relations. This does not mean, however, that the Palestinians are absolved of the burden of finding political solutions. With the right leadership and global support, they could be the first to lay down their arms.

Never Again

When we examine the discourse of victimhood in Israeli society, we find evidence of the same moral power and reprieve from responsibility granted to the Palestinian as victim. While we often hear of the culture of martyrdom growing in Palestinian society, backed by images of grieving but proud families holding up the photos of their martyred loved ones, we hear less of the culture of victimhood in Israeli society. "Never again" is the sentiment that symbolizes the response to Jewish victimhood—the standard by which all victimhood is measured, at least in the West. It is the Holocaust victim of Nazi Germany, particularly the camp survivor, who symbolizes absolute victimhood—pure innocence—for us today.

It is not my intent to trace the history of the status of victimhood in Israeli society. I can only gesture to a development we rarely hear about, despite the number of Israeli writers and academics who seek to analyze it, particularly since the current demand for security against terror has become a dominant discourse. Avraham Burg, a prominent Israeli politician, describes the constant presence of the Shoah in his life as a "buzz" in his ear. "The list of Shoah manifestations in daily life is long," he explains. "Listen to every word spoken and you find countless Shoah references. The Shoah pervades the media and the public life, literature, music, art, education. These overt manifestations hide the Shoah's deepest influence. Israel's security policy, the fears and paranoia, feelings of guilt and belonging are products of the Shoah. Jewish-Arab, religious-secular, Sephardi-Ashkenazi relations are also within the realm of the Shoah. Sixty years after his suicide in Berlin, Hitler's hand still touches us." Burg goes so far as to suggest that the Shoah has caused Israel to become "the voice of the dead, speaking in the name of those who are no longer, more than in the name of those who are still alive."[32] It is a powerful comment about victims living in the grip of history, unable to escape the prison of a victim's worldview.

Burg and others make clear the relationship between this ever-present history of victimhood and Israel's military response to its neighbors and to the people of its occupied territories. According to Yael Zerubavel, it was the 1973 Yom Kippur War that transformed an earlier perception of Holocaust victims in Israel, altering the meaning of victimhood for Israeli Jews. The shocking discovery of the state's own vulnerability during this war "weakened earlier condemnation of the [Holocaust] victims for 'going like sheep to the slaughter.'" A new identification with Holocaust survivors grew out of the embrace of survival as a form of resistance to the Nazis, and of "evidence of inner, if not physical, strength."[33] The victim became the new model of moral and spiritual strength to inspire Israeli soldiers. This transformation is reflected, Zerubavel believes, in changes over the final several decades of the twentieth century in the Israeli commemoration of one of their most important historical events. Masada is the name of the site where approximately nine hundred Jews allegedly committed suicide to avoid being captured by the invading Roman army in the first century C.E.[34] In the early years of Israel's existence as a Jewish state, Zerubavel explains, narratives based on the ghetto uprisings and other forms of Jewish resistance were promoted, while the traumatic aspects of the Holocaust or of Masada were downplayed. In recent decades, however, these narratives have been transformed into tragic histories. They have turned vulnerability into strength. The determination never to allow such deadly events to recur—captured in the expression "Never again!"—turns victimhood into victory and accepts, even glorifies, the violent retribution of the victim.[35]

This evolution of Israeli identity is corroborated by others. Idith Zertal, an Israeli historian, claimed at the start of the second intifada in 2000 that "there has not been a war in Israel, from 1948 till the present ongoing outburst of violence... that has not been perceived, defined, and conceptualized in terms of the Holocaust." Auschwitz, she maintains, has become "Israel's main reference in its relations with a world defined repeatedly as anti-Semitic and forever hostile." The result is that Israel "has rendered itself immune to criticism, and impervious to a rational dialogue with the world around her."[36] We have only to consider our own responses to the conflict in Israel and Palestine to find evidence of the power of this immunity and imperviousness. The fear of offending Jews and appearing anti-Semitic stifles moral judgment and promotes a complicit silence. There appears to be no such corresponding fear of offending Palestinians and attendant worries about anti-Arab sentiment.

We would do well to heed Mamdani's warning that victor's justice comes with a price: an increased need to secure one's position as victor. The jailor becomes as tied to the jail as the prisoner, and so the victor must live in fear of the next round of battle. A permanent civil war ensues.[37] Burg concurs. The devastating consequences of such a defensive position are clear: "A state that lives by the sword and worships its dead is bound to live in a constant state of emergency, because everyone is a Nazi, everyone is an Arab, everyone hates us, the entire world is against us."[38] It leads to the worst excesses of the self-defense alibi, starkly evident in Arnon Sofer's proclamation in the epigraph to this chapter: "So, if we want to remain alive, we will have to kill and kill and kill. All day, every day. If we don't kill, we will cease to exist." As Giorgio Agamben puts it, the state that promotes a politics of security exercised by violence against terrorism turns itself terroristic, ironically transforming itself into a fragile organism. Security and terrorism then form a single deadly system, mutually justifying and legitimizing each other's actions.[39]

The victim thus occupies a very powerful place—a contentious claim, given that it flies in the face of decades of efforts to bring the plight of victims to our attention and recognize their rights. But the implications and effects of these efforts, particularly concerning questions of moral judgment and responsibility in the political realm, have not been fully explored. We might consider, for example, Israeli accounts of the January 2009 attacks on Gaza, in which we find no reference to the occupation, no acknowledgment of the displacement of Palestinians or of the fact that the living conditions in Gaza—the lack of freedoms, rights, and basic necessities—have anything to do with this occupation. Many responses to those attacks in fact demonstrate a frightening logic: "You forced us to kill you."[40] Thus, while the disproportionate brutality is undisputed, this does not matter in countless discussions of this military offensive. Any mention of factors that tarnish the image of Israel as anything but a victim state is silenced. Israelis must believe that *they* are the victims—displaying willful blindness, as many have argued—in order to carry on the occupation. "In this myopic fantasy land," wrote Seamus Milne in the *Guardian*, as the attacks on Gaza raged, "there is no 61-year national dispossession, no refugee camps, no occupations, no siege, no multiple Israeli violations of UN security council resolutions and the Geneva conventions, no illegal wall, no routine assassinations, no prisoners and no West Bank."[41]

"Never forget" has been the mantra of Jewish and Israeli politics for three decades, according to Baruch Kimmerling, who argues that the obsessive commemoration of Jewish victimhood has blinded much of the Jewish community to Israel's real position in the world. The result has been this willful blindness toward the humanity of Palestinians, and to a reasonable political solution to the conflict. Kimmerling asks whether "the cult of death" in Israel has come to an end, or whether the prevailing ideology will last another hundred years. "To choose the former option is to grant priority to the lives of Israel's citizens, Jewish and Arab. To choose the latter is to remain a community of victims," which can only lead to disaster.[42] Kimmerling wrote these words in late 2004. Seven years later, we are no closer to the better option.

"Something Has to Be Invented"

At the end of Gwynne Dyer's comprehensive account of the history of war, he relates a story about a group of olive baboons in Kenya called the "Forest Troop," a group that Robert Sapolsky and Lisa Share have studied since 1978. Over several years in the 1980s, the most brutal and despotic alpha males of the troop, who ate frequently from the dumpsters of a nearby tourist lodge, became infected with bovine tuberculosis and died. This meant that the less aggressive males—those who steered clear of the dumpster so as to avoid fights with the alpha males—survived. After the death of the alpha males, the normally vicious baboon society changed completely. As Dyer puts it, "the surviving members relaxed and began treating one another more decently."[43] The males still fought, but aggression was more likely to occur between males of equal rank rather than between the strong and the weak. At the same time, an increase in grooming was observed, and hormone samples revealed far lower stress levels in even the lowest-ranking males than in other, more aggressive troops.[44] Females stopped being attacked at all. Years later, when the range of male personalities in the Forest Troop had returned to the normal distribution of dominant alphas and submissive, timid types, the behavior of the troop still had not returned to normal: the new behaviors had become entrenched in the troop's culture. As one biologist put it, the aggressive new males were obviously learning that "we don't do things like that around here."[45]

This marvelous anecdote, about animals typically seen as "shackled by their genes to viciously aggressive norms,"[46] unsettles our assumption that violence is necessary or inevitable, particularly as a response to violence. It is easy to forget that there are alternatives to violence when violence is normalized. During the trial of Adolf Eichmann, which Hannah Arendt covered for the *New Yorker*, stories were shared of Germans who assisted Jews during the Nazi years. Arendt recalls the story of a German sergeant, Anton Schmidt, who helped members of the Jewish underground for five months before his arrest and execution. While other German soldiers testified that their own disobedience would have led to a useless sacrifice, since they would have died in anonymity, Arendt argues that such dissent would not have been practically useless, at least not in the long run. Someone always lives to tell the story. The lesson is simple: "Politically speaking, it is that under conditions of terror most people will comply but *some people will not*, just as the lesson of the countries to which the Final Solution was proposed is that 'it could happen' in most places but *it did not happen everywhere*. Humanly speaking, no more is required, and no more can reasonably be asked, for this planet to remain a place fit for human habitation."[47] We spend an inordinate amount of time considering the cases of those who do comply rather than looking for the cases of those who resist. For Ted Honderich to be right that terrorism is the Palestinians' only recourse would mean that every nation or people *without exception* must turn to violence in the struggle for freedom. If even one person or group chooses another path, then nonviolent action remains a permanent possibility. Arendt is making a forceful claim: all that is required for this planet to remain fit for human habitation is the knowledge that some people will dissent under conditions of terror. There is always a choice, always agency, even if severely restricted. And as the anomaly of the Forest Troop baboons tells us, alternatives can establish new patterns and unsettle long accepted norms. If the baboons can do it, why can't we?

A direction out of the quagmire of the Israeli-Palestinian conflict, then, is to start with those dissenting voices and actions that *do not comply*. Like Arendt's anecdote about the German soldier, we have numerous examples, rarely drawn to our attention, that prove that this planet is fit for human habitation. Rami

Elhanan, in a documentary called *ScaredSacred*, relates the terrible story of the day his daughter was killed by a suicide bomber in Jerusalem. There is no blame in his response, but a conscious and concerted effort to accept mutual responsibility for a different kind of future. After hearing about a bombing in the center of Jerusalem, Elhanan finds himself running through the streets in search of his daughter. Later that evening he is at the morgue, witnessing a sight that he "will never, ever be able to forget for the rest of [his] life." From that moment on, he explains, he became a different person:

> You change completely—set of values, perspectives, everything, your genes change. You come back home and you are alone and you have to look yourself in the mirror. Where are you going to take this new and unbearable pain? What are you going to do with the rest of your life, now that you are a different person? And there are only two alternatives. The one is the obvious and the natural and the way most people choose, which is the way of retaliation and revenge because when someone kills your fourteen-year-old little girl and you are very, very angry and you want to get even. This is natural, this is only natural.
>
> You start to think, will killing someone else bring back my baby? Will causing pain to someone else ease my pain in any way? Of course not. And it takes time, a long time, to choose the other way. The other way is the way of understanding. Why did it happen? How could such a thing happen? And the most important thing: what can you do, now that you have the burden on your shoulders to prevent it from happening to others?[48]

This is an extraordinary and powerful passage. Elhanan acknowledges that the loss of his daughter, Smadar, who was killed by two Palestinian suicide bombers while shopping for schoolbooks with friends on September 4, 1997, provoked in him "an urge for revenge that is stronger than death."[49] It was a meeting with others who had lost beloved family members that changed his perspective. Elhanan became one of several hundred members of an organization called the Parents Circle–Families Forum (PCFF) that has brought together bereaved Palestinian and Israeli families since 1995 in order to promote peace and reconciliation, provide mutual support, influence the public and policymakers, and "prevent the usage of bereavement as a means of expanding enmity between our peoples."[50] The organizing principle is that the unbearable pain of losing a family member is an experience common to all human beings. Such suffering establishes common ground by rendering everyone who loses a loved one a victim of the conflict.

There is no dearth of similar stories in Israel and Palestine of individuals who attempt to reach out across the multiple barriers—both material and psychological—thrown up by the occupation, to establish contact with those on the other side, or of groups who work tirelessly to bridge the gaps of understanding between two peoples.[51] They provide us with examples of those who do not comply, often at great risk to their own lives. Like Elhanan, they decide that hostility and revenge are not the destiny of the Israeli and Palestinian people. "Nowhere is it written that we must continue dying and sacrificing our children forever," Elhanan declares in *ScaredSacred*, in what has become a vicious circle of violence and retribution. The intolerable pain of losing a family member can lead to cooperation and strength. "Our blood is the same color, our pain is the same pain, the taste of our tears are as bitter," Elhanan insists. "If we can talk to one another, then anyone can. And this really gives you a reason for existence." It is a dramatic rewriting of the script: from "victory for us is to see you suffer" to "victory for us is to feel your suffering." This is a critical starting point.

It is important to note that the effectiveness of groups like the PCFF depends on the destabilization of the victim/perpetrator opposition, mapped onto the identity of one group in conflict with another. Members of the PCFF exemplify the kind of inventiveness Balibar alludes to when he calls for a postnational politics. Suffering is the unifying factor; it no longer matters whether the parent who grieves the loss of her child is an Israeli Jew in Jerusalem or a Palestinian Arab in the Gaza Strip. Their pain is the same.

The "way of understanding," however, must extend into the realm of politics. Groups that seek to educate for peace by bringing hostile individuals and communities into dialogue provide us with essential examples of non-compliance, examples that make it impossible to ignore the agency of victims and perpetrators alike and allow us to see the dehumanized other as human. It introduces empathy into the equation. But we must be wary of projects and analyses that do not challenge the imbalance of power. Unfortunately, individual change and empathy are not enough if there is no corresponding change at the political and institutional level. What is required is the opportunity for a people to organize and act as a political entity. There must be allowances for dissent, and the acknowledgment of grief before it turns to grievance, and this must occur at all levels of political decision making. Groups like PCFF and individuals like Rami Elhanan demonstrate that identities can be transcended, but without a corresponding change in the structures of power that keep these identities in place, the way of understanding won't help much. The Palestinian and the Israeli, sharing tea in friendship, return to drastically different political and economic realities when they go home.

Could we not make the quest for political solutions, rather than violent ones—taking for granted Arendt's distinction between these terms—the common denominator when working toward a resolution of conflict? Mamdani elaborates an idea he calls "survivor's justice," which does not mean justice only for the surviving victims but for all those who have survived a civil war or genocide. It is a notion he uses to transcend the bipolar terms of victim and perpetrator. He asks, in the context of Rwanda today, whether we couldn't invite into the community of those concerned with political transformation and the creation of a future *only* those willing to forgo violence. It is the victor who must reach out to the vanquished, as only the victor can transcend the opposition between the two by defining both as survivors. The crucial point here is to destabilize the binary opposition between victim and perpetrator, give up the right to hate, as Fanon urged, relinquish claims to being the first and most aggrieved victim, and come to terms with the fact that power is not the precondition for survival. As Mamdani puts it, we must consider the opposite possibility "that the prerequisite to cohabitation, to reconciliation, and a common political future may indeed be to give up the monopoly of power."[52]

Those who exist under the conditions imposed on Palestinians in the occupied territories, who survive a suicide bomb attack and live with the perpetual fear of terror, or who live through genocide, may scoff at this suggestion. Mamdani is aware of this when he writes that we cannot ignore the fact that "must weigh like a nightmare on the minds of the Tutsi survivors": that they are an imperiled minority living under a dark cloud of fear that they will once again have to submit to the very majority that attempted to eliminate them.[53] How dare we ask a victimized population to make themselves vulnerable again, to give up the balance of power that leads to the perception of greater security?

The enormity of this request hit home when I participated in what turned out to be a politically contentious conference (contentious for all the wrong reasons) in 2009 at York University in Toronto called "Israel/Palestine: Mapping Models of Statehood and Paths to Peace." An Israeli academic spoke eloquently and sincerely about the terrible fear that governed the everyday lives of his fellow Israelis. There was a loud chorus of both sympathy and protest from the audience, activists and academics alike. We who are personally untouched by the conflict could perhaps understand this man's plea, could try to put ourselves in the shoes of those who live with political insecurity and instability. But the Palestinians were enraged and hurt. How could you be so audacious, they cried, as to ask for understanding for your security needs when we (or our families) live under the occupation of your government? They found it outrageous that the Israeli occupiers could portray themselves as a victim nation bobbing precariously in a sea of Arab hostility. But Israeli fear is nurtured on a daily basis—its only antidote, political and military power.

In effect, Jeff Halper is asking Israelis to work toward survivor's justice. An Israeli anthropologist and the coordinator of the Israeli Committee Against House Demolitions (ICAHD), Halper advocates a "reframing" of the conflict that stresses three points: first, that an occupation exists and is the center of the conflict; second, that Israel is the strong party in the conflict and thus the only one that can actually end the occupation and be held accountable for its policies and actions; and third, that the occupation is "not defensive or reactive" but a vehicle for establishing Israel's permanent control over the entire country. Central to ICAHD's reframing is the rejection of Israel's security reasoning and its result: the casting of itself as a victim in what Israeli prime minister Benjamin Netanyahu calls "a tough neighborhood of bullies." "This is a crucial part of the security framing," Halper writes, "since it relieves Israel of all responsibility. A victim, after all, is a victim and cannot be held accountable, since his or her actions come merely out of self-defense. Being a victim, however, is a very powerful place to be. Israel can be a regional superpower and an occupying power, yet have responsibility. Indeed, it is the flight from responsibility that impels the security framing." Halper explains the distortion that must occur for Israel to cast itself as a victim, given that Zionists have held disproportionate power since the turn of the twentieth century, when the Zionist movement gained international support denied to Palestinians and other Arabs. It also gained economic and military superiority. Israel is now a regional superpower, with an economy three times larger than those of Egypt, Palestine, Jordan, Syria, and Lebanon put together (it is more than forty times the size of the Palestinian economy), and receives more than $3 billion annually in military aid from the United States. In addition, it is the world's fourth-largest nuclear power and an occupying power. This asymmetry of power, Halper insists, demands an asymmetry of responsibility from Israel.[54]

ICAHD defines itself as "a non-violent Israeli direct-action organization" established in 1997 to end the occupation. The focus of its resistance is the demolition of Palestinian homes in the occupied territories by the Israeli military. Since 1967 more than twenty-four thousand Palestinian homes have been destroyed, more than 95 percent of them for political reasons having nothing to do with security. The intent is "to either drive the Palestinians out of the country altogether, or to confine the four million residents of the West Bank, East Jerusalem and Gaza to small, crowded, impoverished and disconnected enclaves, thus effectively foreclosing any viable Palestinian entity and ensuring Israeli control." Members of ICAHD operate on several levels. They physically block bulldozers about to demolish homes and raise funds abroad to facilitate the rebuilding of new homes; advocate within Israel and internationally for a just peace by disseminating information and networking; and collaborate with Palestinian organizations and communities, providing strategic practical support, including legal assistance to families facing demolition.[55]

Once again we encounter an organization whose focal point is shared human need and a concerted effort to work together on a common project. In this case it is not the emotional work of grief that is shared but the construction of homes. But "reframing" the conflict is a challenge, given that in any debate, the party that succeeds in framing the issue and determining the terms of the discussion inevitably wins. Israel has a great advantage, Halper points out, since it determines the logic of the debate, leading to its desired conclusions. The Israeli peace camp and the Palestinians themselves lack the support of the state agencies, public relations agencies, professional spokespersons, and access to the media that Israel enjoys. "We are thus thrust into the weak position of refuter," Halper concludes, "left only to respond to Israel's charges yet without the space to present a coherent, credible and persuasive alternative framing of our own. Confined to countering the arguments of the 'framer,' respondents (called the 'negative side' in debates) invariably come across as defensive, inarticulate and unconvincing."[56] The problem is not how to make peace—Halper sees viable solutions and an overwhelming will for peace among Israelis and Palestinians—"but how to overcome the fear and obfuscation by which Israel's gatekeepers deflect all attempts to arrive at a just peace, manipulating the thought and feelings of peoples and governments that don't, or won't, 'get it.'" It isn't about taking "sides," then, but about generating critical political discussion and effective action that will help Israelis, Palestinians, peoples of the wider Arab and

Muslim worlds, and all others affected by this conflict to get out of "this mess we share and suffer from."[57]

Dreams

We can conclude from this brief discussion that in the case of Israel/ Palestine, *which* victim's worldview we defend depends on a number of factors, including which side of the political spectrum we find ourselves on and whose interests are being promoted. There is compassion for Israel as a nation of victims—both historically, as the victims of genocide in Nazi Germany, and currently, as the victims of terrorism—and a corresponding apology or acceptance of the need for violent security measures. There is compassion for Palestinians as an occupied people, displaced by the creation of the state of Israel and collectively punished for existing at all, and accompanying excuses for the acts of revenge on the part of Hamas. What they have in common is that they respectively stake their claims to ultimate victimhood and justify their actions with the moral power these claims confer. What the Palestinians do not share with Israel is military strength; the economic, military, and political support of the United States, Canada, and other Western nations; wealth; readily available water and electricity; freedom of movement; basic human rights; and a thriving civil society.

Our responses to the conflict are already conditioned by a conceptual framework that is not easy to question. While victim discourses on both sides have very different origins, they share an oppositional understanding of victim versus perpetrator that sabotages every attempt to refuse to take sides and demand responsibility—albeit to different degrees—of all actors. This is why, at teach-ins or academic panel discussions, the audience is immediately sucked into choosing sides by an almost irresistible competition for ultimate victim status. I am always shocked by what happens at these events—how reasonably intelligent, otherwise considerate and level-headed faculty and students can be seen hurling insults at one another, or crying while others hiss and boo. The impulse to defend and justify oneself or one's political cause is powerful.

Rather than continue this failed dialogue between two sides, unequal in power yet equally entrenched in a victim's binary worldview, we need to reframe the conflict in a way that will lead to alternative political solutions. No one is suggesting that such alternatives are easy to carry out, but we who merely write about them are the first to complain about our own armchair thinking and throw up our hands in despair that there are no solutions. Alternative examples of a different political path are not hard to find if we only look. This is the challenge we need to meet: to sift through the misinformation and the dogma, resist the invitation to believe only in dualistic identities, and listen to those voices of sanity that are no less in the midst of the crisis than many of those who mislead us. We must not forget that there are world leaders and people in positions of power who want us to believe that there are only military solutions. Some of the best critical analyses of the Israeli occupation of the Palestinians, and of this seemingly irresolvable conflict, are coming from extraordinarily courageous Israeli Jewish and Palestinian scholars and activists. We need to keep in mind that Israelis and Palestinians are not necessarily who we think they are, and may not hold the views we think they do, especially since most of what we know of them comes from media and government sources, all promoting a particular agenda. We are led to believe that Israelis present a united front in support of their government policies, and that Palestinians are united in their support of terrorism and their desire to eliminate the state of Israel. While it does not look good for Israeli activism against the occupation at the moment, thousands of Israeli citizens protested the war on Gaza in early 2009—voices we did not hear in the mainstream media.

I return to my opening point that humans are capable of carrying out extraordinarily evil deeds while feeling righteous. Each time I hear the demand that the perspectives of "both sides" be presented in any discussion of the Israeli-Palestinian crisis—from intelligent, compassionate individuals who are normally severely critical of the use of violent means to end conflicts—I am struck anew by the terrible power of this righteousness. This power is the result of the moral status we give to victims. But it is not only as victims of one of the worst genocides of the twentieth century that Israeli Jews benefit from the support of the United States, Canada, and other complicit or indifferent states the world over. It is as victims of terrorism.

The "globalization of terror" gives Balibar reason to believe that the Palestinian struggle is "a universal cause." Israel, he notes, long ago began to identify Palestinian armed resistance with "international terrorism," and the globalization of terror has become the common goal of both Islamic fundamentalists and the U.S. administration since 2001. Halper draws our attention to the global implications of what he calls a new "global system of pacification" that includes extensive surveillance and control measures. It is a system promoted and perfected by the Israeli government in collusion with governments like our own, a system in which the brutal quelling of insurgency, in the name of security for a people under attack, is not only tolerated by the world but confidently justified.[58] The conflict is not the "Palestinian problem," as it is often called by the world's leaders and media, but has an impact far beyond the Middle East. Halper cites Martin Luther King's famous dictum that "injustice anywhere is a threat to justice everywhere." Like all conflicts, Halper concludes, the Israel-Palestine conflict ultimately affects all of us, especially in that the occupation could not be maintained without the active complicity of our own governments, wherever we are.[59]

A world in which the paradigm of terror and security structures all our global relationships will ultimately become unlivable. What we need instead is to focus on forming a new community of political subjects that is not founded on victimized identities that righteously secure themselves from vulnerability and accountability. We really have no choice but to find a way to live together. Neither the Palestinians nor the Israelis are going anywhere. The dream of an end to the Jewish state is as unviable and catastrophic as the desire to eliminate all Palestinians.

3

INDELIBLE WOUNDS

Twenty-two years later I am still dangling over the ground by
dislocated arms, panting, and accusing myself.

I am not the same person who set off, singing, on that sunny
Fourth of July in the French countryside. I left her in a rocky creek bed at
the bottom of a ravine. I had to in order to survive.

These are the words of victims who have survived brutal acts of violence.[1] They provide heartrending glimpses into what it means to be reduced to a suffering body, and to survive the betrayal, exposure, and humiliation of another's dehumanizing act. Listening to a victim recounting an experience of violation invites a profound identification with the suffering of another, the vulnerability we share exposed on the face of the speaker or the white of the page. Those of us who have never been victims of violence are unsettled or perhaps frightened by the knowledge that we too could be tortured, murdered, or raped. We may imagine the sensations of pain in our own bodies, or entertain for a brief, terrible moment what it would feel like to witness the victimization of someone we love. While we may never be able fully to comprehend suffering we have not ourselves experienced, we can identify with another's pain at some level; we can attempt through imagination to feel as others feel. This is empathy—imaginatively inhabiting the other's body and emotive being. Without it, we appear less than human, able to witness or perhaps even commit acts of cruelty without compunction.

The loss of trust in another's capacity for empathy and assistance when we are in need is critical to the experience of victimhood, no matter what the cause. For Jean Améry, who survived torture in a Nazi camp, the certainty of receiving help from another is indeed fundamental to the constitution of the human psyche. We expect that others will be concerned with our plight, will respond to our pain and injury or rescue us from danger. Responses to the disappointment of this expectation are as varied as the acts of violation that destroy our trust in others. We do not all draw from the same wellspring of emotional or mental strength.

Our need to comprehend, to truly identify with a victim's pain, and to respond humanely, with compassion, necessitates listening to the narratives of victims. This is not, however, passive listening. We may be moved by the loveless childhood of the person who grows up to become a murderer or sexual predator, but without appropriate moral judgment we ignore the fact that many unloved children do not murder and that our compassion—if it provides an alibi for inaction—could put the lives of others at risk. We may feel immense sympathy for a colonized or enslaved people, but this sympathy must not occlude reasoned judgment against retributive enslavement, or we will forget that new victims will in turn claim their right to retribution. There is no end to this bitter cycle.

Should the injury of a victim-turned-perpetrator be a mitigating factor in making legal, moral, or political decisions? In this and following chapters, I argue that, yes, we should take into account the pain and suffering of wrongdoers who are or have been victims. This does not entail a blind veneration for victims we believe are no longer responsible for actions that may have been *reactions* to their own victimization but a recognition that "some fates are simply too agonizing to endure."[2] If we take into account the elaborate defense systems an individual psyche can erect to protect one's consciousness from harm or even destruction—defense systems that may rely on preemptive attacks—we throw into question any simple rational account of the self recovering from injury. To understand the condition of victimhood, we need to understand that these defenses may prevent the victim from assuming her own responsibility. What one victim may heroically overcome may be another's undoing; there is no equality at the psychic level.

In chapter 6 we will confront more explicitly the tension often perceived between compassion and judgment, between, on the one hand, our empathic response to a victim's suffering and, on the other, the need for moral judgment and accountability. When these are considered mutually exclusive, the victim is left without the very agency necessary for survival. First, we need to explore in more detail the condition of victimhood, attending carefully to the ambivalence of victims toward this condition and to the ambiguity of their experiences. What follows, then, is a phenomenology of victimhood based on the narratives of several victims we have come to know quite well through their own writings. But it is more than a phenomenology of experience; these narratives are explored in the context of a developing discourse on trauma that began in the twentieth century, informed by psychology, psychoanalysis, feminism, anticolonialism, and military psychiatry. My arguments in this chapter rest on the assumption that victimhood—how it is experienced, how it is interpreted by others, and how one recovers from it—must be investigated in a context that is at once intellectual, political, and historical. This means taking into account the development of ideas about trauma and post-traumatic stress disorder (PTSD) in particular, ideas that have been instrumental in shaping the meaning of victimhood.

Who is a victim? In any given situation it is not always clear who the victim is, but this need not lead to a paralyzing relativism that defines and classifies victims solely on the power of their testimony and the intensity of their suffering. We may be able to isolate certain features of the experience, but there is no universal response to the condition of victimhood, no static "victim identity" unmarked by cultural beliefs and political ideas or movements. I wish to show here that the ambiguity and complexity of victimhood should inspire in us a deeper reflection on the condition and the terms of its survival.

The Seeds of Decay

The final chapter of *The Wretched of the Earth* begins with these lines: "But the war goes on. And for many years to come we shall be bandaging the countless and sometimes indelible wounds inflicted on our people by the colonialist onslaught."[3] What follow are case studies from Frantz Fanon's psychiatric practice, descriptions of the symptoms of psychosis, homicidal impulses, and anxiety disorders—"the seeds of decay," as he calls them (181). Whether it is the torturer who "has a constant desire to give everyone a beating" (197) or the Algerian refugee children who exhibit noise phobias and sadistic tendencies (206), the origin of the psychic injury is evident: "Because it is a systematized negation of the other, a frenzied determination to deny the other any attribute of humanity, colonialism forces the colonized to constantly ask the question: 'Who am I in reality?'" Beyond being victims of domination, a colonized people is a people bereft of its humanity (182). This is the source of immense psychic suffering.

Fanon has bequeathed to us an intimate description of the effects of colonization on the Algerian victim of French occupation. The colonized subject experiences his victimization psychically and corporeally; he expresses symptomatically on his body the mental disturbances that result. The "fact of blackness" stamped on the colonized body is an "epidermal racial schema"—the black man is reduced to a body only, "sealed into crushing objecthood." The colonized self is fragmented, dislocated, constructed as something despicable by the white man who batters him down with the weight of racial stereotypes and gives back his body "sprawled out, distorted, recolored." Thus imprisoned by the white man, the colonized man in turn makes himself an object. He experiences a split, alienated consciousness; enslaved by the colonizer, he ends up enslaving himself in the belief that he is truly inferior. "What else could it be for me but an amputation, an excision, a hemorrhage that spattered my whole body with black blood?"[4] This alienated consciousness, elaborated by many others interested in the effects of racism on the body and psyche, is a crucial manifestation of the worldview of the victim that Mamdani urges us to take into account.

Central to the experience of colonization, then, is an alienated relationship to oneself, a self reduced to the inhuman—a body somehow bereft of the life that defines it as human—a colonized subject "fabricated" by the colonist that nevertheless becomes the colonized subject's only identity (2). When the Manichean nature of the colonial situation reaches its logical conclusion, the "native" is reduced to the state of an animal. The violence the colonist inflicts on the colonized causes an aggression turned first against the colonized subject's own people and perhaps even against himself (15). Given the numerous examples that confront us today—of violence that begets other forms of violence, from perpetrator, to victim, to other victims, back to the perpetrator—the alienated consciousness Fanon describes is applicable beyond colonial situations.

The colonial situation sows and nourishes "seeds of decay." Fanon the psychiatrist never loses sight of the indiscriminate distribution of this rot, as the psychic strife of colonialism spreads easily between victim and perpetrator, but it is clear who is responsible and who will suffer the most. "In the colonial world, the colonized's affectivity is kept on edge like a running sore flinching from a caustic agent. And the psyche retracts, is obliterated, and finds an outlet through muscular spasms that have caused many an expert to classify the colonized as hysterical" (19). The particular psychoses and neuroses of the colonized are difficult to "cure," difficult to fit into the social environment of colonization. Fanon calls the defensive position born of this violent confrontation a "colonized personality" or "sensibility" (182). But at some point, if colonization remains unchallenged and a certain threshold is passed, the defenses of the colonized collapse, and mental disorders proliferate. The triggering factor is "the bloody, pitiless atmosphere, the generalization of inhuman practices, of people's lasting impression that they are witnessing a veritable apocalypse" (183). The effects are hardly benign, Fanon writes: "These disorders last for months, wage a massive attack on the ego, and almost invariably leave behind a vulnerability virtually visible to the naked eye" (184).

Case studies from Fanon's own practice demonstrate the challenges of eradicating these seeds of decay. We read of the Algerian man who becomes impotent following his wife's rape by French soldiers. Initially, he feels anger, followed by acceptance, until a few weeks later, when he realizes that his wife was raped because the soldiers were looking for *him*. It was the rape, he explains, "of a tenacious woman who was prepared to accept anything rather than give up her husband. And that husband *was me*. That woman had saved my life and had protected the network. It was my fault she had been dishonored" (188). Yet he has trouble overcoming the feeling that "everything that had to do with [his] wife was rotten" (189). Fanon also tells the story of this man's compatriot, a thirty-seven-year-old Algerian who survives the massacre of all the other men in his village, afterward becoming "overexcited with violent mood swings and shouting." He admits that he is lucky to be alive, and vehemently claims his life at the expense of other lives: "In life, it's kill or be killed . . . . There are some French among us . . . . They're disguised as Arabs . . . . They've all got to be killed . . . . Give me a machine gun. Everyone wants to kill me. But I'll fight back. I'll kill them all, every one of them" (191).

The seeds of decay are sown but also reaped by the perpetrator. We read of the European police inspector who suffers from his work as a torturer. For some weeks he has felt that something is wrong; he loses his appetite, experiences nightmares and "fits of madness," the desire to punch anyone who gets in his way. He violently assaults his children, including a twenty-month-old baby, and decides to get help after he turns on his wife, tying her to a chair, beating her, and shouting, "I'm going to teach you once and for all who's the boss around here" (197). He explains to the "nerve specialists" that he is being used as a foot soldier and describes in dreadful detail the challenges of working in the interrogation rooms. What bothers him, however, is his aggression at home. Fanon tells us that the young man had no intention of giving up his job as a torturer but wanted to get help in order "to torture Algerian patriots without having a guilty conscience, without any behavioral problems, and with a total peace of mind" (198–99).

It is curious that *The Wretched of the Earth* is read as a call to revolution, *necessarily* violent—its first chapter, "On Violence," garnering the greatest interest—with little acknowledgment of the conclusions that follow from Fanon's psychiatric practice. In the final pages he eloquently demands of his comrades that they "reach for the light," abandoning dreams, beliefs, and old friendships. He appears to be urging them to abandon an ideological identity politics, since it is impossible to dissociate that identity from the one conferred on the black body by the white colonizer. He elaborates this in *Black Skin, White Masks*, in which he criticizes those who seek refuge in an absolute black identity in the name of empowerment, those who, with rage in their mouths and abandon in their hearts, bury themselves in "the vast black abyss." "We shall see," he warns, "that this attitude, so heroically absolute, renounces the present and the future in the name of a mystical past."[5]

It is an uncompromising position: the refuge sought in an absolute black identity—in this case an essentialist victimhood—however justified by the injury of injustice, forecloses a healthy future. There is no future possible in clinging to the identities—colonized or colonizer, victim or perpetrator—forged in a colonial past through the imposition of violent, Manichean relations. Thus, despite Fanon's appreciation for the empowerment of the colonized subject through counterviolent tactics, he recognizes that there is no future for the victim if the victim neglects his own responsibility for it. Despite the moving description of the wretched condition of the colonized subject, Fanon stresses that the colonized must resist becoming the slaves of the slavery that dehumanized their ancestors, must refuse to lock themselves into a world of retroactive reparations. "Let us not lose time in useless laments or sickening mimicry," he writes, referring to the Europe that rules over the world with cynicism and violence. Humanity must be taken to another level, a step forward rather than backward. In words that strike the reader as a condemnation of violence, revolutionary or not, Fanon writes that it is a question "of not dragging man in directions which mutilate him, of not imposing on his brain tempos that rapidly obliterate and unhinge it. The notion of catching up [to Europe] must not be used as a pretext to brutalize man, to tear him from himself and his inner consciousness, to break him, to kill him."[6] The indelible wounds of war—gaping on the torturers as well as the tortured, the killers as well as their victims—is argument enough that another way must be found.

Fanon's antidote to this renunciation of a future is not to accept the amputation of victimhood but to claim a future in the name of simple being in relation to other beings. "Superiority? Inferiority?" Fanon asks. "Why not the quite simple attempt to touch the other, to feel the other, to explain the other to myself?" The alienation suffered by the colonized is reversed neither in the celebration of an empowering black identity nor in the attempt to be white, for both of these projects are defined within the context of white colonialism. Fanon frames this response in the language of rights—rights that he *will not claim* as a man of color—such as the right to hope that the white man will feel guilt, the right to destroy white pride, to claim reparations, or to "cry out [his] hatred at the white man." The only right that Fanon does claim is "that of demanding human behavior from the other."[7]

The Melancholic Victim

Fanon's renunciation of the "amputation" of victimhood might be considered unusual in the context of current views of victimhood. His attention to the agency of the victim, whether he is making an apology for revolutionary violence or urging the colonized to refuse both the mentality of victimization and the inhumanity of the European, provides a provocative opening into the potentially problematic or even pathological response of the victim to the condition of victimhood. Fanon anticipates more recent work by scholars interested in contemporary formulations of racial identity and relations, wary of the naturalization of injury and the neglect of the victim's own investment in the condition of victimhood. The term "melancholia" has become important in this discussion; whether in the context of colonialism or of racism, the idea that grief can turn to grievance rather than resolution recalls our discussion of *ressentiment* in chapter 1. Nietzsche's attention to the narcissism that leads to *ressentiment* in the victim, to what Wendy Brown describes as the attachment to one's subordinate status or wounds, has some affinity with Freud's explanation for this attachment, underscoring the ambivalence of the experience of victimhood. The "diminution" of self-regard that results from mourning gone wrong, according to Freud, has contributed to the understanding, evident throughout Fanon's work, of the "double consciousness" of the victim of racism or colonialism.

In his 1917 essay "Mourning and Melancholia," Freud distinguishes melancholia from mourning as a state of dejection, a pathological form of grief unlike the healthy, normal response to loss. In mourning a beloved object, lost through death or abandonment, the libido must do the work of withdrawing its attachment to the object. Naturally, this incites fierce opposition, Freud points out, an opposition so intense that sometimes a turning away from reality occurs. In the normal case, the work of mourning is carried out bit by bit, requiring "a great expense of time and cathectic energy" during which the existence of the lost object is prolonged in the psyche through memories and expectations. When the work of mourning is completed, however, the ego becomes free and uninhibited again.[8] Through the finite process of mourning, the lost object is relinquished and eventually replaced.[9]

Successfully completing the work of mourning thus involves a narcissistic directing of energies inward in order to assimilate the lost object and the feelings of loss associated with it, in an effort to rebuild the ego.[10] In melancholia, however, this attempt at assimilation fails. Freud describes the mental features of melancholia as identical to those of mourning—"painful dejection, cessation of interest in the outside world, loss of the capacity to love, inhibition of all activity"—but adds to this "an extraordinary diminution" of self-regard. The melancholic displays "an impoverishment of his ego on a grand scale." While in mourning the world has become poor and empty, in melancholia the ego itself becomes "worthless, incapable of achievement and morally despicable." Instead of being assimilated, the lost object is swallowed whole, a paralyzing process for the melancholic that ironically gives rise to what Freud calls "critical agency." Stuck with the object, the melancholic begins to criticize himself for attributes associated with the lost object, for the subject does not know or recognize what has been lost.[11]

Whether one agrees with Freud's analysis, and the psychoanalytic framework it assumes, what remains fascinating is the recognition that victims may internalize the beliefs that lead to their subordination, and the description of this internalization as undesirable, even pathological. Much has been written about this split or alienated consciousness in the field of race studies.[12] W. E. B. Du Bois notes that the double consciousness of the black man, who sees himself through his own eyes but also through the eyes of the white man, leads tragically to shame and to "a hesitant and doubtful striving" that makes him appear powerless and weak. Prejudice, Du Bois explains, inevitably brings about self-abnegation on the part of the black man, echoed and enforced by the larger culture, "the Nation." "We are diseased and dying ... we cannot write, our voting is vain; what need of education, since we must always cook and serve?" And the Nation responds, yes, be content to be servants, and nothing more."[13]

With supreme irony, then, the melancholic in effect feeds on the lost object—manifesting the curiously nurturing feature of the impoverishment of melancholia. But the nourishment works both ways; the victim is not alone in this strange entanglement. Anne Anlin Cheng remarks that in the context of contemporary racial dynamics, as in the colonial world, this "feeding" means that the identity and authority of whites are secured through the melancholic introjection of racial others, which can't be completely relinquished or accommodated. Equally troubling, the "racial other" suffers similarly from a melancholia in which his racial identity is imaginatively reinforced through "the introjection of a lost, never-possible perfection, an inarticulable loss that comes to inform the individual's sense of his or her own subjectivity."[14] Evidently, these two "sides" are deeply entangled.

In Cheng's words, this process reveals "an intricate world of psychical negotiation that unsettles the simplistic division between power and powerlessness." "Like melancholia," she writes, "racism is hardly ever a clear rejection of the other. While racism is mostly thought of as a kind of violent rejection, racist institutions in fact often do not want to fully expel the racial other; instead, they wish to maintain that other within existing structures. . . . Segregation and colonialism are internally fraught institutions not because they have eliminated the other but because they need the very thing they hate or fear." We have moved from recognizing injury to naturalizing it, as Cheng astutely concludes, failing to attend sufficiently to the ways in which individuals and communities remain invested in maintaining certain identity categories "even when such identities prove to be prohibitive or debilitating." We naturalize injury by jumping from psychic injury to inherent disability and from descriptive to prescriptive psychological analyses.[15] An example is instructive here: Cheng reflects on a scene in Ralph Ellison's novel *Invisible Man*. After complaining that whites refuse to see him, the black narrator relates an incident in which he accidentally bumps into a white man at night who then glares at him insolently with his blue eyes and curses him. The narrator yells at him, demanding an apology, then beats the stranger, who continues to curse and struggle. "I kicked him profusely," he admits, but then realizes "that the man had not seen me, actually; that he, as far as he knew, was walking in the midst of a walking nightmare ... a man almost killed by a phantom."[16]

Is the white man the only one suffering from not seeing? Cheng asks. Could the white man also be invisible to the black man? The narrator accuses the other of blindness, but it may be that the white man was only cursing the black man for his clumsiness, and that the narrator's perception of his "insolence" was itself a melancholic response, evidence of self-denigration and wounded pride. The passage is ambiguous, according to Cheng:

> That invisibility is rarely a one-way street is one of its most insidious effects. In this confrontation, there is potential mutual invisibility and mutual projection. Indeed, the racial moment is born out of this dynamic locking of the two men in mutual projection. In a response that is both macho and hysterical, the narrator demonstrates that he is trapped, not by having been seen as invisible but by suspecting himself to be so. This is racial melancholia for the raced subject: the internalization of discipline and rejection—and the installation of a scripted context of perception.[17]

Cheng's analysis of the psychology of race relations corroborates Mamdani's argument for the necessity of scrutinizing the victim's "worldview." It provides an insightful, if contentious, psychological explanation for points made in previous chapters of this book. These conclusions do not mean that we should dismiss the suffering of the victim whose mourning turns into melancholia; on the contrary, we need to address the ambivalence and complexity of the process, arresting the development of grief into grievance before further violence occurs. In order to do this, we need to scratch below the surface of conscious desires and behavior to the desires and attachments of the unconscious. Ultimately, we will find many victims who are capable of the long, patient work necessary to alleviate psychic injury, as well as a few who may be incapable of it, whose lives are permanently maimed, or even threatened with destruction if their defense systems are disabled. But since we can never know this in advance, we must act *as if they can* overcome the obstacles to survival.

The Birth of Trauma

Fanon's description of the psychopathology of colonial racism was written at the height of anticolonialism and already presupposed a certain cultural acceptance of the effects of trauma. The history of this acceptance is important for understanding how our ideas about what constitutes victimhood have developed, and how we have come to naturalize injury.

According to Didier Fassin and Richard Rechtman in *The Empire of Trauma: An Inquiry into the Condition of Victimhood*, psychological trauma of the sort Fanon depicts has acquired global status. No longer confined to psychiatric vocabulary, they argue, it has "created a new language of the event."[18] Trauma has become normalized as a scar or imprint on an individual or collective victim, the means of relating present suffering to past violence. We speak of rape, genocide, torture, slavery, terrorist attacks, and natural disasters using the same language of trauma, whether clinically or metaphorically.

Fanon's emphasis on the psychological effects of colonization, following what amounts to an apology for revolutionary violence, cements an association we have come to take for granted between violent events and psychological trauma. We are familiar with the idea that acts of violence cause not only physical injury but psychic wounds that may be more irreparable, more indelible, than the wounds of the flesh. This point has not always been taken for granted. In the five decades since Fanon's death, attention to these indelible wounds, caused by political turmoil, racism, ethnopolitical conflict, and genocide, has burgeoned. The key term in this discussion is *trauma*. But Fassin and Rechtman warn us of two points obscured by this discourse: first, we forget that the idea that a person exposed to violence may be traumatized and consequently recognized as a victim is quite recent; and second, the pathos attached to the violence that causes trauma, understandable though it may be, "leads us to ignore the fact that social agents are not passive recipients of the label 'traumatized.'"[19] Damage, as Cheng reminds us, does not take away agency. The concept of trauma has political uses.

Consider the opening examples of Ruth Leys's genealogical study of trauma. In the spring of 1998 the story emerged that a group of young Ugandan girls had been abducted by members of the Lord's Resistance Army, a rebel group fighting government forces. The girls were forced to serve as "wives" and to assist in the killing of those captured, including girls who tried to escape. Eventually, the survivors were sent to trauma centers to recover. That same spring, in the United States, Paula Jones claimed that she suffered PTSD after her alleged sexual harassment by President Bill Clinton, including long-term symptoms of anxiety, intrusive thoughts and memories, and sexual aversion.

According to Leys, these examples illustrate the spectrum of issues raised by the notion of trauma, pointing to the "absolute indispensability of the concept," on the one hand, but, on the other, to the "debased currency" that the concept has acquired when applied to truly horrible events, as well as "to something as dubious as the long-term harm to Paula Jones."[20] That a reader may immediately protest that we cannot judge Jones's claim to have suffered trauma simply makes the point: trauma has moral and political currency.

Interest in the conceptualization of trauma has waxed and waned since the 1860s, when the British physician John Erichsen identified the symptomatic fear and nervous disturbances of railway accident victims, attributing them to the shock of the spine. The term acquired a more psychological meaning when Freud and his contemporaries Jean-Martin Charcot, Pierre Janet, and Josef Breuer used it to describe the wounding of the mind caused by sudden emotional shock. "Railway spine" or "railway brain" became "trauma neurosis," a concept that Charcot used as a model to confirm his hypotheses regarding hysteria. Freud came up with his own theory, famously linking female hysteria with an infantile experience of sexual trauma. Trauma neuroses had in common with hysteria a fixation on the moment of the traumatic event, for Freud, through dreams that replayed the event. It was the symptoms that testified to the existence of a forgotten or repressed trauma. No matter that Freud rejected his own theory that hysterics had experienced sexual trauma early in life; his ideas were instrumental in placing trauma definitively into the arena of the psyche.[21] Extreme terror or fright—whether the result of an external event like sexual abuse or the "internal force" of an already traumatic sexuality shared by all developing subjects—was thought to shatter the personality or psyche.[22]

The history of the modern concept of trauma is not a coherent story but one riddled with controversy. Disagreement persists on the most significant factors in the development of the concept, as well as on the definition and diagnosis of trauma. It is clear, however, that attitudes toward victims of traumatic events have shifted considerably over the course of the twentieth century.[23] Historical accounts of the concept point out various critical moments in its development: the passage of labor laws regarding financial compensation for victims of trauma; military psychiatry during World War I; the Nazi Holocaust and postwar psychoanalysis; colonial wars such as that in Algeria; the Vietnam War and the naming of PTSD as a clinical condition in 1980; feminist interventions in child abuse; and, most recently, the terrorist attacks of 9/11 and the global war on terror.

While it is impossible to trace in detail this compelling history here, a few critical moments are worth highlighting. It is particularly interesting to note the change in attitudes toward what was once called "shell shock." Recognition of the war neuroses of soldiers in World War I exposed the fact that men could exhibit the same symptoms of psychic suffering as the women Freud diagnosed as hysterics.[24] At that time, however, these soldiers did not receive much sympathy from the medical establishment, the military, or the public. Physical wounds were the marks of heroes, while psychological wounds were regarded with suspicion and treated with contempt. Traumatic neuroses among soldiers were thought to lower troop morale by conveying weakness and a pathetic submission to fear. Combat illness was thus the fault of the weak soldier, the antithesis of the heroism and sacrifice required of the man who fought and died for his country, the embodiment of a selfish desire to escape enemy fire and claim reparations if possible.[25] The patriotic ideal was too strong during World War I to permit any recognition of, or sympathy for, the effects of horror and violence on the soldier's psyche.

This attitude did not change much during World War II, according to Fassin and Rechtman.[26] Military psychiatrists continued to see traumatic neurosis as a consequence of the desire for compensation on the part of the weak, deficient soldier. Their objective was to treat shell shock and send the men back to the front. The image of psychologically destroyed men, Fassin and Rechtman tell us, "was intolerable in American eyes. The heroic ideal of the freedom fighter setting out to save old Europe and returning victorious, crowned with glory, did not match up with the haggard faces, the accounts of nightmares, of waking drenched in sweat, and of paralyzing fear, even far from the front." To demonstrate this fact, these authors ask us to consider the difference between the reaction to John Huston's documentary about the treatment of traumatized soldiers, *Let There Be Light*, when it was made in 1946 and when it was presented decades later, in 1981, at the Cannes Film Festival. The film is an honest exploration of the daily life of former World War II combatants living in a military hospital on Long Island. While their courage and sacrifice are featured, so are their fear, shame, and tears, as well as the brutality of some of the psychiatric methods used to treat them. The documentary was originally commissioned by the U.S. military as a propaganda film on the psychiatric treatment of soldiers. When military officials saw the reality the film portrayed, however, they refused to broadcast or distribute it. By 1981 a dramatic shift had occurred. By that time audiences were looking for new revelations about military and medical practices during and after World War II. They were already quite familiar with the fact that war can destroy the lives of survivors, who are scarred for life by the horrors of their experience, and they judged the film conventional and unoriginal.

Fassin and Rechtman conclude that in 1946 the nightmares of former combatants "had not yet come to represent traces of a collective memory that would persuade those with power in the world that such things must never again be allowed to happen." The suffering of a few men psychologically destroyed by war did not imply anything about the war itself. Traumatized soldiers were not victims to be honored for their sacrifice but frail men who needed to be cured at an early stage of their neuroses and returned to normal life. Objects of contempt and shame, they were to be pitied.

What happened in the intervening decades? It was not until after the Vietnam War that the long-term effects of combat became the subject of large-scale studies. Political pressure to recognize the predicament of soldiers psychologically harmed by war was instigated by the soldiers themselves, who refused to be stigmatized or forgotten and organized themselves into "rap groups." By the end of the 1970s these groups had put enough political pressure on the Veterans' Administration that a psychological treatment program called Operation Outreach was initiated. The impact of participating in war became a subject worthy of research. Studies of returning veterans raised awareness of the psychological disturbances caused by war, lending moral legitimacy to the antiwar movement. In 1980 the hard work of psychiatrists, social workers, and activists in acknowledging the psychic trauma of war veterans resulted in the official recognition of PTSD by the American Psychiatric Association.[27]

While the Vietnam War is often pinpointed as having the most significant impact on attitudes toward the soldier as a victim of war—particularly by raising the profile of PTSD—this trend began with World War II and the Nazi Holocaust. (I will say more later about the feminist movement, also a crucial influence at this time.) According to Fassin and Rechtman, the Holocaust was the starting point for the contemporary public manifestation of collective trauma. Although remembering was a gradual process—occurring not immediately after the discovery of the camps but through the narratives of survivors and the work of historians—it was the memory of the Holocaust that became a paradigm for trauma. The Holocaust, Fassin and Rechtman explain, represents "the most extreme reach of violence" and has thus become the reference point for all suffering. That this process of remembering developed after a period of silence attests precisely to its traumatic nature.[28]

The universalization of the pain and suffering of the Holocaust has led to a kind of "communion in trauma" through empathy. Cathy Caruth is a proponent of this idea, suggesting that "in a catastrophic age . . . trauma itself may provide the very link between cultures."[29] There is an urgent need, she argues, to speak and listen from the site of trauma and to cultivate a collective sensitivity to the misfortunes of the world from our own wounds. Fassin and Rechtman rightly complain that this kind of universalization trivializes trauma. From the perspective of thinkers like Caruth, they observe,

> every society and every individual suffers the traumatic experience of their past. Not only do scales of violence disappear, but their history is erased. There is no difference between the survivor of genocide and the survivor of rape; this is in any case the clinical view. . . . This tension between universalization and historicization shows us that the notion of "trauma" has become a general way of expressing the suffering of contemporary society, whether the events it derives from are individual (rape, torture, illness) or collective (genocide, war, disaster). (19–20)

Fassin and Rechtman conclude that the testimonies of Holocaust victims provided an unprecedented perspective, one "we can now consider the universalization of victim status in the last three decades" (76). Unlike the traumatized soldier, whose admission of shell shock was quite unwelcome, the testimony of the camp survivor was gradually recognized as offering the ultimate truth about the human condition.

> It was the mark of trauma that revealed the extraordinary persistence of humanity among the survivors of the Holocaust; and it was the pain of trauma, inscribed in the collective memory, that would prevent a repetition of the horrors. The persistence of the psychic scar guaranteed that the memory of the intolerable would never be erased. But the meaning of that trace was still inextricably linked to the moral qualities ascribed to survivors—their innocence and their weakness in the face of the brutal forces that overwhelmed them—and to the empathy they inspired. (95)

The Holocaust marked a dramatic shift in attitudes toward the victim, from the stigma of cowardice or duplicity in World War I soldiers, to the more acceptable weakness of World War II veterans, to the perception of trauma as a normal response to an abnormal situation. This new attitude entered the public arena, and trauma became a household term.

At the Mind's Limit

Now, more than sixty years after the Nazi death camps closed, we are very familiar with the haunting testimonies of their Jewish victims. Hans Mayer was one victim of German National Socialism whose legacy is a poignant phenomenological description of the victim of torture, written under the name of Jean Améry—the name he chose in denial and rejection of his hated German heritage. Améry was imprisoned and tortured in a concentration camp in Belgium for his participation in the resistance movement, and was then sent to Auschwitz, Buchenwald, and finally Bergen-Belsen, where he was released when the camp was liberated in 1945. Despite the difference in historical contexts, Améry's reflections share with Fanon's a focus on the reduction of the victim to flesh—to a dehumanized body or object—and on the destruction of human reciprocity. In both accounts we witness an antagonistic relationship between self and other originating in the sovereign destructive power of the victimizer, but one for which the victim bears some responsibility. For Améry, the other never ceases to be the "antiman." His response to the condition of victimhood, however, is quite divergent from Fanon's. We must keep in mind that Fanon, unlike Améry, was not the victim of torture.

After twenty years of silence, Améry began to write what he calls a "phenomenological description of the existence of the victim." Suddenly, he tells us, "everything demanded telling."[30] In one of his most moving essays, he gives an intimate and reflective account of what it means to be tortured, after being caught distributing anti-Nazi flyers at Fort Breendonk. The first blow from a policeman's fist, he writes, "contains in the bud everything that is to come" because it signifies the utter helplessness of the prisoner (27). Suspended by his arms until his shoulders became dislocated, he was left to dangle without hope of assistance. Améry describes this moment: "Frail in the face of violence, yelling out in pain, awaiting no help, capable of no resistance, the tortured person is only a body, and nothing else beside that" (33). It is an experience that never leaves him, for whoever is tortured stays tortured; it is burned into the tortured, even when all objective traces have disappeared. Twenty-two years later, he confesses, "I am still dangling over the ground by dislocated arms, panting, and accusing myself" (36).

At the first blow, Améry loses trust in the world, defined as "the certainty that by reason of written or unwritten social contracts the other person will spare me—more precisely stated, that he will respect my physical, and with it also my metaphysical, being" (28). For the boundaries of the body are also the boundaries of the self, and if one is to have trust in the world, Améry tells us, we must feel on our bodies only what we want to feel. "It is my skin surface that shields me against the external world," he explains (28). Thus already at the very first blow—a corporeal force he compares to rape—this trust in the world breaks down. There is no prospect of successful resistance against this border violation by the one who has become an "antiman," or "counter-man." The expectation of help—even the *certainty* of help—is therefore one of the most fundamental experiences of human life, as fundamental to the constitution of the psyche as the struggle for existence. With no defense against that first blow, and no assistance, Améry writes, "a part of our life ends and it can never again be revived" (29). In fact, no "subsequent human communication" can compensate for this new foreignness in the world, after the antiman's sovereign power to inflict suffering and destroy (39).

We are left with a very bleak view of the world from the perspective of the victim. "Whoever has succumbed to torture can no longer feel at home in the world," Améry declares, and certainly we have no reason to doubt his sincerity, given that he took his own life in 1978, thirty-three years after his liberation from the camp. The shame of destruction cannot be erased, he insists, nor can trust in the world be regained: "That one's fellow man was experienced as the antiman remains in the tortured person as accumulated horror. It blocks the view into a world in which the principle of hope rules . . . . It is *fear* that henceforth reigns over him. Fear—and also what is called resentments" (40).

Améry elaborates on the theme of resentment in an essay by that title, reacting to what he believes is the common assumption that Nietzsche had the last word on the matter. While Nietzsche believes that *ressentiment* is a negative response to victimization, Améry describes it as a valuable, even a morally necessary reaction, despite the fact that, as he writes, "it nails every one of us onto the cross of his ruined past" (68). He calls his own resentment a "personal protest against the antimoral natural process of healing that time brings about" (77) and remains resentful not only of the SS man who tortured him but of all Germans. Forgiveness and forgetting—immoral when induced by social pressure, according to Améry—simply allow what happened "to remain what it was" (72). There is a fascinating resistance to healing in these words; moving on would mean forgetting about justice. I will return to this point in chapter 6.

Yet Améry insists that his response to victimization is not about the lust for revenge. When the SS man who repeatedly beat him with a shovel is executed, Améry expresses a moment of strange elation that he insists is not the satisfaction of revenge. Rather, he explains that at the moment of execution, they met—victim and perpetrator—in the extreme loneliness of persecution, torture, and death. It was a moment in which the antiman became a fellow man once again: "He was with me—and I was no longer alone with the shovel handle" (70). Améry even imagines that before dying the SS man desired the same turning back of time, the same undoing of what had been done. Resentment is experienced, he concludes, "in order that the crime become a moral reality for the criminal, in order that he be swept into the truth of his atrocity" (70). It is difficult to interpret this as anything but a paradigmatic example of a victim's hunger for vengeful "justice."

As the years went by, and Germans talked less of remorse and Jews talked more of forgiveness, Améry tells us that he stubbornly bore his grudge. "I preserved my resentments," he writes, "and since I neither can nor want to get rid of them, I must live with them and am obliged to clarify them for those against whom they are directed" (67). But at the end of this enigmatic defense, Améry is more ambivalent. He admits that his resentment— "a morality for the losers"—has little or no chance at all to make the antimen feel the bitterness of their evil work. He asks only for patience in the face of such grudges (81). But what do we forgive or deny in that patience? Reading Améry is emotionally wrenching; it is all too tempting to believe that he had no choice but to respond to extreme suffering with bitterness and resentment. We are reticent to criticize or judge the wounded. It is easier to deny their moral agency.

Améry appears to make the choice that Fanon warns his compatriots to avoid at all costs. He accepts victimhood as an "amputation" and views the world as a hostile place that he must forever secure himself against. Shortly before he took his own life, Améry wrote that to belong to oneself, one must maintain an aggression against the outside world, a hostile world that has to be held apart "in order to exist, to endure."[31] In a word, he dissociates himself—from the world, from others, from himself. Fanon, by contrast, refuses the resentment that demands reparations or rights, refuses to remain imprisoned by the worldview of the colonizers, which defines both victim and perpetrator, and focuses on the reciprocity that opens up a future. In a third victim's narrative, to which we will turn shortly, it becomes clear why the vulnerability that Fanon alludes to when he speaks of "the quite simple attempt to touch the other" is ironically essential for the victim who desires security above all. This is an excruciating fact of the human condition: we are fundamentally vulnerable to violence and perpetually crave security from it. The condition of victimhood increases the stakes, often rendering vulnerability so unbearable that the craving for security becomes all-consuming. In the process of building our elaborate defense systems, we may ward off harm, but we may also destroy the vulnerability we need if we are to relate to one another.

Sexual Trauma

The feminist movement of the 1960s and 1970s in North America benefited from the victim discourses that arose from growing interest in Holocaust survivors. Feminists attempted to raise public awareness of sexual abuse against women by comparing it to what went on in the Nazi death camps. The psychic symptoms caused by the abuse bore testimony to the violation; they became evidence and attested to its reality. Bearing witness to the unspeakable—a central theme in the discussion of Holocaust survival—gave feminists a new perspective from which to assert that the suffering of sexual violence was similar to that of concentration camp survivors.[32] Even "the problem that has no name"—as Betty Friedan called the experience of the unfulfilled American housewife in the 1950s, whose identity and self-determination were destroyed in the *ennui* of domesticity—was compared to the predicament of the Jew in a concentration camp.[33]

Judith Herman, who was instrumental in shaping the field of trauma studies, argues that feminism assumed a central role in the victims' rights movement and in the recognition of the lasting effects of the trauma of abuse. The 1970s witnessed a veritable explosion of research and activism on sexual assault. The first public "speak-out" against rape was organized by the New York Radical Feminists in 1971, and five years later the first International Tribunal on Crimes Against Women was held in Brussels.[34] Previously ignored, sexual assault was eventually defined as an atrocity, owing to this flurry of activity, a crime of violence rather than a sexual act, even a method of political control to subordinate women through terror. As Susan Brownmiller famously put it, "Man's discovery that his genitalia could serve as a weapon to generate fear must rank as one of the most important discoveries of pre-historic times, along with the use of fire and the first crude stone axe. From prehistoric times to the present, I believe, rape has played a critical function. It is nothing more or less than a conscious process of intimidation by which *all men keep all women* in a state of fear" (emphasis added).[35]

Herman writes that only after 1980, when the concept of PTSD had been legitimized by combat veterans, did it become clear that survivors of rape, domestic abuse, and incest experienced essentially the same syndrome. The symptoms experienced by rape victims were similar to those described by combat veterans and colonized subjects: insomnia, nausea, startle responses, nightmares, dissociation, and emotional numbness (31). The implications are as horrifying now as they were a century ago, according to Herman: "the sub-ordinate condition of women is maintained and enforced by the hidden vio-lence of men. There is war between the sexes. Rape victims, battered women, and sexually abused children are its casualties. Hysteria is the combat neurosis of the sex war" (32).

The importance of Herman's work, and that of the feminist movement in general, for raising awareness of the traumatic effects of sexual abuse and assault, should not be underestimated. We need to consider carefully, however, how the experience of victimhood is framed by this movement and what are its political effects. Herman defines trauma as "an affliction of the powerless. At the moment of trauma, the victim is rendered help-less by overwhelming force" (33). In fact, she adds, "the salient characteristic of the traumatic event is its power to inspire helplessness and terror," and harm to the victim is more likely if she is taken by surprise, or by other experiences, like being trapped or exposed to the point of exhaustion. Threat arouses the sympathetic nervous system and concentrates a person's atten-tion on the immediate situation. Threat can alter ordinary perception and invoke intense feelings of fear and anger, "mobilizing a threatened person for strenuous action, either in battle or in flight" (34). When there is no possibility of action, when resistance and escape are impossible, the human self-defense system becomes overwhelmed, and a kind of fragmentation or dissociation often occurs. Herman claims that the core experiences of psychological trauma are disempowerment and disconnection from others. Therefore, recovery is based on the empowerment of the survivor and the creation of new connections (133).

This definition is in keeping with Fanon's work in the context of colonial-ism and with Améry's response to his betrayal by the "antiman." The question of how to respond appropriately—how precisely to "empower" and create new connections—may not be helped by a strictly victim-centered approach, if with this approach we forget the critical qualification in Herman's definition: *"at the moment of trauma*, the victim is rendered helpless by an overwhelming force" (emphasis added).

Kristin Bumiller draws attention to several negative consequences of a feminist movement that "initially characterized sexual violence as a social problem."[36] Focusing on individual victims and perpetrators and exaggerating women's vulnerability to the sadistic exploits of men, feminists created a fateful characterization of the issue as a gender war (160). Bumiller cites surprising research that suggests that the situation of women who experience intimate violence has not improved much since the introduction of reforms targeted at improving the treatment of victims. These reforms include victim "shield" laws, victim advocacy, support and counseling, and improving the attitudes of police, prosecutors, and judges. Nor has it helped to expand the definition of rape by redefining assault or changing the requirements of consent, or by increasing the levels of reporting, prosecution, and conviction of perpetrators (158–59). Overall, Bumiller concludes, "rape law reform has brought about limited change in regard to increasing the likelihood that a victim will be vindicated by the courts"; at the same time, the courts' increased demand for the "expressive justice" of celebrated cases has perpetuated negative stereotypes about victims and perpetrators (159).

Bumiller encourages us to consider women's responsibility and agency, to make connections "between the plight of individual women and the larger responsibilities of democratic communities" (161). The most desirable solutions, in her view, are "neither perpetrator nor relationship focused but directed to addressing the most persistent problems causing and created by sexual violence—the social and economic disadvantage experienced by women and their dependents" (163). We must promote, she insists, the emotional well-being and economic sustainability of women who suffer repeatedly from sexual violence throughout life. This includes not only the emotional, material, and communal support women need to empower themselves but also the kind of advocacy that focuses on systemic issues and unfavorable state action. In fact, Bumiller concludes, "when women reject the psychological construction of victimhood, romantic notions of returning to the confines of private patriarchy, and unending war with hostile state agencies, they open up possibilities for demanding respect and autonomy in all aspects of their lives" (164).

One could argue that Bumiller places too much emphasis on the victim's responsibility, leaving her vulnerable to the accusation of blaming the victim. Like Fanon, however, her focus on the agency of the victim is motivated by the attempt to overcome victimhood. Without the acknowledgment of one's own responsibility, this overcoming is impossible, for the impetus for change will remain with the perpetrator—the one whose actions and attitudes we cannot control. Significantly, Bumiller demonstrates that the most important strategy of *response* to the condition of victimhood is one that also *prevents* it, for the demand for respect and autonomy may both help to overcome previous abuse and also ward off future abuse.

The Shattered Self

Susan Brison gives us a remarkable account of the experience of victimhood and recovery after being violently raped and beaten almost to the point of death while on leave from teaching philosophy in the United States. In *Aftermath: Violence and the Remaking of a Self,* she describes how violence shatters the self and our "fundamental assumptions about the world, including beliefs about our ability to control what happens to us."[37] In the months following the attack, the world ceased to make sense to her—it became "profoundly disorienting," "utterly strange and paradoxical." During this time she led "a spectral existence," not sure whether she had died and the world had continued without her, or whether she was alive, "but in a totally alien world" (9). When asked a few months later whether she had recovered, she replied, "I am not the same person who set off, singing, on that sunny Fourth of July in the French countryside. I left her in a rocky creek bed at the bottom of a ravine. I had to in order to survive" (21).

Brison expresses the pain of displacement, of exile from the body, the human community, and the world—the same dissociation from which Améry never recovered. She describes an "undoing" of the self that assumes the same antagonistic relation between self and other that we read in Améry and Fanon. When the trauma is inflicted intentionally, she states, "it not only shatters one's fundamental assumptions about the world and one's safety in it, but it also severs the sustaining connection between the self and the rest of humanity" (40). The victimization occurs in this shattering and severance. It is not, then, strictly a violation of the boundaries of an enclosed, autonomous self but a violation of human reciprocity. For rape victims in particular, Brison argues, this violation is repeated every time the account is not believed, a denial she claims is "an almost universal response to rape" (9). Each time someone failed to respond to her attempts to talk about the assault, she explains "I felt as though I were alone again in the ravine, dying, screaming. And still no one could hear me. Or, worse, they heard me, but refused to help" (16). Brison's analysis of her own victimization and recovery process is focused on what it means to have one's self completely shattered and how to reconstruct it. Central to this process is regaining the autonomy and control that the violation destroyed—at least in the limited sense that we can exercise control in an unpredictable universe. Significantly, Brison observes, recovery requires reestablishing vulnerability to the other, and accepting the risk that entails.

This cannot, however, take place in the immediate aftermath of the assault. In the part of the book written within two years of the attack, Brison makes frequent allusions to a shattered self, the loss of security, a unified sense of the body, as well as self-esteem, love, and work (20). "In order to recover," she writes, "a trauma survivor needs to be able to control herself, control her environment (within reasonable limits), and be reconnected with humanity" (60). This control, particularly control over fear of future attacks—of walking alone, for example—and of the symptoms of PTSD, permits the return of a sense of autonomy, which Brison claims is the most apparent transformation in survivors of trauma. She stresses, however, that this control or autonomy is "fundamentally relational," for it is the need to speak to others about her attack that profoundly demonstrates the vulnerability of one's life in relation to another (41). The self can be destroyed by others, but it is also created and sustained by them (62). The dire need for this control appears to lessen as Brison's narrative continues. Over time, she is able to accept that absolute control is never possible, and that life will continue to be unpredictable.

Of critical importance for Brison in this process of developing control is the construction of a narrative, one to which others listen empathically. What she calls a "trauma narrative" transforms the ever-present memories into narratives, and this process both accomplishes the integration of the trauma into the survivor's sense of self and her view of the world and reintegrates the survivor into a community, reestablishing her trust in others and permitting renewed vulnerability (x–xi). In other words, a narrative permits the victim to regain some modicum of control. Brison demonstrates that we can accept and nurture the vulnerability that makes us human and yet puts us at risk of violation and suffering: vulnerability is what makes human life bearable and enjoyable.

We are fortunate to have an addendum from Brison, seventeen years after her assault and six years after the publication of *Aftermath*, for it provides a rare opportunity to see the progress of recovery and receive the benefit of her own hindsight. She acknowledges that she no longer has the same need to tell her story—in fact, she is "bored by it" (188). In spite of having claimed that she died in the ravine where she was attacked, Brison now admits she has "more in common with [her] preassault self than with the person [she] became for more than a decade afterward" (189).

> I really am over my assault. Other things distress me much more now, and rightly so: the war in Iraq, the torture our government is inflicting with apparent impunity, devastating and inexcusably unjust global inequalities. This is not to say that my assault has left no traces. I still have lingering symptoms of posttraumatic stress disorder. I have fractured speech and a disordered brain in stressful situations. I have claustrophobia (which I never had before) that prevents me from taking elevators unless absolutely necessary. I still take antidepressants and sleeping pills (which I'd never taken before), and I won't go for walks in the woods by myself (which used to be one of my favorite activities). But these things are pretty trivial. I *have* regained my lost self. (195)

Brison concludes by throwing into question Améry's assertion that "whoever is tortured stays tortured" (131). It is possible, she says, that she is able to "embrace life so wholeheartedly now" *because* of her assault (196).

To Endure

The intimate narratives of victims demonstrate the unique condition of victimhood, characterized by the reduction to suffering flesh, the humiliation of dehumanization associated with this reduction, the betrayal of others whom we expect to come to our aid and consequent inability to trust, and a shattered or dissociated self. At the phenomenological level it seems that some or all of these features are universally experienced by victims of violence. Responses to the condition vary, however, as we can see from these few examples. Some seek to justify resentment and the desire for retribution; others demonstrate a melancholic diminution of self-regard; still others struggle to regain trust in humankind. In any community subjected to violence, we need to keep in mind that there is no equality at the psychological or psychic level. Not every victim of assault can say, with Brison, "I have regained my lost self." What we do with the resources we are born with and the events we live through helps to determine how well we will cope with future events, but we struggle against powerful, sometimes unconscious impulses. This is not to say that we are entirely determined by them, but the challenge of changing them may be, for some, too agonizing to endure.[38]

It is senseless, however, to end with a relativistic understanding of victimhood and recovery. We must do more than point out the ambivalent and diverse responses to victimization. Some responses are better than others; some victims have the personal resources or support from others that enable them to recover, and refuse to take refuge in an identity based exclusively on a victimized status. This means that victims' *needs* must be distinguished from their *desires*. There is more to the truth of their condition than the emotions and longings they express. Victimhood is not politically innocent, and its moral power can be immense. The scripts we have inherited from twentieth-century discourses on trauma have lent moral and political weight to human suffering at the hands of another, clouding our judgment at times, rendering it difficult to know what victims need in order to recover.

If some responses are better than others, how do we judge them appropriately and create the conditions that enable the better responses? In the next chapter we turn to Hannah Arendt, for whom judgment and responsibility are central to political action and moral thought. There is a twofold requirement here: we respond to the suffering of victimhood at the same time that we act to prevent it. Our response must be proactive rather than simply reactive, for the birth of new victims could depend on it. This work cannot occur without judgment.

4

ARENDT IN JERUSALEM

From killing so much, we forgot to think about you.

*Nothing strikes us more forcefully than the utter innocence
of the individual caught in the horror machine and his utter
inability to change his fate.*

In the early 1960s Hannah Arendt argued that there is a "widespread fear of judging" in our society.[1] Behind this fear, she added, "lurks the suspicion that no one is a free agent, and hence the doubt that anyone is responsible or could be expected to answer for what he has done." She wrote these words in response to the furor over her reportage and analysis of the Adolf Eichmann trial in Jerusalem in 1961. Eichmann, once an ordinary German bureaucrat, was tried and executed for crimes against humanity during the Nazi regime. While he told the court that he had nothing to do with the killing of Jews, he was in fact responsible for transporting thousands of Jews to their death. The idea that he could have chosen and acted otherwise was a postwar legend created in hindsight "and supported by people who did not know or had forgotten how things had actually been."[2]

Given Eichmann's refusal to accept responsibility for his monstrous actions, Arendt's concern over "the suspicion that no one is a free agent" seems well founded. The controversy over her coverage of the trial, however, was caused not by her claim that Eichmann could have chosen otherwise but by her bold insistence that the Jewish Councils, or *Judenräte*, that cooperated with the Nazis could also have chosen otherwise. For Arendt's close friend Gershom Scholem, this was a contentious, disappointing claim. He vehemently protested her criticism of the Jewish Councils: "I do not know whether they were right or wrong," Scholem wrote to Arendt, "nor do I presume to judge. I was not there."[3]

Arendt hit a nerve with her insistence that members of a victimized group must not be exempted from the demands of responsibility and accountability, that the same reticence to believe one could have chosen and acted otherwise can be exhibited by both victim and perpetrator. To speak of responsibility and victimhood in the same breath may strike us as an appalling *lack* of judgment, equivalent to blaming an innocent victim and presuming agency in one who lacks it. Judgment is perceived as exercised from a lofty position of moral authority, disqualified by virtue of the fact that the one who judges from a distance cannot understand the experience of the victim and therefore is in no position to judge. It morally offends the victim, whose sole power may now arise from embracing her identity as a victim.

Consider the outrage directed at Victoire Ingabire Umuhoza, a Hutu woman who was arrested in Rwanda in April 2010 for allegedly collaborating with a terrorist organization and denying the 1994 genocide. She was accused of "divisionism" for speaking out about Hutu grief for Hutu deaths during and following the genocide that claimed approximately eight hundred thousand Tutsi lives. Some twenty-five to forty-five thousand Hutu deaths—including Ingabire's brother (mistaken for a Tutsi)—remain a taboo subject. Although she condemns the genocide and advocates reconciliation, mutual respect, and justice for all, regardless of ethnicity, Ingabire has been called a "genocide denier." She has been refused permission to register her political party, the Unified Democratic Forces, and has suffered harassment and vilification at the hands of the press and police. An investigation into her "genocide ideology" has begun. "We have to understand the pain of others," Ingabire maintains. "When I condemn the genocide, I'm also thinking of my brother. Not all Hutus are killers, and not all Tutsis are victims."[4] But as a Hutu, considered to represent the perpetrators of a savage genocide, Ingabire has crossed a line considered sacrosanct in her call for Tutsis to acknowledge their own specific responsibility.

When the magnitude of the killing perpetuated by one segment of a population on another is as great as it was in Rwanda and Nazi Germany, focusing on the responsibility of those comparatively few perpetrators among the victims seems to violate a fundamental belief in the pure innocence of the victim. We must ask what is at stake here. Who or what are we protecting when we refuse to acknowledge any responsibility the victim may bear for events? It is at once a refusal to make appropriate moral judgments and a denial of agency, whether our own or a victim's. This chapter seeks to probe these issues, inquiring into the responsibility of the victim and articulating the grounds for judgment. These tasks go hand in hand, especially when we consider judging well an act of responsibility. Arendt's concerns are as relevant today as they were fifty years ago in postwar Europe. "Who am I *not* to judge?" is perhaps the vexing question we need to ask.

The Responsibility of the Victim

As we have seen, drawing attention to the responsibility a victim may bear for the circumstances that led to his or her victimization is often equated with blaming the victim, and blaming the victim—any victim—is considered unambiguously wrong. Most of us would not dare to suggest, for example, that victims of rape or abuse bear any responsibility for the act of violation that rendered them victims.[5] The vehemence with which we accuse someone of blaming the victim, however, should give us pause. The claim implicitly assumes an abstract entity extracted from any historical circumstances, presumed to be absolutely innocent. But we need to be wary of assuming that all victims are equally and purely innocent. That victims are not all the same does not mean that someone deserved to be victimized, but it does mean that some victims take risks that increase that possibility. When we are reticent about acknowledging agency in a victim, even the most limited agency, we neglect to consider any acts or events leading up to the victimization for which the victim *was* responsible. To continue with the example of rape, we could consider the responsibility women bear for the conditions that contribute to a patriarchal culture in which there is a certain level of indifference to, or acceptance of, rape. Feminist discourse continues to place the responsibility for male domination (and therefore for rape, which is generally considered one of its effects) exclusively on the shoulders of men, absolving women of any responsibility for inequality or patriarchal ideology, even though mothers wield considerable power in the raising of children, and despite women's complicity in, and reproduction of, patriarchal power relations. We could speak here of women's responsibility, though it is shared unequally around the globe, which nevertheless does not entail blaming the individual victim for being attacked. The fact that women are not the only victims of rape (a fact often ignored in discussions of rape) supports this point, for if men are to be held solely responsible for violence, then the individual male victim cannot be absolved of that responsibility.

The issue, then, is one of historicizing responsibility. As Arendt discovered, however, the historicization of the responsibility and agency of victims is a contentious project. She begins this project in *The Origins of Totalitarianism*, her bewildering, wide-ranging work of 1951. In the first part, which describes the rise of modern, secular anti-Semitism up to the turn of the twentieth century, Arendt complains that European Jews did not take the birth and growth of anti-Semitism seriously enough. Instead, they proffered "hasty explanations," attributing anti-Semitism to rampant nationalism and xenophobia. One of these explanations, the "scapegoat theory," claimed that because Jews were entirely powerless, caught up in the insoluble conflicts of the time, their oppressors could make them appear "the hidden authors of all evil."[6] *Anyone*, this theory holds, could have taken the place of the Jews. From the perspective of the victims, Arendt argues, the scapegoat theory upholds their perfect innocence, "an innocence which insinuates not only that no evil was done but that nothing at all was done which might possibly have a connection with the issue at stake" (5).

When it comes to a regime of terror, Arendt notes, we are even more tempted to fall back on the scapegoat theory, because terror strikes with no provocation. Its victims are innocent even from the point of view of the perpetrators. "Nothing strikes us more forcefully," she writes, "than the utter innocence of the individual caught in the horror machine and his utter inability to change his fate" (6). The Nazis targeted Jews not for specific behavior but for sharing certain common characteristics; regardless of what they may or may not have done, they were *chosen*. Modern state terror thus appears to support absolving victims of responsibility: since nothing they did or failed to do has any connection with their fate, they are objectively and absolutely innocent. The victim in this equation is a scapegoat, chosen arbitrarily.

Even under these circumstances, however, Arendt pushes the issue of responsibility. The temptation to see the victim as an arbitrary scapegoat should trouble us, she warns, because of the character of modern terror. Unlike previous tyrannies, modern terror is used not as a means to exterminate or frighten its opponents but as "an instrument to rule masses of people who are perfectly obedient" (6). It does not begin as a full-fledged form of government but develops out of a specific ideology that must win mass adherence. Totalitarian regimes are made over time, Arendt explains, and only after winning the consent of the majority do they employ state terror. Furthermore, any ideology that has to persuade and mobilize people "cannot choose its victim arbitrarily" (7). In Nazi Germany, the Jews were made the center of an ideology before they became the primary victims of a terror regime; anti-Semitic slogans proved to be "the most effective means of inspiring and organizing great masses of people for imperialist expansion and destruction of the old forms of government" (10). It follows, for Arendt, that clues are to be found in the previous history of the relationship between the Jews and the state that will help explain the growing hostility toward them. For this history, all Germans bore some responsibility, albeit to varying degrees.

There is thus a historical context to terror and its choice of victims, one in which all individuals exercise agency. One group "does not simply cease to be coresponsible because it became the victim of the world's injustice and cruelty" writes Arendt (6). What is remarkable about the scapegoat theory, or the assumption of "eternal antisemitism," for Arendt, is that these notions deny "all specific Jewish responsibility" and refuse to address the historical context (8). In *The Origins of Totalitarianism* Arendt singles out Jews' self-destructive alliance with state power. The nation-state from its inception depended on the financial resources and political loyalty of Jews, and in return rewarded wealthy Jews with social privileges that made them dependent on state power and prevented their assimilation into the broader society.[7] To make matters worse, Arendt points to a lack of political ability and judgment caused by the nature of Jewish history, a people without a government, country, or language, who "avoided all political action for two thousand years" and thus became even more dependent than other nations or peoples on unforeseen or accidental historical developments (8). Arendt was criticized harshly for this exaggerated claim.

It is not my intention to investigate here the historical reasons Arendt provides to substantiate her claims regarding the specific responsibility of the Jews for their own history. I am more interested in her argument for the necessity of historicizing the responsibility of victims, which is significant for a number of reasons. The claim that in the "moment of terror" the victim is absolutely innocent, but that in the events leading up to this moment *all are co-responsible* for the making of history, as well as her elaboration of the specificity of this history in the case of European Jews, enables us to consider not only the past but the future as well—a future not constrained by the conditions of victimhood. It locates victimhood in a specific historical moment—one in which individual agency was *for a time* radically reduced or destroyed altogether—rather than defining it as an absolute identity that both precedes and follows the act of victimization, signifying pure, timeless innocence and thus procuring a great deal of moral capital.

Considering responsibility in a historical context permits us to understand it in a less derogatory sense than blame or culpability and acknowledge that there are degrees of responsibility. But Arendt's criticism of the Jewish Councils cannot be sugarcoated. Richard J. Bernstein cautions us against misinterpreting her claim, "for the issue is not one of blame, guilt, or even *moral* responsibility. It is, rather, a question of political responsibility: of how the Jews have (and have not) responded to the concrete political situations in which they have found themselves."[8] The moral and the political, however, are not easily disentangled. Arendt *is* making a moral judgment against those who did not act politically to prevent an atrocity, German Gentiles and Jews alike, and who failed to make the right moral decisions in the moment of crisis.

Justifications

A survivor of the 1994 Rwandan genocide named Innocent Rwililiza tells the following story to Jean Hatzfeld in *Life Laid Bare: The Survivors of Rwanda Speak*. Along with hundreds of other Tutsis, Rwililiza had spent weeks running from the Hutu killing bands who roamed the hills from morning to dusk, hacking to death with machetes any Tutsis they could find, singing all the while. One day while on the run, Rwililiza and a few other Tutsis surprised three Hutus resting from their macabre job. The Tutsis told their hunters that now their luck had turned. When the Hutus protested, the Tutsis asked them why they shouldn't be killed: "You spend your days cutting us—and now you're crying so you won't be stuck full of arrows?" One Hutu responded, "It's not my fault, it's the commune that wants this. It's down there that they make us do all this." If that's true, Rwililiza asked him, then "why don't you come pass the whole time until the evening in the shade—without killing, in any case—and then go back down to Nyamata all rested and so keep the approval of the authorities?" The Hutu replied, "That is a good idea, I hadn't thought of that." Rwililiza describes what followed: "I started to yell, I was incensed: 'It never occurred to you that you could simply not kill us?' He answered, 'No: from killing so much, we forgot to think about you.'" This response persuaded Rwililiza "that this Hutu harbored no savagery in his heart."[9]

We observe here the same thoughtlessness that Arendt captures in her account of Adolf Eichmann's trial, *Eichmann in Jerusalem: A Report on the Banality of Evil*, first written as a report for the *New Yorker* in 1963. In reflecting on the objections to the report, Arendt confesses that she had taken it for granted that "we all still believe with Socrates that it is better to suffer than to do wrong." This turned out to be a mistake, she decides, and she goes on to describe what she calls the "widespread conviction" that none of us can withstand temptation of any kind or be trusted in hard times to do the right thing, and thus that to be tempted and forced are one and the same.[10] Here again we are struck by the implications for both perpetrators and victims: Eichmann believed that he was simply following orders and could not have chosen another path—that he was merely a cog in a monstrous wheel, a victim of the system—while defenders of the Jewish Councils maintained that Jewish leaders were simply doing what they had to do, what amounted to "the lesser evil." Nowhere does Arendt suggest that sending Jews to their death is morally equivalent to Jewish cooperation with the Nazis, but she does claim that the moral justifications given for their actions are similar. "What needs to be discussed," she writes, "are not the people so much as the arguments with which they justified themselves in their own eyes and in those of others."[11] The lesser evil is still evil, Arendt reminds us.

Arendt is responding here to accusations that her report exonerated Eichmann and blamed the Jews for their own extermination. She was condemned for being "soulless," "malicious," "arrogant," "flippant," and a "self-hating Jew."[12] These condemnations were the outcome of her elaboration of the idea that evil is banal, without content or depth, and that Adolf Eichmann—a superficial, thoughtless man who cared only for his career—epitomized this banality. Arendt describes her impressions of Eichmann:

> I was struck by a manifest shallowness in the doer that made it impossible to trace the uncontestable evil of his deeds to any deeper level of roots or motives. The deeds were monstrous, but the doer—at least the very effective one now on trial—was quite ordinary, commonplace, and neither demonic nor monstrous. There was no sign in him of firm ideological convictions or of specific evil motives, and the only notable characteristic one could detect in his past behavior as well as in his behavior during the trial and throughout the pre-trial police examination was something entirely negative: it was not stupidity but *thoughtlessness*.[13]

There was no "diabolical or demonic profundity" in Eichmann, Arendt tells us, yet his thoughtlessness and remoteness from reality wrought "more havoc than all the evil instincts taken together which, perhaps, are inherent in man."[14] This was the lesson of the trial that Arendt wanted to convey. The "banality of evil" was often interpreted, however, as trivializing Eichmann's crimes. Jean Améry, a victim of Nazi torture and imprisonment, objects that Arendt saw evil as banal only because she looked at it from the other side of the glass. When face to face with his torturers, their seemingly ordinary faces became Gestapo faces after all.[15] Améry was by no means the only one to accuse Arendt of making a dispassionate judgment from the safety of the "other side" of the glass. To many it seemed that Arendt's judgment of the Jewish leadership, the *Judenräte*, was harsher than her judgment of Eichmann.[16]

Eichmann himself told the court that he received the cooperation of Jews "to a truly extraordinary degree." The Jewish Councils, made up of locally recognized Jewish leaders, were given enormous powers by the Nazis, Arendt explains, until they too were deported to the camps. Their cooperation, she concludes, "is undoubtedly the darkest chapter of the whole dark story." They were responsible for compiling the lists of names and property, getting funds from the deported to cover their own deportation and extermination costs, keeping track of their emptied homes, supplying police forces to help seize Jews and put them on trains, and handing over Jewish assets to the Nazi authorities. Most disturbingly, they had the power to choose who would be deported and who would not. Arendt refers to a Dr. Kastner in Hungary, whose report indicated that out of approximately 476,000 victims he saved 1,684 Jews, specifically, the most prominent Jews of the community, not, as Arendt wryly notes, "little Hans Cohn from around the corner." She goes so far as to argue that "without Jewish help in administrative and police work ... there would have been either complete chaos or an impossibly severe drain on German manpower."[17] If this is true, then it would be grossly irresponsible *not* to judge the *Judenräte*.

That the Jewish Councils were primarily responsible for deciding who would be sent to the death camps was avoided during the Eichmann trial, Arendt claims, in the interest of making a clear distinction between victim and perpetrator. She argues that the lack of a single witness to testify to the cooperation of the Jewish authorities was a grave omission, for the question was never raised: "Why did you cooperate in the destruction of your own people and, eventually, in your own ruin?" The only testimony from a member of a Jewish Council caused the court to erupt in shouting, as the spectators—some of whom claimed that Jewish leaders told them not to try to escape—reacted with outrage. Arendt concludes that while it was true "that the Jewish people as a whole had not been organized, that they possessed no territory, no government, and no army," and that no one among the Allies would represent them, "the whole truth" was that recognized Jewish leaders, "almost without exception," cooperated with the Nazis in one way or another. She adds that "if the Jewish people had really been unorganized and leaderless, there would have been chaos and plenty of misery but the total number of victims would hardly have been between four and a half and six million people."[18]

Arendt insists that we are "entitled to pass judgment" on these matters. The Jewish leaders' decisions to cooperate were not made under the immediate pressure or impact of terror. During the years of the Final Solution, on the other hand, there was no possibility of resistance: "There never was a moment when 'the community leaders' could have said, 'Cooperate no longer, but fight!'" Resistance meant only "We don't want that kind of death, we want to die with honor." The moment of such a decision could have come, Arendt reasons, when the Nazis asked Jewish leaders to prepare the lists for deportation, when these leaders *already knew* what deportation entailed. They could have chosen to attempt to flee, despite the risk of death, rather than take into their hands the matter of who should survive and who should die. The Jewish Councils justified this work primarily with the idea that if some Jews had to die, it was better that Jews themselves make these selections than leave it to the Nazis, for this also gave Jews the power to choose who might live. To these claims Arendt responds that it would have been "infinitely better to let the Nazis do their own murderous business."[19]

While Arendt protests that the criticism of her judgment of the Jewish Councils is misguided and blown out of proportion—in her words she was merely giving a factual report of the trial—the severity of the criticism leaves us with nagging questions. How to deal with the moral problems that arise when we view the issue through an either/or lens is the challenge we face when we consider the victim's responsibility. One is either completely victimized, and therefore innocent and without responsibility, or purely guilty and culpable. Eichmann claimed that he was a cog in the wheel of an efficient system from which he could not be simply released—a victim, therefore, of the Nazi machine. The Jewish leaders were victims who contributed to this system, but whatever wrongful deeds they may have committed, they were exonerated and considered with compassion on the basis of their victimization, viewed as forced, not tempted, by the circumstances. Thus they too were cogs in the wheel of an efficient system, albeit with far fewer choices than Eichmann had. If Arendt's own judgment in this matter was—and still is—unpopular and controversial, it is partly because of our wish to draw this line between victim and perpetrator starkly, along with its attendant line between "us and them" and its variations: self and other, friend and enemy, good and evil. It is easier to sit in judgment against a clearly designated enemy than to judge one's own people, who are "known" in some sense, familiar, possibly loved. Compassion for those we perceive to be "in common" with us helps to explain the fierce resistance to Arendt's criticism of Jews, as is evident in Gershom Scholem's reaction to *Eichmann in Jerusalem.*

Arendt states that we are "entitled" to make moral judgments, but I would argue that this is our responsibility rather than our right. The danger of abdicating this responsibility lies in the tendency of both victim and perpetrator to fall back on the same moral justification for actions—of choosing *the lesser evil* under duress. In this justification there is the tendency to hide under the banner of collective responsibility, like the German soldiers who testified at the Eichmann trial that their own disobedience would have been a useless sacrifice, since any number of others would have taken their place.[20]

We need to remain aware of the risks of this justification. The suppression of personal responsibility or individual agency when performing collective evil, Arne Johan Vetlesen explains, is a crucial psychological precondition for genocide. The individual starts behaving as though he is not responsible for his actions, "having internalized the ideological notion that the individual's agency-based freedom counts for nothing, and his or her collective identity-cum-destiny for everything, whereby (collective) evil is made out to be imperative and necessary, not optional and avoidable."[21] Of course, not all who insist that they are merely victims of evil systems will participate in genocide—this is only one extreme—but it is a good reason to be wary of the justification of wrongdoing on the basis of one's innocence and another's blameworthiness.

Arendt gives us reason to believe that behind this wish to claim innocence and render the lesser evil an imperative is "contempt" for human freedom. In a perceptive passage in *The Human Condition*, she explains:

> That deeds possess such an enormous capacity for endurance, superior to every other man-made product, could be a matter of pride if men were able to bear its burden, the burden of irreversibility and unpredictability, from which the action process draws its very strength. That this

is impossible, men have always known. They have known that he who acts never quite knows what he is doing, that he always becomes "guilty" of consequences he never intended or even foresaw, that no matter how disastrous and unexpected the consequences of his deed he can never undo it, that the process he starts is never consummated unequivocally in one single deed or event, and that its very meaning never discloses itself to the actor but only to the backward glance of the historian who himself does not act. All this is reason enough to turn away with despair from the realm of human affairs and to hold in contempt the human capacity for freedom, which, by producing the web of human relationships, seems to entangle its producer to such an extent that he appears much more the victim and the sufferer than the author and doer of what he has done.[22]

Jean-Paul Sartre was right: we flee our freedom, unable to cope with the abyss of choice and responsibility. One of our greatest defenses against this unbearable freedom is the claim that we are victims, fervently believing ourselves to be without agency, facing a world of necessity and lesser evils. Likewise, we seem devoted to upholding the absolute innocence of victims. We identify easily with the innocent, believing them to be without recourse, rendering their innocence pure and absolute, so as to avoid the possibility that we too might have to answer for deeds we have done. Conversely, we perceive the perpetrator as savage rather than human; otherwise, we would be able to identify with him and face this same possibility—that we too could act without thinking, commit terrible deeds when we actually had a choice. The contempt for human freedom necessitates this distinct division between absolute innocence and absolute guilt. We might ask, however, whether Arendt's emphasis on the contempt for freedom misses other relevant factors that are not framed as negatively—affects like fear, for example, and the profound sympathy it can invite.

What Is Judgment?

To judge means to assess, to evaluate or discern. Our daily lives are filled with judgments, whether moral, aesthetic, or intellectual. We make decisions based on our assessments of an issue or situation. We judge a book excellent, mediocre, or terrible; we judge a work of art beautiful, competent, or crude;

we judge an action right or wrong, good or evil, appropriate or inappropriate. I am mostly concerned here with moral judgment, in which we evaluate our own and others' actions and make decisions about what is right or wrong in a given situation. Judgment should be distinguished from *moralism*, which evokes an obsession with moral regulations, particularly as they relate to others' behavior rather than our own. The moralist focuses on a narrowly circumscribed code of behavior, leaving no room for contingency or ambiguity, but judges only on the basis of superficial attention to rules. The religious moralist, like the political ideologue, condemns another for not "toeing the party line," not living up to the precepts of Christianity, feminism, leftist politics, neo-Nazism, and so forth. This is not judging in the sense of discernment that relies on thinking and respect for persons—this is only policing.

Even without religion or ideology, however, we may balk at being judged, perceiving the one who judges to be claiming moral and epistemological superiority. In recent years, when I have broached the neglected matter of judgment in my university classrooms, the response inevitably takes the form of the questions: Who has the authority to judge?[23] To whom should we grant that authority? Whose judgment counts? The underlying assumption is always the same: judgment works vertically and hierarchically, not horizontally. This is judgment as moralism, concerned only with who has the authority to make the rules. In an academic and cultural climate governed by the principle of tolerance for what is considered to be "other"—or perhaps more aptly, "othered"—whether we speak of culture, race, gender, sexual orientation, or any number of other categories of identification, judgment usually implies the self-righteous arrogance and paternalism of the privileged. When I ask students why we are willing to use the value of tolerance as an alibi to avoid making moral judgments, the response is invariably, but who are we to judge? The assumption is that differences of culture, race, gender, and economic privilege necessitate different moral codes and, for those who live in the West, an attitude of humble self-denigration and guilt, a mindfulness of the imperialism from which we continue to benefit. In the first chapter of this book, I described this as the veneration of an essentialized other. Inevitably, it leads to a refusal to judge practices that we would not accept in our own society in the name of "cultural sensitivity" or tolerance for groups we deem to be victimized by our imperialist or hegemonic practices. It seems a dangerous formula of cultural sensitivity indeed that renders us silent in the face of genital mutilation, yet it is frequently argued that categorically judging this practice as wrong imposes Western values that ignore the desires and beliefs of women perpetuating the practice. Note, however, that we are not expected to be sensitive to the desires and beliefs of pedophiles when we condemn the harm they cause to their young victims' sexual development and expression.

Slavoj Žižek calls this the "antinomy of tolerant reason" in a discussion of the West's fraught relationship with Islam. In our "tolerance" of the "other," whether cultural, racial, ethnic, religious, or geopolitical, liberal-minded citizens of Western democracies become tolerant of *intolerance*. Apologies for our own cultural beliefs and practices proliferate, while those who remain steadfast in their intolerance of or hostility toward the West are not expected to be apologetic. Žižek's primary example is the international response to the Danish newspaper *Jyllands-Posten*, which published caricatures of Muhammad in 2005, spurring mob violence and the stigmatization of an entire country. "Even if we reject the caricatures in disgust," Žižek maintains, their publication in no way justifies such a response. The Western partisans of "multiculturalist tolerance" who attempt to be understanding of this outrage, he insists, are not respecting the Muslim other but rather demonstrating a "hidden and patronizing racism."[24] This is precisely why we must judge—why we have a responsibility to judge. Mere tolerance for practices that may be wrong means that we do not recognize the other's agency and ability to make the right choices.

While he does not explicitly use the term "judgment," Žižek's conclusion makes it clear that this is what is missing from such a perspective.

> Respect for others' beliefs as the highest value can mean only one of two things: either we treat the other in a patronizing way and avoid hurting him in order not to ruin his illusions, or we adopt the relativist stance of multiple "regimes of truth," disqualifying as violent imposition any clear insistence of truth. What, however, about submitting Islam—together with all other religions—to a respectful, but for that reason no less ruthless, critical analysis? This, and only this, is the way to show true respect for Muslims: to treat them as serious adults responsible for their beliefs.[25]

Reticence to renounce practices about which we ought to be outraged demonstrates one of the worst effects of moral relativism: the abdication of our responsibility to judge and to judge well. But what does it mean to *judge well*? And on what basis do we know that others have *not* judged well? Does judgment lead to truth? In other words, how do we judge judgment? In this passage, Žižek refers to a respectful yet ruthless critical analysis that does not negate agency or responsibility. In this he is close to Gayatri Chakravorty Spivak, who urges us to "earn the right to criticize." Spivak refers to the American student in her classroom who says, "I am only a bourgeois white male, I can't speak," when discussions on "the Third World" arise. The assumption here is that the student is not qualified to make a criticism, as he has the proximity of neither experience nor knowledge. Spivak demands that we learn what is necessary to learn in order to take this "risk ... of criticizing something which is *Other*." The refusal to engage in this critical operation, she explains, amounts to "salving your conscience, and allowing you not to do any homework." The nature of this risk is no doubt the risk of being unpopular. While Spivak says that if we take this risk, we will "probably be made welcome, and can hope to be judged with respect," it didn't turn out this way for Arendt.[26]

Žižek and Spivak both point to the need for critical engagement and investigation in making judgments. Central to this task is *respect for persons* rather than for beliefs or practices—respect for others' agency and responsibility—combined with doing one's "homework" in order to discover the facts, acquire knowledge, and understand circumstances in order to evaluate them. This is not a show of responsibility *for* the other or her actions but respecting the other enough to expect that she will be responsible for her own actions. And we must also be responsible for ours. Still, we should ask whether judgments necessarily lead to the right outcomes, to truth or justice or the good life.

I am drawn to this perspective and believe that it is enhanced by Arendt's argument that thinking freely beyond any moral code is necessary for judgment. While Arendt died before completing her conceptualization of judgment in *The Life of the Mind*, judgment is a theme throughout her writings. Arendt's critics express some disappointment that a unified account remains a mystery, and much speculation, particularly since she is thought to have made a dramatic shift in her final work from politics and community to philosophy and the solitary act of thinking.[27] Ronald Beiner, for example, argues that Arendt offers two theories on judgment, an earlier theory that considers it from the point of view of the *vita activa*, and a later theory from the point of view of the life of the mind. In the first approach, judging is a feature of political activity; in the second, it is a distinct mental activity, one that privileges the perspective of the "blind poet," at a remove from action and therefore capable of reflection.[28] I am more inclined to agree with Peter J. Steinberger, who suggests that this approach underestimates the relationship between Arendt's work on the life of the mind and her earlier political theory.[29] Judgment, an activity of the mind, occurs in a political world; ideas—the products of thinking—belong to the world. As Max Deutscher puts it, "judgment is required both in the midst of active life and when we take the 'ringside seat' of the spectator."[30]

Arendt defines thinking as "a silent discourse with oneself"[31] and as "the habit of examining whatever happens to come to pass."[32] Despite its solitary nature, thinking depends on its public use, as Arendt's lectures on Kant's political philosophy illuminate. Reason is not made "to isolate itself but to get into community with others."[33] Kant asks, "how much and how correctly would we think if we did not think in community with others to whom we communicate our thoughts and who communicate theirs to us!" It is the freedom to communicate our thoughts publicly that alone provides "a remedy against all the evils of the present state of affairs"—"the only treasure left to us in our civic life."[34] Truth is what we can communicate, as Karl Jaspers put it; without this exposure of ideas to others, thinking would disappear.[35]

Consequently, objections to our own ideas must be approached not merely to refute them, Kant explains, but to weave them into our judgments, give them the opportunity to overturn our "most cherished beliefs." He argues that "by thus viewing my judgments impartially from the standpoint of others, some third view that will improve upon my previous insight may be obtainable."[36] Impartiality comes not from a higher standpoint that transcends the "*melée*" and settles disputes objectively, but from taking the viewpoints of others into account.[37] It is a matter of enlarging one's point of view by adopting every conceivable standpoint, "verifying the observations of each by means of all the others."[38] Kant called this process of thinking the "enlargement of the mind," an idea that plays a crucial role in the *Critique of Judgment*. This doesn't mean passively accepting what another thinks, which would entail a mere exchange of another's prejudice for one's own. Arendt calls this "representative thought": "I form an opinion by considering a given issue from different viewpoints, by making present to my mind the standpoints of those who are absent; that is, I represent them." It is a question neither of empathy nor of joining a majority, she insists, but of "being and thinking in my own identity where actually I am not." The imagination thus plays a critical role in thinking and judging. Even if I am alone with myself in solitude, Arendt writes, "I remain in this world of universal interdependence, where I can make myself the representative of everybody else."[39]

In *The Life of the Mind*, Arendt's analysis of thinking is inspired by the question, Could the activity of thinking be "among the conditions that make men abstain from evil-doing or even actually 'condition' them against it?" She contends that the absence of thought she encountered in Adolf Eichmann was neither because he forgot moral habits nor because he was uncomprehending and stupid. It was due to an absence of thinking.[40] As a result, Eichmann's judgment was skewed. Thus thinking, not principles, intuitions, or habits, prepares us for moral judgment: thinking makes it possible to judge, and knowledge prompts the thinking that judgment requires.[41] This silent discourse with oneself is a reflective, deliberative examination of what comes to pass, required for the "ruthless, critical analysis" of which Žižek speaks.

All human beings with their mental faculties intact are capable of this kind of thought and therefore of moral judgment. It is the freedom of the human mind that gives rise to both thinking and judging, according to Arendt. We are bound not by commandments but by the freedom to deliberate, evaluate, and create the improbable. And the mind's freedom "can survive even in the midst of the most unfree political conditions."[42] Those who did not collaborate with the Nazis, although they could not and did not rise in rebellion, were thinking and judging, not from an automatic conscience—a prejudgment based on "a set of learned or innate rules" applied to a particular case— but from the desire to live at peace with themselves. "They decided that it would be better to do nothing, not because the world would then be changed for the better, but simply because only on this condition could they go on living with themselves at all."[43]

Thus the criterion for right and wrong depends not on moral habits and customs or on a set of commands or principles, Arendt tells us, but "on what I decide with regard to myself."[44] Moral judgment is about refusing to do wrong, which she suggests is far less difficult than we are often led to believe. It is by declaring "I can't do this," because I don't want to live with a murderer or a thief or a liar, that I judge. The onus falls squarely on my own shoulders; it is *my* responsibility to live well and govern my own behavior. Of course, we are still required to judge the deeds of others, but this is also out of a refusal to comply. Doubters and skeptics are more reliable in times of trouble than those who "hold fast to moral norms," Arendt says, for the former are accustomed to making up their own minds rather than obeying orders. Refusing to support a dictatorship, for example, would be an effective weapon if enough people joined in.[45]

One must judge as a member of a community, guided by one's *sensus communis*, or community sense. Arendt means by this not only a local community but a global one: "In the last analysis, one is a member of a world community by the sheer fact of being human; this is one's 'cosmopolitan existence.'" To judge and to act politically means to take one's bearings from the idea—not the actuality—of being a world citizen. But the idea of *sensus communis* or enlarged thinking doesn't help us to understand how to make good judgments when everyone else is making bad judgments. Arendt maintains that individuals must be capable of formulating judgments independently of prevailing opinion and yet in concert with others. In the end, we must rely on our own judgment regardless of what everyone else thinks.

This is unsatisfying for critics like Steinberger, who argues that Arendt does not provide "anything approaching a criterion on the basis of which we might reliably distinguish good from bad judgment" or give us any explicit idea as to "how the faculty of judgment might be cultivated and nurtured."[46] Indeed, judgment is not something we can learn, according to Arendt; nor is it a cognitive skill or a "highly developed intelligence." For Kant, it emerges as a "talent" that can be practiced but not taught. It deals with particulars, in a realm in which being "learned" does not necessarily result in good judgment.[47] We must think, examine, assess, refuse to comply, imagine other perspectives, take into account other opinions and judgments, but ultimately make our own moral judgments. What makes some individuals better at the kind of thinking required for judgment than others isn't, therefore, entirely clear. Deutscher uses the analogy of a musician rehearsing for a concert: "It would be bad judgment to stop in the midst of a concert to rehearse a *bravura* passage even if that would improve one's playing. Forging ahead, hoping for the best may be the only thing to do, but emphasises the need to have already rehearsed, thoughtfully, technically difficult passages. Only after practice and rehearsal can one act with good judgment in launching into the passage under the spotlight of an audience's attention and expectation."[48]

This "rehearsal" may be implicit in Arendt's description of Karl Jaspers as exemplary with regard to judgment, although at times it seems that he was simply born exemplary. Responsibility was not a burden for Jaspers, or a moral imperative, but flowed naturally out of an innate pleasure in "illuminating the darkness." Indeed, "he has loved light so long that it has marked his whole personality," Arendt writes, "and whatever stands up to light and does not dissolve in vapors under its brightness, partakes of *humanitas;* to take it upon oneself to answer before mankind for every thought means to live in that luminosity in which oneself and everything one thinks is tested." Like the Jewish pariahs Arendt highlights in "We Refugees," Jaspers is "inviolable, untemptable, unswayable," and she finds this both admirable and fascinating. There is no succumbing to the temptation to support evil by choosing the lesser evil. Experience—going beyond the solitude of thinking—is essential, for a lack of exposure to temptation, Arendt warns, can lead to inexperience and uncover the danger of such "unerring certainty of judgment and sovereignty of mind." Jaspers bears a kind of "indigenous self-assurance," a "cheerful recklessness" with which he exposes himself to "the currents of public life while at the same time remaining independent of all the trends and opinions that happen to be in vogue." Here is the crux: Arendt believes that within Jaspers's own "small world," created between himself and his wife, he learned what is "essential for the whole realm of human affairs." "Within this small world he unfolded and practiced his incomparable faculty for dialogue, the splendid precision of his way of listening, the constant readiness to give a candid account of himself, the patience to linger over a matter under discussion, and above all the ability to lure what is otherwise passed over in silence into the area of discourse, to make it worth talking about. Thus in speaking and listening, he succeeds in changing, widening, sharpening—or, as he himself would beautifully put it, in illuminating."[49]

Jaspers's "small world" does not sound like a global *sensus communis*, but it appears as a kind of microcosm of the stage on which thinking must occur through experience and reflection. In these passages Arendt describes her own personal version of one who judges well, highlighting respect for others and the desire to "illuminate," both critical elements in the human interactions for which she praises Jaspers: dialogue, listening, patience, and the rigorous testing of thoughts.

One must think, alone and with others, must imagine and listen to as many perspectives as possible, but must remain unswayed by the majority when it is not thinking well, when it is lured by the lesser-evil argument or lulled by indifference. In the absence of categorical imperatives and in the presence of unrelenting contingency, we must rely on human judgment, in concert with others, motivated by respect and the desire to know what is the best course of action, for we share a world in which we are all fundamentally vulnerable to risk and injury.

What is missing from Arendt's effusive admiration for her friend is any mention of the love or compassion Jaspers might bear for others that would motivate his pleasure in "illuminating the darkness." Arendt's emphasis on the role of thinking in judgment neglects the part that affect plays in the moral life. Even if judgment is a talent or skill that can be practiced, her version of judgment remains too exclusively in the cognitive realm. Highlighting the freedom of the mind and the thinking that determines whether one is able to say, "I do not want to live with a murderer," ignores the effects of fear, empathic identification, trauma, or powerful parental instincts. These effects may lead one to make moral judgments and act in ways we would normally consider unethical. Emotions, as Kathleen Taylor reminds us, are the force behind every act of cruelty, fueling the urge to act.[50]

Arendt's confidence in the power of the human mind to make the right judgments if one is actually thinking explains why she passes judgment on the Jewish Councils *before* the years of the Final Solution, when they were not, as she put it, under the pressure and impact of terror. Implicit in this distinction is the acknowledgment that when the choice is between loading bodies into furnaces or being thrown into the furnace oneself—in other words, when one acts under unbearable pressure with little or no choice—the terms of responsibility and judgment change. Thinking may take a back seat to acting out of sheer emotion—to terror, resignation, or rage. Habituation may then also come into play. The musician rehearses for a concert only after years of training. Against Arendt, I would argue that we learn from the example of others how to treat one another with respect, how to engage in the speaking, listening, and "illuminating" for which Arendt praised Jaspers.

Even the best kind of thinking, if empathy for another and compassion for human fallibility are lacking, will not be enough. Had Arendt chosen to discuss the predicament of those already dying in the camps without means of resistance, rather than the Jewish leaders, she might have addressed this point. Her claim that actions can be "undone" to some extent through the gesture of forgiveness does not detract from her argument that the Jewish leaders were responsible for their actions, but it does suggest that compassion, love, and friendship play a larger part in judgment than Arendt is willing to admit here.

Judgment, then, is only partially about engaging in "ruthless, critical analysis," to use Žižek's phrase, which means not only thinking within a social context but also informing ourselves about those whose actions or opinions we are judging. Earning the right to criticize means becoming knowledgeable about a particular event or phenomenon. It is not only an imaginative or representative exercise—at least not one that can forgo the necessary work required in representative thinking of the kind Arendt describes. If we are to imagine another's perspective, something of the context, the environment in which the other is situated, is required. We can point to horrific examples of what happens in the absence of such thinking, when the order to kill your neighbor with a machete is piped over the morning radio, or when you are persuaded to blow yourself up in a crowded shopping mall for the cause of freedom. It is too simple to say that moral judgment is premised on knowing right from wrong, for wrong actions are often thought to be right. There must also be respect for others, born of compassion.

The Blind Poet

We need to keep in mind that two aspects of judgment are being consid-
ered here simultaneously: the judgment we exercise when we deliberate, make choices, and act, and the judgment we perform when we assess the actions and decisions of others. In both there is a tension between distance and proximity. The role of time and objective distance in the matter of judgment is important, for only in hindsight can we recognize the part that actors—whether victims or perpetrators—play in the unfolding of history, enough to call ourselves and others to account. We are often considered to be making imprudent choices simply because we are too close to any given situation; we are unable to view our circumstances with some modicum of objectivity. When immersed in a crisis, we don't see the whole picture; we are lost in the trees, unable to see the forest. There is no time to deliberate, to weigh our options, so *we act;* we do not decide. In the midst of a crisis there is usually little time to stop and think about what is the best thing to do based on moral codes or principles. We do not often find ourselves in a boat adrift on an open sea, deliberating about who should be thrown over the side so as to prolong the lives of others. This is not to suggest that we dispense with principles but that we recognize their limits in a crisis. We don't have the benefit of hindsight when we act, and we can't anticipate in advance the consequences of our actions.

When we assess the actions of others, we experience the quandary of being too close or too far, vilified for judging—and therefore betraying—those whom we love, or condemned for judging those whose experience we do not share. Here we do have the benefit of hindsight, a distinct advantage over the person whose actions we are judging.

Arendt herself shifted in later writings from describing judgment as a feature of political life—as the decision of the actor on how to act in the public realm—to judgment as a faculty of the mind, requiring the objective distance of a spectator. The symbol of judging becomes for her the "blind poet," removed from action and more capable of disinterested reflection and retrospective judgment. This is the position of the spectator, whose advantage is that "he sees the play as a whole, while each of the actors knows only his part or, if he should judge from the perspective of acting, only the part of the whole that concerns him. The actor is partial by definition."[51]

In "Truth and Politics," Arendt states unequivocally that "the very quality of an opinion, as of a judgment, depends upon the degree of its impartiality." Opinions are not self-evident truths, but neither are the contingent "facts" of human affairs. Furthermore, factual evidence is established through the testimony of witnesses, which is notoriously unreliable. Discrepancies are usually settled through the majority interpretation of other eyewitnesses, and there is nothing to prevent the majority from bearing false witness.[52] If this is true, then we cannot demand the same impartiality and retrospective judgment from the victim immersed in an event in the present that we demand from the spectator who reflects in hindsight. Yet we can't wait for hindsight to clarify where our responsibilities lie, for it is in the midst of a crisis that we most need to make wise choices, to remain fully aware of our responsibilities. This may be difficult for us to accept, for it is in the moment of crisis that our moral and political responsibilities are often too great to bear. In crisis, fear and pain can overwhelm us.

The requirement that the observer remain impartial has fallen out of fashion, however, in the movement to recognize the importance of the victim's experience and voice in the account of an event. Our current reticence to judge has much to do with our unwillingness to speak for others. Vetlesen addresses the contradiction implicit in the desire to judge impartially and at the same time privilege the victim's experience. To judge impartially, he argues, "means to be able to take into account the views of all parties without identifying with any of them." Such judgment presupposes that the judge is a spectator, not a participant, one who has the privilege of hindsight. But where is the victim's own voice in this operation? Vetlesen suggests that we can make the case that only the victim—the survivor, rather—knows the reality of evil, because she is the one who has suffered it. But it is also true, he adds, "that victims have a great need to find ways to deceive themselves about the sheer horror of the suffering that has been visited upon them so as to deny it, forget it, minimize it, sensing that their very survival as human beings depends upon some measure of such self-deception. Or alternatively, victims may be tempted to exaggerate the evil they have suffered to such an extent that these evils entirely escape human comprehension, thus disconnecting them from the ambit of judgment—*anyone's* judgment." Vetlesen recommends a middle road: we must be "as attentive as is practically possible" to the sufferings of victims while the actions responsible for their victimization are occurring, in order to stop them. It is the character of the deed, he argues, not the identity of the victim or the perpetrator, that matters in impartial judgment.[53]

Arendt does not shirk the problem of proximity versus distance. How "troubled men of our time are by this question of judgment" is obvious to her given the controversy over *Eichmann in Jerusalem:*

> The argument that we cannot judge if we were not present and involved ourselves seems to convince everyone everywhere, although it seems obvious that if it were true, neither the administration of justice nor the writing of history would ever be possible. In contrast to these confu- sions, the reproach of self-righteousness raised against those who do judge is age-old; but that does not make it any the more valid. Even the judge who condemns a murderer can still say when he goes home: "And there, but for the grace of God, go I." All German Jews unani- mously have condemned the wave of coordination which passed over the German people in 1933 and from one day to the next turned the Jews into pariahs. Is it conceivable that none of them ever asked him- self how many of his own group would have done just the same if only they had been allowed to? But is their condemnation today any the less correct for that reason?[54]

There is little patience here for the criticism against her judgment of the Jewish Councils on the basis of her distance from the Nazi horrors. The "self-righteousness" of the judge who stands at a remove from the events she judges does not negate the necessity of the judgment. It does make the judge unpopular, however. The one who exercises judgment must be prepared to be vilified.

And vilified Arendt was. Although she saw herself as something of a "blind poet" analyzing the case of the Jewish Councils in her coverage of the Eichmann trial, others accused her of betraying her own people. In a famous exchange of letters, Gershom Scholem complained of her "heartless" tone and lack of love for the Jewish people, and accused her of benefiting the Germans more than mourning the fate of the Jews. She showed not balanced judgment, according to Scholem, but "demagogic will-to-overstatement."[55]

Who can say what the Jewish elders should have decided? he asks. There were many compelled to make terrible decisions in circumstances that we cannot reproduce or reconstruct.

Walter Laqueur echoed these sentiments when he expressed to Arendt his unease with her criticism against the Jewish establishment for its lack of judgment: "There has been and is great reluctance to pass judgment on certain Jewish leaders. They may have failed, they may have to be condemned; and yet, who does not feel that there but for the grace of God, go I?" Both Scholem and Laqueur express a deep compassion for the Jewish people as victims, and a reluctance to judge their misdeeds in light of the much greater evil of a clearly defined perpetrator. Like Scholem, Laqueur suggests that Arendt was attacked not for what she said but how she said it. Her "cardinal sin" lay not in telling the truth in the hostile environment of the Jewish establishment—as she thought she was doing—but in her conviction that a conspiracy had formed against her, with "dramatic and sinister" causes, that led to the polemicization of the entire discussion.[56]

These sentiments arise from profound discomfort with the criticism of a community by one of its members. The question "Who am I to judge?" may have less to do with the meaning Arendt gives it—that we are all alike and equally bad—than with our empathic proximity to others familiar to us in the face of a common enemy. After all, the Germans, as Arendt informs us, were also reluctant to judge their own Nazi criminals—who might be neighbors or friends—hiding them in their midst after the war. Scholem chastised Arendt for disloyalty, calling her "a daughter of our people" who exhibited a shocking lack of "*Ahabath Israel*," or love of Jewish people. But a defiant Arendt responded, "You are quite right—I am not moved by any 'love' of this sort, and for two reasons: I have never in my life 'loved' any people or collective—neither the German people, nor the French, nor the American, nor the working class or anything of that sort. I indeed love 'only' my friends and the only kind of love I know of and believe in is the love of persons."[57] This is a powerful statement of Arendt's beliefs regarding her own belonging to the Jewish community in particular, and belonging to an identity category in general. As she later wrote to Samuel Grafton, she identified with those Jews "with no strong connections to the Jewish community, for whom, however, the fact of their Jewishness is not a matter of indifference."[58]

The exchange between Scholem and Arendt is significant, for it exposes the dangers of a community built on the solidarity of those who have been victimized. It is this solidarity in the face of oppression and violation that can lead to the very same abdication of responsibility and reluctance to judge that we find in perpetrators, which is why Arendt urges us to think about the reasons used to justify actions, not about the persons who employ them. She describes these dangers in other writings. In an essay on the need for Arab and Jewish cooperation in the newly created state of Israel, she notes "the dangerous tendencies of formerly oppressed peoples to shut themselves off from the rest of the world and develop nationalist superiority complexes of their own."[59] She relates these tendencies to a lack of political responsibility and accountability unique to pariahs like the Jews. Indeed, such groups are in this sense *privileged*. In "dark times," Arendt explains, humanity manifests itself in "brotherly attachment" or "philanthropic feelings" among historically persecuted peoples and enslaved groups. This kind of humanity "is the advantage that the pariahs of this world always and in all circumstances can have over others." It is dearly bought, however, "often accompanied by so radical a loss of the world, so fearful an atrophy of all the organs with which we respond to it . . . that in extreme cases, in which pariahdom has persisted for centuries, we can speak of real worldlessness. And worldlessness, alas, is always a form of barbarism."[60]

Arendt turns on its head the worldview we have come to accept after several decades of theorizing "otherness"—one in which the victim (the oppressed) is granted an unmediated access to moral truth, the truth of experience and of pure innocence. In these passages it is the victimized who share a kind of privilege, a solidarity that nonpariah peoples desire for themselves but can only experience through compassion for the suffering pariahs, and a certain freedom from responsibility. This "warmth of persecuted peoples" can bring a "sheer goodness," as Arendt puts it, often otherwise lacking in human beings. It can be the source of vitality or joy in simply being alive, "rather suggesting that life comes fully into its own only among those who are, in worldly terms, the insulted and injured." But, she warns, the feelings of "fraternity" that accompany the victimized community manifest themselves only in darkness, and threaten to "dissolve into nothingness like phantoms" as soon as conditions change. "The humanity of the insulted and injured," Arendt concludes, "has never yet survived the hour of liberation by so much as a minute. This does not mean that it is insignificant, for in fact it makes insult and injury endurable; but it does mean that in political terms it is absolutely irrelevant."[61]

When it comes to the solidarity of friendship, however, Arendt's certainty in these passages gives way to ambivalence. What happens when we must judge the actions of friends? In a review of the edited collection of letters between Arendt and Martin Heidegger, Mark Greif argues that Arendt may have betrayed her own principles in the matter of judgment when she failed to judge someone who was very close to her personally. Arendt's intimate friendship with Heidegger was cut off after 1933, when he became the rector of Freiburg and a member of the Nazi party, at the same time that Arendt was fleeing the Nazis. Their prewar correspondence ended with Arendt questioning Heidegger about his anti-Semitism and the rumors she had heard about his abandonment of Jewish colleagues and students, a challenge from which Heidegger defended himself with the retort that it was all "slander." After an impromptu visit several decades later, Arendt wrote to Heidegger that her visit saved her from committing the "inexcusable act of infidelity" of abandoning her friend. Greif calls this Arendt's own "lesser evil," an inexcusable refusal to judge Heidegger as she had judged others and as she demanded that we all must judge. "What Arendt did not know about Heidegger, and what she excused, one hesitates to separate," Greif states. "The clear thing is that she made her choice. Her philosophy of judgment, together with her one key refusal to judge, can be understood in human terms but never reconciled."[62]

But was this a refusal to judge, or did Arendt in fact judge well, with compassion? If the latter, then perhaps she would have judged the Jewish Councils differently had her close friends been among them. Greif's example highlights the tension I am describing here between proximity and distance in the matter of judgment. Friendship, love, or loyalty to one's own should not prevent judgment, but they may render it more challenging, evoking a stubborn tension between compassion and judgment. Arendt recognizes this, and she introduces friendship as a "subjective" criterion in moral judgment and philosophy.

In "Some Questions of Moral Philosophy," for example, she quotes Cicero in the context of a discussion on the conflicting opinions of philosophers. When deciding which philosopher was right and which was wrong, Cicero "suddenly and quite unexpectedly introduces an altogether different criterion," Arendt states, the subjective criterion of the kind of person with whom he wishes to be associated. "By God I'd much rather go astray with Plato than hold true views with these people [the Pythagoreans]," Cicero declares. Elsewhere she explains that our decisions concerning right and wrong will depend on our choice of company, "of those with whom we wish to spend our lives."[63]

Of course, we may love and choose to spend our time with individuals who are capable of doing harmful things. There is nothing surprising in this fact. Friendship does not let us off the hook when it comes to judgment. For

Arendt, the greatest evil is perpetrated by "nobodies, that is, by human beings who refuse to be persons." Those who refuse to think by themselves about what they are doing, about their wrongdoing retrospectively, or to remember what they did, have failed to constitute themselves into somebodies.[64] If we forgive the person but not the crime, then we cannot forgive those who fail to become somebodies. Did Heidegger become a "somebody" for Arendt in private? While he remained silent publicly on the question of his involvement with the Nazi party, we will never know whether he vindicated himself to Arendt privately. If the humanity—the vulnerability—of the perpetrator must be evident in order to forgive him, then we will be tempted to refuse to judge, for no human being, not even the most violent perpetrator, is without some good. If we witness that fragment of goodness, of *humanitas*, in the perpetrator, then we are always in danger of excusing his or her wrongdoing. What is the alternative? If we refuse to see it, we are in danger of the opposite risk, of judging too harshly.

In a discussion of the political function of collective memory in the context of the Eichmann trial, Eyal Sivan writes that in the great tradition of documenting, collecting, and archiving images and stories of victims, perpetrators are rarely represented. Victims fascinate us, Sivan notes, and we defend the emphasis on their stories and images as a duty of memory.[65] But perpetrators are more often fictionalized as inhuman; they become quasi-mythic representations—monsters, beasts, maniacs.

> It is true that to focus on the perpetrator is to risk making us identify with him; as he explains and justifies himself, tells us about his work, his joys, his sorrows, he looks like anyone else and we grant him our understanding. The technical problems he has had to resolve, his problems with his conscience, the "duty" that obliges him to follow orders—these are experiences that all of us can recognize. But it is precisely on this familiarity with him that we should count. It is in this small space, which involves identification, comprehension, and indulgence, that we can choose to evaluate him.[66]

Images of horror and its victims, Sivan points out, can replace thought with mere spectacle. "Pity paralyzes thinking" when the political event is reduced to a pathetic current affair.[67] "Identification, comprehension, and indulgence" constitute an essential emotional response to an event or action, and these responses are more likely when wrongdoers are known or loved by a witness or judge. These are the features perhaps missing in Arendt's judgment of the Jewish Councils but present in her regard for Heidegger. She certainly judged him for his Nazi sympathies, but later decided that he was still someone she did not want to abandon.

Yet "pity paralyzes thinking," as Sivan warns. We could consider this task in terms of a spectrum. Judging well requires some identification or "indulgence"—as the judge who leaves the courtroom thinking "there but for the grace of God go I" does not suggest the condemnation was less necessary. Perhaps the situation is only more tragic. It is difficult to judge those whom we love, but necessary if the harm to others (including ourselves) is at stake. In some cases, the intervention of a third party is crucial. It must be remembered that understanding one's predicament is not the same as condoning a wrongdoing. Rather than believing judgment is compromised when we are too close, we could argue that it is more effective, as Sivan suggests, when it is exercised with understanding and identification.

To Flourish

I have argued throughout this chapter that we must acknowledge the responsibility of perpetrators who were once victims, and of those who ambiguously inhabit both categories. Arendt prohibits any easy association of the victim with moral blamelessness and of the perpetrator with absolute evil. The storm of controversy such a move unleashed speaks to our inability to imagine a future for political communities beyond these binaries. A victimized individual or group, subsumed under the rubric of a generalized "other," is assumed to be without agency, as though the moment of victimization erases both the past and the future of a political actor. Under certain conditions, compassion and solidarity, though necessary, have a paradoxical outcome: they provide comfort yet may perpetuate politically impotent victimhood.

The fact that judgment and responsibility remain thoroughly contingent for Arendt, unbound by prefabricated standards or rules, may be difficult to swallow, but contingency is the necessary precondition for judging at all—otherwise we indulge in moralism. Lack of judgment is related to an inability to learn from experience and to apply categories and formulas "whose basis of experience has long been forgotten." It is necessary to think and more significantly to judge without holding on to preconceived standards, norms, and general rules under which particular cases can be subsumed. Those who are qualified to judge are those who have nothing to fall back on but their experience, "unpatterned by preconceived concepts," or those who have standards and norms that do not fit the experience.[68] This forces us to engage with history and thus with the responsibility and decisions of actors who move it along. We are then governed by respect for others and their particular circumstances, rather than by moral codes.

The emphasis on judgment demands the agency of both victim and perpetrator while enabling us to make moral distinctions between their respective misdeeds. Eichmann, the Jewish Councils, and the rest of us alike are called on to think and judge in such a way that we will be able to live with ourselves. There is nothing to ease the frustration of being unable to program such an injunction. Each historical event, each experience of victimization, must be investigated and analyzed within its own historical context. Rather than throw up our hands in protest—that we do not know, we are not there, we cannot criticize, for who are we to judge?—we take on the responsibility of "earning the right to criticize."

Stressing political responsibility for oneself and one's people is a very different approach from the paradigm of responsibility bequeathed by such philosophers as Emmanuel Levinas, which appears to have led us to a culture of pathos motivated by guilt and lacking in judgment. Many are unwilling to criticize the occupation of the Palestinians for fear of appearing anti-Semitic, and of not being compassionate enough toward a persecuted people—a terrible irony, considering the lack of compassion on a global scale for Palestinians. Similarly, acts of terror are sometimes justified as acts of despair, and although compassionate onlookers attempt to justify these acts—in the most rational of terms—as the necessary self-defense of the oppressed, terror does not tend to garner support from the global community, and its condemnation should not be read as siding with the occupiers.

If we are to move beyond the extremely polarized terrain of global politics today, then we need the courage to take up our responsibility to judge, morally and politically. In drawing attention to the temporal aspect of solidarity and the dangers of perpetuating a community of victims that responds to victimhood by reinforcing the binary logic of victim versus perpetrator, Arendt is neither blaming victims for their own misfortunes nor neglecting to judge the worst evil we encounter. Rather, she enables us to conceive of a future in which the seemingly inevitable transition of victim to perpetrator might be suspended.

We make moral judgments in order to create a world in which we want to live—to flourish, not merely to subsist. It isn't simply to know what is right and wrong, as though all we needed were a list to follow, a tablet of commandments, but to choose with whom we want to live in proximity and what kind of life we will share in our communities. We teach our children to emulate the kind of behavior that will foster this flourishing, not merely so that they know what is right or wrong but so that they will acquire the habits they need in order to get along with others, to act with integrity, honesty, kindness, creativity, or reason, and so on. We judge our own behavior in order to live with ourselves; we judge others in order to live among our fellow human beings and cultivate community. Accounting for our actions, acknowledging our freedom to make decisions and to act, and taking responsibility for this freedom are all inextricably linked to judgment. That there are limits to this responsibility and accountability—limits that reveal a blind spot in Arendt's emphasis on thinking and judging—is the subject of the following chapter.

5

TO KILL OR BE KILLED

I consider myself a victim. I was forced to take part [in] that war.
I didn't have a choice. I had to kill or be killed.

Maybe war is the strongest narcotic in the world.

That war has the seductive allure of a narcotic is a surprising admission to those of us who more easily imagine youthful soldiers sucked into a world of relentless mud and blood against their will as pawns, cannon fodder, or victims of a war they didn't want.[1] These epigraphs were written by Ishmael Beah and Arkady Babchenko, two young men who were still teens when they participated in wars characterized by particularly heinous acts of cruelty. Their stories have become best-sellers. Beah was a child soldier in Sierra Leone, forced to participate in a vicious eleven-year civil war, whose eventual rescue led him to write *A Long Way Gone: Memoirs of a Boy Soldier*. Babchenko was conscripted to fight in Chechnya in 1995 while an eighteen-year-old law student, and he returned voluntarily to fight in the second Chechen campaign in 1999. He wrote a memoir of his experience called *One Soldier's War* that has been hailed as possessing "a touch of Tolstoy."[2]

Unflinchingly grim, Babchenko devotes a good part of his book to describing the brutal violence unleashed by the army leadership on its own untrained recruits and volunteers. Given the beatings and deprivation that he suffered repeatedly, it is difficult to think of Babchenko as anything but a victim in this story—for the Russian state is responsible and must be held accountable, not the soldiers. Explaining his voluntary return to the front four years later, he says only, "I just couldn't help it. I was irresistibly drawn back there." But he flatly concludes, "there is no blood on my conscience."[3]

In Babchenko's case it may be appropriate to recall Arendt's suggestion that we are "tempted," rather than forced, to do wrong. Beah, however, identifying himself as a victim whose agency was stolen by a "kill-or-be-killed" ultimatum, tells us that he was only twelve when he was forced to fight against rebel groups after being captured and repeatedly drugged by the government army in Sierra Leone in 1993. In the introductory paragraphs of this book, I referred to Beah's story as an example of the kind of excruciating moral dilemma that is at the heart of this project. In the case of the child soldier especially, we find it impossible to move between discrete categories of victim and perpetrator. If Beah is a pure victim, as he is most often considered, then it seems necessary to erase all consideration of *his* victims and focus on those who forced his hand. This ignores the fact that those who recruited him may also have been child soldiers whose hands were forced. We have to acknowledge that Beah, and all child soldiers in combat—even those who choose to participate in order to survive—are killers as much as they are victims, neither purely guilty nor purely innocent.

What Beah's and Babchenko's declarations have in common is the view of the victim as caught helplessly in the machinery of war. Both killed innocent people while literally or figuratively narcotized by war. Both arouse our sympathies with their heartrending accounts of the misery of killing and of the fear of being killed. There may be a world of difference in their respective experiences and in the conditions under which they had to make choices, but in both cases the public response has been to view them as pure victims in need of compassion, or as heroes worth celebrating. It is a troubling compassion that remains willfully blind to the victims of victims, for when there is no choice—or at most a choice to kill or be killed—to raise the question of responsibility, to acknowledge the victims of victims, is to tarnish the purity of the victim's innocence and blame the sufferer.

This boy and this young man were rendered victims in the act of killing. They were not victims-turned-perpetrators—not yesterday's victims who killed today—but victims and perpetrators simultaneously. They were victims *as* killers, a fact that almost no one is willing to acknowledge. And why should we? What good will come of an investigation into the agency and responsibility of a child or youth forced to take up arms and participate in a cruel war? Why not focus instead on the accountability of the government and rebel leaders who recruit, train, torture, and rape these children? I have been arguing that identifying with, and living within, a victim's worldview leads to the denial of agency, the manipulation of sympathy, and the rationalization or justification of wrongdoing. In the case of child soldiers—of victims *as* killers—we face the particularly difficult problem of trying to delineate clearly who is a "victim" and who a "perpetrator." As we will see, child and adult soldiers are ruled by an ideology committed to vengeful violence in the name of security against an enemy. Too little attention is paid to the agency of these actors, whether children, youth, or adults, and to their complicity in the process of learning to kill.

The problem, once again, is that innocence and guilt, victimhood and culpability, are not discrete categories. We are considering wars in which there is no "good" government protecting purely innocent civilians from evil rebels. These groups and their actions are hardly incommensurable—and neither are their motives. The claims made by child soldiers are often the very claims made by their captors; they are acting in self-defense for a just cause. Most important, these children may in turn become other children's captors, rendering political analysis and moral inquiry all the more challenging and all the more necessary. One of the most effective ways to seduce masses of people into the job of killing is to convince them that it is the right, and the only, solution to a problem. If those trained to kill for the "right" reasons already view themselves as victims, so much the better. The victim who kills out of revenge and in the name of reclaiming dignity and humanity can be the most vicious killer of all.

There is little point in investigating questions of moral responsibility and judgment with respect to victims if we cannot account for the most excruciating case of the victim as killer. In the previous chapter we witnessed the challenges Hannah Arendt faced when she grappled with the question of judgment and responsibility in the case of Jewish leaders who collaborated with the Nazis. The uproar she provoked speaks to our commitment to upholding the circumstances in which a human subject can claim immunity from personal responsibility for events seemingly out of his or her control. But even if we were willing to grant that an adult in extraordinary circumstances, under duress, is still responsible to varying degrees for his own actions, can we say the same about a child? While we face in this instance the same challenges that Arendt faced, we are dealing with a very different historical and political context. Are the children, some of them as young as seven or eight, who are recruited and coerced into killing emblematic of absolute and pure innocence? How should we judge these children if we judge them at all?

War's Children

While the number of children acting as soldiers at any one time around the world is impossible to determine, various organizations have attempted to make a calculation. A 1996 United Nations report claimed there were approximately 250,000 child soldiers in the world, with the largest numbers in Africa and Asia.[4] A few years later the estimate increased to 300,000, although today, another decade later, this figure is outdated.[5] In Africa, Asia, and Latin America, child soldiers have become a major part of military forces, and in the Middle East they play an increasingly important role strategically. Rebel forces are not solely responsible for this increase, although the recruitment of child soldiers is calculated to be greater among rebel groups than in state armies.[6] Although not a significant decrease, it is slightly encouraging to note that the number of governments using child soldiers appears to have declined from ten in the period 2001–4 to nine in the period 2004–7.[7] Among these are Israel and the United Kingdom. Meanwhile, the number of states ratifying the Optional Protocol to the UN Convention on the Rights of the Child, which prohibits child soldiers, has risen from seventy-seven in 2004 to 125 in 2010.[8]

The vast majority of child soldiers serve in the ranks of nonstate armed groups. In recent decades, dozens of armed groups in at least twenty-four countries have recruited children under eighteen years of age. The best known of these are the Revolutionary Armed Forces of Colombia, the Liberation Tigers of Tamil Eelam in Sri Lanka, and the Lord's Resistance Army in Uganda. But numerous other groups receive less international attention, including the separatist National Revolution Front-Coordinate of southern Thailand, Maoist groups in India, and other insurgent forces in the Philippines and Myanmar. In countries such as Kenya, Nigeria, Afghanistan, Iraq, and the Occupied Palestinian Territories, groups are shifting in their alliances, and their activities are often characterized as criminal rather than political. Children used in these countries—in suicide attacks, for example—are considered terrorists rather than soldiers.[9]

Despite humanitarian efforts, the 2008 global report of the Coalition to Stop the Use of Child Soldiers laments that "a near global consensus that children should not be used as soldiers and strenuous international efforts have failed to protect tens of thousands of children from war." While there has been a decrease in the number of conflicts in which children are directly involved—from twenty-seven in 2004 to seventeen by the end of 2007—the 2008 report indicates that this decrease is due to the end of a number of significant conflicts (in Burundi, Côte d'Ivoire, the Democratic Republic of Congo, Guinea, Liberia, and elsewhere) rather than the impact of initiatives to end the use of child soldiers. In fact, where there is armed conflict, child soldiers will most certainly be involved, primarily but not exclusively participating in nonstate armed groups.[10] No estimate at a particular point in time can reflect the total number of children who have been in armed groups, since these groups function like revolving doors. The global scope is staggering when we consider that as child soldiers die or escape, new children are recruited to fill the ranks; likewise, as one conflict dies and another begins, new groups spring up to replace old ones. Between 2001 and 2004 children were involved in armed conflict in twenty-seven countries, but the list would be much longer if we went back to the 1960s.[11]

That children become soldiers and participate in war is not new. If we define a child as a person under the age of eighteen, as is typically the case in Western culture, we could name countless wars throughout history in which children went to battle. In the Middle Ages, boy soldiers were regularly recruited into the British military, and by the nineteenth century, institutions such as the Royal Military Asylum and the Royal Hibernium Military School were founded to organize this recruitment. Significantly, these institutions evolved out of orphanages for poor boys—even twelve- and thirteen-year-olds—where the need for a sense of belonging and purpose would have been acute. While most military service in the West was voluntary, the recruitment of child soldiers continued as schools and military apprenticeship programs encouraged boys to join. The American Civil War was a war of boy soldiers, some of whom lied about their age and managed to fool recruiters because they looked older. While these boys began in support roles, they often became combatants; some as young as nine or ten fought and killed in battle.[12] It is estimated that more than a million of the 2.7 million soldiers serving in the Civil War were under the age of eighteen, but according to David Rosen this is exaggerated; the figure is more likely to be between 10 and 20 per cent of the recruits. Despite the official age restrictions, young boys continued to enlist during both World Wars.[13]

The public perception that the child soldier is an abused and exploited victim of war, however, is rather new. Boy soldiers in nineteenth- and twentieth-century wars were respected for their bravery and patience, their lives considered "ennobled" by the experience of war rather than destroyed by it. Childhood has not always been considered a salient cultural or social category, nor have children always been considered innocent or weak. We must note that changes in the way we view childhood have transformed the perception of children's involvement in war. Our perceptions are notably contingent on culture, evidenced by the fact that the Western view of childhood as constituting the population under eighteen years of age is not universal. In rural sub-Saharan Africa, for example, a person is considered an adult once certain rites of passage into adulthood have been completed. This can occur at age fourteen or sometimes younger.[14] Practices that challenge accepted international humanitarian and legal assumptions about childhood in Angola and Mozambique include identifying children by the roles they assume rather than by age.[15] Girls who marry as early as thirteen or fourteen, for instance, are considered young adults ready to assume the responsibilities of motherhood. In these societies, children may be portrayed as strong and resilient rather than in need of protection. While this shouldn't lead to the neglect of protection, it does render the definition of the child soldier as "any person under eighteen years of age who is recruited or used by an army or armed group" (known as the "Straight 18" position) somewhat arbitrary.[16]

Contributing to this perceptual shift regarding child soldiers is increased global humanitarian concern with children as a distinct category. Humanitarian groups have been extremely influential in shaping the international legal treaties that currently attempt to ban the use of child soldiers.[17] Graça Machel's 1996 report on child soldiers for the UN was particularly important in initiating this influence. Machel complained that peace agreements rarely attend to child soldiers and their interests. In fact, at the time, no peace treaty had ever formally recognized the existence of child combatants, and their needs had not been taken into account in demobilization and reintegration programs.[18]

The United Nations Children's Fund, or Unicef, has broadened the definition of a child soldier to "any child—boy or girl—under 18 years of age, who is part of any kind of regular or irregular armed force or armed group in any capacity, including, but not limited to, cooks, porters, messengers, and anyone accompanying such groups other than family members."[19] Child soldiers are not only boys or combatants, according to this definition. It is understandable that children who are recruited into military groups should be acknowledged even if they are not used in active combat, but defining them as soldiers poses a dilemma. Such an acknowledgment may recognize the suffering that both combatants and noncombatants experience, but it does not acknowledge the killing that only soldiers carry out, again failing to consider the victim as killer. Today, the predicament of child soldiers has become a cause célèbre, and it is difficult to find any reference to the crimes committed by these children, however horrific. Any violence committed by the child soldier is perceived as though it were committed against the child soldier himself; those individuals *victimized by victims* are ignored.

Consider a letter to the UN Security Council from the Coalition to Stop the Use of Child Soldiers, written in 2009. The Coalition urged the UN to consider that although there is a "wide consensus" that children should be treated as victims, in practice many are detained "on the basis of their alleged association" with armed groups. In some cases they are even tortured for this while in detainment facilities. The letter also complains of the impunity regularly granted to those who recruit children into armies, and refers favorably to the recent International Criminal Court indictments against commanders in the Lord's Resistance Army of Uganda and in the Democratic Republic of Congo for war crimes, including the recruitment of children.[20]

Nowhere in this document do we find even a nod to the fact that these children and youth are also capable of horrific acts. The child soldier is described in the abstract as a pure victim of adult cruelty. As Rosen puts it, "Like the concepts of the 'child laborer,' 'child bride,' or 'child prostitute,' the 'child soldier' is conceived of as a deviant product of adult abuse; such a conception presupposes that children are dependent, exploited, and powerless." These children cannot therefore be held responsible or accountable for the war crimes they commit. They are considered to have no legally relevant agency, which contradicts "the real-world experience of the victims of crimes committed by child soldiers and also may violate local understandings of blameworthiness and justice."[21]

Suffering and Agency

Humanitarian and human rights discourses have thus encouraged certain assumptions about what it means to be a child soldier, barely distinguishable from the child noncombatant victim of war—part of the nebulous category Cynthia Enloe calls "womenandchildren." The almost exclusive public focus on the child soldier in Africa contributes to this view; a young African boy holding an AK-47—detached from any geographical, historical or ethnic context—is the paradigmatic image. It is an unsettling one, according to Rosen, because it confounds two fundamental and unquestioned assumptions of modern society: that war is evil and that children are innocent.[22] This innocence is further hyperbolized by the Western stereotype of the victimized African—starving, impoverished, and seeking refuge from war.[23] The context and history of various conflicts in Africa are glossed over, allowing the moral currency of pure innocence to be affixed to a generic African child without any hesitation.

Contrast this with Rosen's example of the Jewish children and youth—for whom there was no safety during the years of the unfolding Holocaust—who fought with the partisans against the Nazi occupation. Joining the armed resistance was a matter of life or death for them, kill or be killed, as it has been for child soldiers throughout history. Rosen claims that these children played a major role in partisan resistance against the Germans, usually serving directly in combat. Resistance provided the possibility of maintaining dignity and honor in the face of horror. These young people preferred to die in a way that would be meaningful if they were to die anyway. But Rosen argues that dignity and honor—even the need to survive—were not enough to sustain resistance. Older Jews could not match the "energy, flexibility, and brazenness of children and youth." These qualities grew out of youth movements in which self-determination, egalitarianism, and ideals of universal justice helped to sustain the children and youth—a testament, Rosen concludes, to the remarkable capability of children and youth to shape their own destinies.[24] Children are often prized today by military groups for this brazenness.

Young Palestinian suicide bombers, for example, demonstrate a fierce desire for self-determination and an end to the humiliation and suffering of the Israeli occupation. Ayat al-Akhras was a Palestinian teenager who blew herself up outside a Jerusalem supermarket on March 29, 2002, killing two Israeli citizens. A month earlier, Noura Shalhoub, the fifteen-year-old daughter of a veterinarian in Tulkarm, was shot and killed after attacking a soldier at an Israeli military checkpoint with a kitchen knife. Both girls were described as having become politically militant after the death of a family member or neighbor.[25]

In the testimonies left behind on videotapes, these youth give us a chilling glimpse into their own motivation for killing. Here are the words of al-Akhras: "I am the living martyr, Ayat Mohammed al-Akhras. I do this operation for the sake of God and fulfilling the cry of the martyrs and orphans, the others who have buried their children, and those who are weak on earth. I tell the Arab leaders, don't shirk from your duty. Shame on the Arab armies who are sitting and watching the girls of Palestine fighting while they are asleep. I say this as a cry, a plea. Oh, al-Aqsa Mosque, Oh, Palestine. It will be *intifada* until victory."[26] These are not the words of a young, innocent victim but of a killer with no concern for her victims. But she is also a victim of the Israeli occupation. In both of these examples, we note that the sheer will for one's people to survive is the engine behind the violence of self-defense and revenge empowering those who otherwise have very limited power.

The child soldier—because her suffering is immense—exemplifies probably better than any other victim as perpetrator that victims are not without agency. If we can isolate moral agency in these children, we can't argue that suffering negates it. The most significant harms that child soldiers experience in places like Sudan and Sierra Leone are witnessing killing, being beaten, raped, or sexually assaulted, and being forced to kill and to rape. In one 2005 study of 169 former child soldiers, eleven to eighteen years of age, from rehabilitation centers in Uganda and the Democratic Republic of Congo, the most commonly reported traumatic experiences were the witnessing of shooting, wounding, and being seriously beaten. Slightly more than half of these children reported having killed someone, and nearly one-third reported that they were forced to engage in sexual contact. Furthermore, the study concluded that higher scores of PTSD symptoms corresponded to an increased desire for revenge in the children and greater difficulty reconciling and reintegrating into society.[27] An earlier study in Angola, during the period from 1996 to 1998, focusing on boys whose median age of recruitment was thirteen to fourteen and whose average time with the armed group was nearly four years, established that an overwhelming majority of the boys had shot someone, lost family members or close friends in the war, witnessed others being killed, and said they had been in life-or-death situations. Similar rates have been found in Mozambique and Somalia.[28] Girls recruited into military groups often face sexual enslavement, repeated rape and beating, and pregnancy and motherhood at young ages. Those who become "wives" of commanders are often the more fortunate girls because they receive better care, while others are forced to have sexual relations with a different soldier every night. Giving birth is generally a grueling experience, because of the harsh conditions of military camps, with food and water shortages, a lack of adequate hygiene, and the frequent need to flee the camp when an attack is imminent.[29] Sexual violation has devastating, sometimes lifelong, effects. These experiences are common to most child soldiers who survive atrocity; innumerable others die from the torture and suffering inflicted on them. No one could reasonably argue that these children, no matter what age, are not victims of horrific events.

Not all child soldiers, however, are affected by war in the same way. Contrary to what we learn from humanitarian discourse, Michael Wessells points out, recent research in fact challenges the view of child soldiers as "scarred for life." It is a position that he believes is "out of touch with most former child soldiers' resilience and ability to function." Although children certainly experience war trauma, this is only one element of a larger and more complex mosaic of psychosocial impacts.[30] A child who is abducted and forced to do labor at an army base will have a different psychological response to her experience than a child who witnessed or participated in killing. A greater concern than these psychological effects could be the loss of education, lack of training and job skills, stigmatization and social exclusion, disability and health problems, and poverty. Consequently, studies that measure suffering in terms of PTSD must be interpreted carefully, as no data are collected *before* the conflict for comparison. Trauma, defined as "a sense of profound helplessness in the face of overwhelming danger, anxiety, and arousal" associated with life-threatening experiences, is a concept that must be carefully scrutinized. Not only does the trauma concept pathologize a normal response to severe experiences; it can lead to an identification with victimhood.[31]

Wessells argues that in order to understand the phenomenon of child soldiering, we must consider these children's experiences in relation to the wider suffering of all children in war zones. Children who become soldiers are not necessarily worse off than those who do not. In fact, they often have better access to food and protection than other children do.[32] This helps to explain why many choose to join rebel or government military groups. Much of the information on child soldiers that we receive through media sources and from humanitarian organizations focus on coercive child recruitment practices, but not all children are recruited. Of course, we need to understand "choice" when options are heavily circumscribed. Nevertheless, children speak of their willingness—even eagerness—to join. Parents may be dead, homes set on fire, and entire villages destroyed. The army provides some protection and provisions that others may not enjoy. This aspect of survival should not be ignored. Children who grow up in war zones may no longer occupy a positive place in society, Wessells explains; they are oppressed, have little or no access to education, feel powerless and alienated, and have been denied positive life options. As a result, violence becomes an acceptable way to replace the existing social order with one offering social justice and positive economic and political opportunities.[33] Recall Frantz Fanon's emphasis on self-determination, on re-creating the self through violence when there appear to be no other options. Like the young Palestinian suicide bomber who expresses a search for dignity and autonomy through violence, the child wants to take revenge against those who destroyed his family and community. Revenge is empowering, if only momentarily. We have seen this expressed repeatedly.

These facts dispel the myth of the powerless victim. They point to the political agency that suffering often activates. Given this suffering, however, and the young age of many of these soldiers, can we speak meaningfully of their responsibility? We cannot be held responsible for the conditions into which we are born, if by responsibility we mean a causal connection between the actor and the event or deed. But children can be responsible for actions they have committed by claiming ownership of these actions. They are responsible in the sense that they will experience the consequences of their actions. Indeed, as the deed cannot be undone, these consequences are inescapable.

Alcinda Honwana observes that questions of responsibility pervade the narratives of child soldiers, attesting to a very engaged sense of moral agency. Some are defensive and reiterate their blamelessness over and over again. "I was living with this big pain inside my heart, but I couldn't say anything. I just did what I did, because I was forced to do it. I didn't fight because I wanted to," one nineteen-year-old ex-combatant told her. Ben, at seventeen, lamented, "During the war I was very sad because of all the violence and killings we had to do. Now I continue to be sad because some people here in the village say that I was responsible for the people killed in the war because I belonged to UNITA [National Union for the Total Independence of Angola]. They despise me. I am afraid of them." Ben felt powerless both as a soldier who could not avoid killing and as an ex-combatant who could not avoid being punished for his deeds. Nelito, a nineteen-year-old boy, admitted, "I didn't want to fight; they forced me to fight and kill people ... Now I am not well; I act like a crazy person ... The spirits of those I killed in the war are haunting me and making me ill."[34]

Honwana is unequivocal in her response to the ambiguity of the child soldier's victim/perpetrator status. In the situation of the child soldier, whose circumstances and emotional state vary significantly from child to child, we are not concerned with a war crimes tribunal or trial for crimes against humanity, she insists, but we are called to account for civil wars that enlist children in horrific violence. From this perspective, Honwana argues, the soldiers are both victims and perpetrators, not fully responsible for their actions but not entirely deprived of agency, either. They have what she calls limited or weak agency, demonstrated by their decisions to minimize violence when they could—by pretending to be sick, for example. Child soldiers create their own world within the political violence and terror in which they have to operate. They make escape plans, try to deceive their supervisors, pretend to be stupid, or act indirectly to thwart their superiors' plans when a direct refusal would mean certain death. Honwana concludes, "They acted in the moment, without a strategic logic that would make sense of their wandering trajectories. They might kill on one occasion and show mercy on another."[35]

Furthermore, from her research with former child soldiers, Honwana believes that a "substantial" number were fully aware of the atrocities they had committed. "Some acted out of vengeance, greed, immaturity, impulsiveness, or jealousy, while others did so with the expectation of being rewarded by their commanders. Aggressive acts against the enemy could be recompensed with the friendship and protection of commanders. Although few would admit to it, some soldiers undoubtedly found a thrill in killing, in wielding weapons and exercising life-and-death power over others more powerless than themselves."[36] In short, when it comes to moral agency, child soldiers do not appear to differ significantly from adults faced with the extreme conditions of war and terror, forced to make moral choices in drastically constricted circumstances. They feel the same reticence to kill, the same repulsion toward death, the same difficulty in accepting that they were the authors of horrific deeds. With less life experience than adults, however, they are more susceptible to ideological indoctrination. This may also explain their extraordinary capacity for resourcefulness and resilience within these tragic circumstances. As Charles London puts it, they are protagonists, not "vehicles for suffering" or passive victims.[37] They require the gift of mercy rather than veneration, judgment rather than punishment.

Complex Victims

Beah's story, remarkable for the way it depicts the complexity of his victim status, supports the conclusions of child soldier research. *A Long Way Gone: Memoirs of a Boy Soldier* has generated an outpouring of sympathy from readers in the West. On the *New York Times* and *Globe and Mail* best-seller lists, Beah's emotionally wrenching personal account of his life as a child soldier has given rise to an extensive publicity network, including a website with public statements, excerpts from the book, information on his tours, a list of Beah's NGO involvement, and videos of speaking engagements. The full extent of its mainstream popularity is summed up in its 2008 status as a "Starbucks Featured Book." More than seven hundred thousand copies have been sold in the United States alone.[38]

Beah's narrative is an engrossing read. The boyish innocence that emerges in stories of his childhood in a village in Sierra Leone, his love of rap music, his affection toward family members, and his friendship with the boys who accompanied him endear him to us from the start. In 1992, at the age of twelve, Beah and his friends leave their village for a musical event in a neighboring village and are unable to return home because of a rebel invasion of their hometown. This is the beginning of a year of wandering, sometimes alone, sometimes in groups, fleeing the violent rebel attacks on villages until they are forced to join the government army. On the dust cover we read that Beah, "at heart a gentle boy, found that he was capable of truly terrible acts"— a statement that sums up the reason for the story's fascination.

After their capture by government soldiers, Beah and his companions believe they have found safety.[39] At first they work in the village as any children would, cooking, cleaning, and doing other chores. There are evening soccer games and movies to watch with the soldiers, or marble playing with the thirty-some other orphaned boys. All this changes overnight when a nearby village is attacked by rebel forces. From then on Beah becomes a soldier fighting to avenge the deaths of his family and community; pumped up on drugs and the ideological rhetoric of the commanders, he participates in the killing and pillaging for several years, until he is rescued and rehabilitated by Unicef at the age of fifteen. Eventually, this intelligent and articulate boy is invited by the United Nations to the United States for an interview and conference on child soldiering. On the last day of his stay, Beah makes a speech to diplomats in the UN Economic and Social Council chamber:

> I am from Sierra Leone, and the problem that is affecting us children is the war that forces us to run away from our homes, lose our families, and aimlessly roam the forests. As a result, we get involved in the conflict as soldiers, carriers of loads, and in many other difficult tasks. All this is because of starvation, the loss of our families, and the need to feel safe and be part of something when all else has broken down. I joined the army really because of the loss of my family and starvation. I wanted to avenge the deaths of my family. I also had to get some food to survive,

and the only way to do that was to be part of the army. It was not easy being a soldier, but we just had to do it. I have been rehabilitated now, so don't be afraid of me. I am not a soldier anymore; I am a child.[40]

In numerous accounts, by child and adult soldiers alike, we find this ambivalence toward their participation in violent actions. Beah gives the reasons for why he "joined" the army: to avenge the deaths of loved ones, to create a safe place to call home when forced to flee his family and community, and to survive. This reasoning implies agency. And yet, Beah concludes, "we just had to do it." It is a testament to the reticence to comprehend and accept one's own complicity in violence.

Dominic Ongwen was about ten years old when he was abducted by the Lord's Resistance Army (LRA) of Uganda on his way to school. He was one of eight children, born around August 1980, to two schoolteachers who transferred him to a better school only months before his abduction. Described as "too little to walk," he was apparently carried by other captives to the LRA's main military bases. He gave a false name to his captors as he was taught to do by his parents in order to protect his family and village in case of such an event.

The LRA has terrorized Uganda and neighboring countries for several decades, supporting its ranks by the abduction of some twenty to sixty-six thousand children in the past two decades, according to conflicting sources.[41] Joseph Kony is their leader, having taken over the remnants of a quasi-Christian army led by his cousin, Alice Lakwena, in 1988.[42] His followers believe that Kony has "omnipresent powers," according to Erin Baines, and the ability to read minds, take the form of animals in order to spy on those who are considering escape, and predict the future.[43] Ongwen's story might be similar to Beah's except that he did not have the good fortune to be saved by Unicef or adopted by an American woman living in New York. He steadily rose in the ranks of the army and has been indicted by the International Criminal Court (ICC) for committing crimes against humanity, including the abduction and slavery of children and cruel treatment of civilians.[44] At twenty-seven years old, Ongwen is close to Kony and one of the most respected leaders in the LRA. He is described by people who know him as having exhibited a natural ability as a fighter from a young age, successfully conducting raids on military attachés, capturing soldiers and weapons, and abducting children. Reportedly a field commander (lieutenant) at eighteen, he was promoted a few years later to a senior rank in the high command of the LRA. Ongwen was described by those who knew him as "without mercy," promoted rapidly because he was an exceptional and loyal killer and managed to outlive his superiors.[45]

It is doubtful whether anyone would question the ICC indictment unless it was known that Ongwen was abducted as a child. Baines calls him a "complex political victim"—a concept she borrows from Erica Bouris, who defines this type of victim as one "who is no longer chained to characteristics of complete innocence and purity, but remains a victim nonetheless"—but he could as easily be called a complex political perpetrator.[46] Like countless other children in Uganda, Sierra Leone, Sudan, and elsewhere, Ongwen was initially forced to commit the very acts of brutality he experienced as a victim. The unique status of such victims is not recognized in current justice debates at the international level, Baines argues, "yet they represent precisely the kind of complex political victims who, if excluded from justice pursuits, could give birth to the next generation of perpetrators in Uganda; generations marginalized by the judicial sector and who have nothing to gain from citizenship and nothing to lose from war." Baines, along with her research group, insists that she does not want to exonerate Ongwen for his crimes, which she has no reason to doubt: "Our point is not to prove his innocence or guilt, but to place his life into historical context and to complicate his status, urging current justice pursuits in Uganda to do likewise. We argue a legal approach is limited in this regard, and that the ICC may have been incorrect in identifying Ongwen as one of the 'most responsible' given his ambiguous political status. To be clear, this does not deny that Ongwen committed heinous crimes, but to complicate his status as a perpetrator, as well as a victim."[47]

Here we have the crux of the problem: the birth of the next generation of perpetrators is contingent on how we respond to leaders like Ongwen. Beah is also a complex political victim, although perhaps less complex than Ongwen. In Beah's case, suspicion regarding the truth of his story sheds light on the impact of public sympathy on the question of moral agency. Bob Lloyd, an Australian mining engineer who traveled to Sierra Leone in 2008, claimed to have found Beah's father—a man who was killed by rebels, according to Beah's account in the book—working in a mine close to his home village. The mine employee turned out not to be Beah's father, which was confirmed after the story was investigated by Peter Wilson, the London-based correspondent for the *Australian*. But Wilson found other reasons to doubt Beah's story, after conversations with a number of individuals from Beah's hometown, Mattru Jong, including the village chief, a Catholic priest, the school principal, former neighbors, local miners, and medical staff. They confirmed that the attacks Beah describes as occurring in January 1993 actually took place in January 1995. This means that Beah would have been fourteen years old, not twelve, when he was captured by the rebels and forced to fight, and would have served in the army for only a few months rather than two years. Unicef staff confirmed that he entered Benin House, where he began a rehabilitation program for boy soldiers, at the age of fifteen. Teachers at Beah's school have also established that he was in school for two years longer than he states in the book, and that the school was not attacked at the time he claimed it was.[48] Whether Beah's account is factually accurate or was written with a certain amount of poetic license is important to know, but I am more interested here in what the public response tells us about the perception of a victim-as-killer in the case of a child.

Beah adamantly stands by the truth of every detail of his story. The public, in turn, with few exceptions, stands by Beah. There are a few cynics—one blogger suggests that if Beah didn't look so boyish at twenty-seven he would not garner so much sympathy—but readers have overwhelmingly expressed outrage that a story told with such anguish would be discredited and a victim of such horrors be so tarnished.[49] Skeptics are told that they must not criticize unless they too have experienced atrocity—an echo of certain responses to Arendt's criticism of the Jewish Councils discussed in the previous chapter. Even if the entire book is a lie, some write, it has done such good in bringing the plight of child soldiers to the world's attention that the lies do not matter. One writer compares the "naysayers" to Holocaust deniers.[50] It is as though questioning Beah's story is tantamount to arguing that child soldiering is not a tragedy. The need to believe in absolute innocence—regardless of the facts—is a powerful one.

Other accounts of child soldiering have appeared since the publication of *A Long Way Gone*, but the "Lost Boys of Sudan"—the subjects of many documentary films and written narratives since 2003—may have acquired the most fame in the West. The name was coined by aid agencies when some twenty thousand boys fled their war-devastated homes during the civil war in Sudan between 1983 and 2005.[51] In 2001 approximately thirty-six hundred boys were brought to the United States from refugee camps in Kenya.

The idea that a Lost Boy would trade "a life of terror for hope and forgiveness" provides the public with a heartwarming story: terrible things can happen to us that are completely out of our control, but human goodness triumphs. This was the headline of a *Globe and Mail* story about Emmanuel Jal, boy soldier turned international rap star, who published a book about his recruitment into the Sudanese civil war, produced a film, and created a charitable organization called "Gua Africa."[52] The article, titled "A Child Soldier Trades Rifles for the Rap Game," begins with Jal's tender comments about his mother, who was killed in a village attack, last seen by Jal when he was seven. A brief outline of his childhood follows: Jal's abrupt loss of innocence as he witnessed the beating and raping of his family, the long journey as a Lost Boy on his way to a school that turned out to be a "vast, disease-ridden refugee camp," and his eventual recruitment into a southern rebel group, the Sudan People's Liberation Army (SPLA). In the end, it is faith that holds him up, not fame. "Faith, you lose it many times, and then it comes back," he says. The interviewer adds, "When he laughs this time, tipping his head back, it seems to be directed at the world, which has held him at its whim, capable of enormous harm and, when he least expected it, surprising grace."[53]

But the excerpt from the book included in the newspaper describes a most vicious killing—intended to maximize suffering—of a "jallaba."[54] In this passage, Jal refers a number of times to "the black hate" that propelled him and his friend to kill despite the Arab's pleas for mercy. Jal writes, "I looked at my hand—my black skin holding the machete. Both Lam and I marked by our blackness, which had made us this jallaba's enemy. I did not think of my God in that moment who had also pitted us against each other." As the others raised their machetes, so too did Emmanuel Jal.

There is no doubt that Jal is a victim who invites our sympathy in this article, despite—or perhaps even because of—its visceral references to the killing he committed. Indeed, the blows of the machete appear to be descending on Jal rather than on Jal's victims. How would we read such an article if the pleading Arab were himself eight years old? Are parts of the story being left out in order to render the victim absolutely innocent? Why is rape never mentioned? Given the high prevalence of rape in ethnopolitical conflicts, it is highly unlikely that none of the boy soldiers whose accounts entrance us were the perpetrators or victims of rape. It might be relatively simple to justify killing as an act of self-defense by a boy forcibly recruited into an army, but rape is not an act of self-defense, and more difficult to justify. The reluctance to confess a rape may have something to do with this difficulty.

The narratives of Emmanuel Jal and Ishmael Beah make compelling reading and bring global attention to the plight of children who have been forced to participate in wars in Sierra Leone, Sudan, and elsewhere, but there is a sensational element to the stories that is disturbing. The sensationalism appears to be at least partly responsible for the lack of interest in the victims of both Beah and Jal. When I pressed the students who read *A Long Way Gone* in my undergraduate philosophy class on the issue of Beah's victims, they insisted adamantly that Beah had no choice in the matter and could not be held responsible.[55] He was simply an unambiguous, uncomplicated victim. It seemed impossible for them to acknowledge the needs of both Beah and his victims simultaneously. On the other hand, Beah and Jal, celebrities now, are devoting their energies and talents to assisting their own people.[56] Is this the only accountability we require?

Yes and no. Their work is admirable, but their victims remain nameless and unknown. There is no rapper stardom for the families of the dead or for the injured victims. The conditions responsible for the hostilities in their own countries are not altered by the perception of these boys as innocent victims and the celebration of their rags-to-riches stories. We cannot treat Beah and Jal and all child soldiers as pure victims, without agency, in need of protective laws that do not address at the same time their actions as perpetrators. This ignores the victims who died by their hands. The inappropriateness of this approach is evident when we consider Ongwen's story. His path could easily have been taken by Beah and Jal had they not been saved by outsiders, although their own choices may have also led them to a better life.[57] Readers do not seem alarmed by the brutality they describe. Jal's story is particularly unabashed in its depiction of the destruction of human life. Yet, unlike Ongwen, he is an endearing rather than abhorrent figure to the public. If responsibility for actions is not acknowledged—if deeds are not *owned*—then we cannot learn from our pasts, and the same excuses will suffice again and again. If this were the only reason we needed to judge the violence of victims, it would be sufficient.

Beah and Jal are only two examples, among thousands, and highly unusual cases at that. What they tell us is that complicating the condition and status of the victim is not enough. The moral and political challenges initiated by the dilemma of the child soldier as a complex victim are evident in the unsatisfying conclusion to Rosen's *Armies of the Young:* "How should we see them [child soldiers]? As innocent victims of political circumstance who should be protected and forgiven? Or as moral agents who should be held responsible for their actions?" Perhaps too obliquely, Rosen's book answers the question for us: we must consider the child soldier both as innocent victim *and* as moral agent—not an easy task. "The crimes these children have committed are terrible, and the systems of law designed to address them are far too inexact and weak to ever fully compensate for this evil. A more nuanced view of both the vagaries of war and the contextual definition of childhood should deepen our ability to wrestle the question." As such, blanket immunity from prosecution for all those under eighteen "clearly falls short of achieving justice for the victims of war."[58] Complicating our view of the victim necessitates a more complicated response, one that renders the usual legal responses inadequate. Ongwen's case demonstrates this inadequacy. If he is incarcerated, there is no change in the conditions of life for his living victims, nor is there any relief for his own past as a victim.

The Making of a Killer

Honwana responds to the challenges of reintegrating child soldiers into community life with the following insight: "What would be required to address the consequences of armed conflict is exactly the same as what would be required to prevent such conflicts from occurring in the first place."[59] She highlights the very practical needs of any war-torn community: shelter, a safe environment, a secure livelihood, political inclusion, and reconciliation and healing. Implied in her discussion is the insufficiency of legal measures to achieve these conditions. Preventive social, political, and economic measures are therefore equally responsive. This is not an either/or strategy. We must devise effective responses at the same time that we come up with preventive measures, which demands that we evaluate the ideological underpinnings of war.

Machel not only broke the silence on the unique suffering of children forced to kill in war in her 1996 UN report, but also initiated a humanitarian discourse that puts children's pure innocence in stark relief against contemporary war as evil beyond measure. Machel writes, the "statistics are shocking enough, but more chilling is the conclusion to be drawn from them: more and more of the world is being sucked into a desolate moral vacuum. This is a space devoid of the most basic human values; a space in which children are slaughtered, raped, and maimed; a space in which children are exploited as soldiers; a space in which children are starved and exposed to extreme brutality. Such unregulated terror and violence speak of deliberate victimization. There are few further depths to which humanity can sink."[60] Throughout human history war has always been brutal, but changes in its methods are evident. Although it is difficult to establish significant trends in post–cold war conflict, one trend that is clear is the decline in the number of *inter*state wars;[61] the predominant type of conflict has become *intra*state, in particular "ethnonationalist" conflict.[62] Like civil wars in the nineteenth and early twentieth centuries, the overwhelming majority of civil wars in the post–World War II era were fought in the name of "ethnonational autonomy or independence,"[63] and since the 1950s these continued to increase, reaching a peak in 1993–94. While identity groups have not replaced the nation-state as the dominant conceptual tool in the field of international relations, identity is a growing focus of global peacemaking, indicating a "new landscape" for international conflict. There is, of course, a corresponding increased desire to understand and manage these conflicts. As Andreas Wimmer puts it, ethnic conflicts have become "a testing ground for a new morality of promoting peace, stability, and human rights across the globe."[64]

This new landscape requires new approaches to the study of violent conflict and its aftermath. Hugh Miall's 1992 study of eighty-one peaceful and violent international and civil conflicts from 1945 to 1985, in Africa, Europe, and the Middle East, concludes that civil wars were more likely than interstate wars to exhibit major violence. The fact that ethnic conflicts mostly involve the rights of ethnic groups to maintain their identity, gain equal recognition, and share equal status with other groups renders traditional interest-based bargaining and negotiation insufficient, according to Miall.[65]

We must be concerned with the circumstances of the participants of ethnopolitical war before it erupts and not merely with the mess left in war's wake. Ideology plays an especially significant role in identity-based conflict, in persuading civilians to join military groups—whether government or rebel forces—and to participate in killing, and often in raping and torturing, members of the "enemy" ethnic group. War is not declared against a foreign enemy outside one's national borders—an unknown stranger—but against one's immediate neighbor, a cousin's Muslim wife, the local Tutsi schoolteacher, or the Serbian down the street. If there is a strong, innate resistance to killing a fellow human being at close proximity, how much more blind adherence to ideology is necessary for this kind of killing to occur?[66] Bludgeoning to death a fellow human being whom you passed by every day for twenty years necessitates a fierce ideological conditioning in which identity becomes the sacrosanct marker determining whether one individual lives or dies.

The power of this conditioning makes ethnic conflict a particularly important phenomenon for investigating a realm in which "normal" morality, along with personal responsibility, is considered suspended—subjects are rendered docile, drugged by the narcotic of war. In accounts by those who participated in killing in Rwanda, Sierra Leone, Liberia, Uganda, Bosnia, and

Croatia—from children to adults—the primary conditioning agent is the perception that violence is necessary for self-defense, to kill or be killed the only choice. Fanon focused primarily on the ideology of dehumanization as the requisite justifying principle for killing the colonized with impunity. The revenge of those bereft of humanity appears in a different moral light for Fanon— a necessary, if dangerous, response to the misery of colonization—but its effects are the same: the dehumanization of both the victim-turned-perpetrator and the perpetrator-turned-victim. Hatred for the politicized ethnic identity of the other is easy to inspire and nurture when one group is convinced that another is ready to kill, maim, and rape its members. From there it is a simple progression to a war of vengeance, motivated by fear. Johan Vetlesen explains, "In all cases of genocide in the twentieth century, the action taken by one's own group typically assumes the character of self-defence. To the extent that aggression is exhibited, it is presented in the propaganda as but a mirror of the aggression once performed—or now about to be unleashed—by the chosen target group. The will to genocide is accompanied by a sense of historical and moral entitlement to what is secured for one's own group. If there is a mentality characteristic of genocidal perpetrators, it is that of self-righteousness."[67] While the child soldiers featured in this chapter were not all participants in genocide, the attitude of self-righteousness and defensiveness pointed out here is similar. They live in their own moral world, their actions excused by the events occurring around them. Arendt underestimated the power of this conditioning in her analysis of moral judgment and responsibility. The soldier is also making judgments, based on knowledge, spurred by thinking, and activated by willing. There is no guarantee that judgment will be kind and nonviolent; compassion, respect, and love for others need to be foregrounded.

We must ask, then, how child soldiers arrive at the psychological state that enables them to kill. Some or even many of these children inflict pain and suffering intentionally, even if initially forced. If violent atrocity is committed in the name of a just cause, then participants must be persuaded to kill by encouraging them to believe that killing is right, just, and necessary in this instance. Thus it is not a question of children not knowing right from wrong and acting blindly on that basis—not of acting outside the realm of moral principles—but of choosing to do wrong in the interests of survival, revenge, and empowerment, and making the necessary justifications. Poor judgment is the problem. They may not even be confused about right and wrong, feeling certain that they are doing the right thing, fighting for a just cause. For those who are recruited, it is an extremely limited choice—to kill or be killed—and certainly a choice that most adults would find equally impossible, but a choice nonetheless. For those children who join, the choice is still heavily circumscribed by ideological conditioning. There is moral agency either way.

Killing another human being at close range is an extraordinary challenge, according to Lieutenant Colonel Dave Grossman, owing to "the existence of a powerful, innate human resistance toward killing one's own species." Throughout history, the majority of men did not attempt to kill the enemy, he informs us, even to save their own lives or the lives of their friends. But "with the proper conditioning and the proper circumstances," he adds, "it appears that almost anyone can and will kill," despite the psychological obstacles.[68]

We learn from the narrative accounts of child soldiers that the conditioning they undergo after abduction or recruitment is terrible, and some do not survive. Military training is designed to break the young soldier's ties to family and community and create a warrior. Survival is dependent on this process. Children are initiated into a life of violence through cruel beatings, often with canes and sticks, forced to carry supplies for days, raped, and forced to be violent themselves. If tasks are not done quickly and without question, beatings often end in death.[69] The physical beatings are only the beginning of a process of disorientation and indoctrination. In short, children are terrorized. Some are forced to kill the first time they encounter a rebel or government army, like Richard Opio, who was ordered by members of the LRA to kill his parents with the blunt end of an ax just after his family was forced to leave their home. Richard refused at first, but after his parents pleaded with him to ensure his survival by carrying out the order, he complied. He was seventeen years old at the time. Subsequently, Richard describes his life, both as an LRA soldier and in the years since his escape in 2002, as "a living hell."[70]

Wessells cites a number of reasons why children become amenable to killing. First and foremost is the will to survive. When given a choice between killing or being killed, they choose the former for obvious reasons. Most would not consider this a choice. Perhaps an adult would be capable of making a choice of self-sacrifice if it were reasoned that such a sacrifice would prevent further deaths, but a child's will to survive is too strong, and there is less foresight. Second, violence becomes normalized. Wessells explains:

> Killing produces a host of emotional and cognitive changes that enable additional killing and blunt potentially inhibiting reactions such as disgust and guilt.... Furthermore, the upside-down logic and morals of

the armed group makes the abnormal seem normal, as killing and worse acts may occur on a daily basis. Having killed, and having seen others kill on a regular basis, children become less responsive to killing and may rationalize their own acts of killing by telling themselves, "I'm only doing what everyone else is doing" or "It's not such a big deal."[71]

More disturbing is the fact that killing can be satisfying.[72] It both solicits respect from the child's peers and commanders and satisfies the fierce desire for revenge. As Honwana points out, while some youth and children join military groups owing to conditions of insecurity, vulnerability, or lack of food and shelter, others join for ideological reasons, fully aware of the strategic objectives of war, for sheer adventure and the desire for the power provided by weapons.[73] Violence is viewed as a legitimate response to violence, killing, an effective and legitimate tool for achieving liberation, justice, or redemption. The enemy deserves to be killed, and any guilt for killing him is waylaid by the moral buffer zone provided by ideology.[74] The conflict is portrayed as a heroic contest between good and evil, and in the process the enemy is dehumanized, excluded from the moral universe. In other words, soldiers kill for moral reasons.

Consider the words of a thirteen-year-old Philippine boy soldier of the Moro Islamic Liberation Front (MILF): "It feels great to kill your enemy. The MILF does not initiate attacks. If the military didn't attack us, there will be no trouble. They are the ones who are really at fault. They deserve to be killed. The other children, they are happy too. They are not sad. I really do not regret killing. If they are your enemies, you can kill them. But if they are not your enemies, you shouldn't kill them." Youth may have the capacity to reason and ponder moral issues in ways that transcend the Manichean dichotomies we witness in these statements, Wessells argues, but "their limited life experience and limited exposure to members of other groups, coupled with political or religious indoctrination and, in many cases, limited education, can make them more susceptible to leaders' ideological manipulation."[75]

The Bitter Taste of Hate

Beah and Jal vividly describe how they were conditioned as child soldiers. When Beah is finally captured by government forces after wandering for months, alone or with other boys, he lives for a time as a noncombatant, cooking and cleaning in the village they have occupied. But as the rebels close in, the leader, Lieutenant Jabati, orders the village people, including some thirty captured boys, to prepare for battle. Beah recalls Jabati warning them that "in the forest there are men waiting to destroy all of our lives." While the lieutenant gives everyone the opportunity to leave, the message is clear that there is no hope of surviving. To prove it, Jabati displays the bodies of two villagers who attempted to escape, allegedly shot by the rebels. Beah recalls this incident:

> The lieutenant went on for almost an hour describing how rebels had cut off the heads of some people's family members and made them watch, burned entire villages along with their inhabitants, forced sons to have intercourse with their mothers, hacked newly born babies in half because they cried too much, cut open pregnant women's stomachs, took the babies out, and killed them.... "They have lost everything that makes them human. They do not deserve to live. That is why we must kill every single one of them. Think of it as destroying a great evil. It is the highest service you can perform for your country."[76]

Jabati gets the response he wants. "All of us hated the rebels," Beah admits, and vowed to stop them from capturing the village (108).

If at first Beah is afraid to hold a gun, it does not take him long to acquire an attachment to it. Again we see that in training it is an ideological conditioning stressing revenge and self-defense that indoctrinates the soldier. Taken to a nearby banana farm, the boys are instructed to practice stabbing the banana trees with a bayonet. "Visualize the banana tree as the enemy, the rebels who killed your parents, your family, and those who are responsible for everything that has happened to you," the corporal screams at them. He demonstrates for them, stabbing a tree and shouting, "I first stab him in the stomach, then the neck, then his heart, and I will cut it out, show it to him, and then pluck his eyes out. Remember, he probably killed your parents worse." This strategy proved remarkably effective, Beah writes. "When he said this, we all got angry and drove our knives in and out of the banana trees until they fell to the ground" (112).

Beah's first experience of combat is depicted in chilling detail. After his exposure to the blood of his friends, the death of the youngest boy in their group, and the screams of the corporal successfully blunt the edges of his fear of holding an AK-47, he writes, "I raised my gun and pulled the trigger, and

I killed a man. Suddenly, as if someone was shooting them inside my brain, all the massacres I had seen since the day I was touched by war began flashing in my head. Every time I stopped shooting to change magazines and saw my two lifeless friends, I angrily pointed my gun into the swamp and killed more people. I shot everything that moved, until we were ordered to retreat.... We went out two more times that week and I had no problem shooting my gun" (119–20). The combination of cocaine and gunpowder ("brown brown") and a nightly diet of Rambo movies further conditions the boys, giving them energy and making them fierce, until "killing becomes as easy as drinking water" (122). Remorse dissipates.

The pleasure in killing that the boys experience is palpable, as they cheer at the brutal murder of a captured rebel, sure of the righteousness of their rebellion. The lieutenant works to maintain this attitude, distinguishing between their own killing and that of the rebels, "riffraffs [*sic*] who kill for no reason." Beah feels the pride of belonging to a serious, moral cause, for the lieutenant tells the soldiers that they kill for "the good and betterment" of their country (123–24). In a disturbing passage, Beah describes how they "practiced" killing the prisoners as the corporal did. Whoever sliced the throat of their assigned prisoner the quickest would win the contest. Beah's own prisoner is described as having a swollen face, and his eyes looked at something beyond Beah; he seemed calm. "I didn't feel a thing for him," Beah admits, "didn't think that much about what I was doing. I just waited for the corporal's order. The prisoner was simply another rebel who was responsible for the death of my family, as I had come to truly believe." Beah's speed made him the winner. The boys clapped "as if I had just fulfilled one of life's greatest achievements" (125). After two years of this, Beah believes that his squad is his family, his gun his provider and protector, and his rule to kill or be killed. Killing becomes a daily activity. "I felt no pity for anyone. My childhood had gone by without my knowing, and it seemed as if my heart had frozen" (126).

Emmanuel Jal's account is similar. His training as a soldier in the Sudan People's Liberation Army began when he was nine and living at the Pinyudu refugee camp. While he was not kidnapped and forced to kill, he describes the indoctrination that led him to want to be a soldier. Jal describes his excitement when the top SPLA command visits the camp and rouses the crowd with the cry of vengeance. "The Arabs have shown no mercy.... They are to blame for every drop of blood spilled, for every child left lying in the dust, for every boy stolen as a slave, for every girl taken. They have destroyed our people, our homes, our land, and our religion. They have starved and murdered us, and now it is time for us to fight. Remember what they have done to each of you, think of what you have heard here in Pinyudu, never forget why you had to leave your homes to come here." Jal feels the desired response. He remembers his village burning, his siblings running, his aunt's rape, and his mother's fear, and feels anger "hot and sharp" inside him. "I felt the bitter taste of hate slide down the back of my throat and burn its way to the tips of my toes." As every boy in the crowd of thousands lifts his arms in response to the rousing speech, Jal is flooded with excitement. "At last I was going to leave Pinyudu, at last I was going to fight to get back home, at last I would be able to do to the jallabas what had been done to me and my family."[77]

In the ensuing pages of Jal's narrative, we hear repeatedly of his boredom in the camp and his longing to fight for revenge. He expresses guilt, remembering his mother's Christian values, after the first battle against civilians who live on the edges of the camp. When forced to punish his friend Malual for losing his weapon—the very friend who was forced to beat him on a previous day—Jal is glad. "Raising the whip in my hand, I brought it down using all my strength. Malual gasped as the whip cut into his back, and each scream he gave made my heart beat a little faster. Now he'd feel as I had when he beat me. I had to obey the command I'd been given. My arm was numb when Malual finally stood up, and I could see he was crying without tears. The worst kind of pain. I was glad." The desire for revenge is as fierce in Jal as his pride in participating in a military group, propelled by a violent hatred of Arabs. When he first confronts the bodies of men he has killed, he discovers with surprise that they are black, like him. Jal is informed that only a third of the army in Juba is Arab; the rest are Sudanese who have joined the "enemies" against them. He no longer sees their "African eyes" but only their "Arab hearts."[78]

We have only glanced at two accounts, whose facts may be tempered with fiction, but they corroborate the historical research briefly reviewed here. Beah's and Jal's stories do not depict children without moral agency or the ability to discern between right and wrong. There is no "arrested" moral development. On the contrary, these boy soldiers believe they are acting morally for a just cause. They are fighting for freedom within an armed group, inhabiting a unique moral space defined by both the moral discourse of the soldiers and the children's discourse and action within the group.[79] This belief has far-reaching implications for rehabilitating child soldiers and reintegrating them into civil society. The child soldier who has lived within this different moral world for some time is not simply going to return to a world in which enemies are not eliminated and killing does not win approval. Beah's own dramatic rehabilitation at Benin House bears this out. After several years of army life, he is taken by a Unicef team with a group of boys all around age fifteen to a rehabilitation center in Freetown Just after their arrival, a vicious fight erupts with another group of boys, who fought for the RUF, leaving several boys injured and a few dead.[80] Regarding the incident, Beah says, "It was war all over again. Perhaps the naïve foreigners thought that removing us from the war would lessen our hatred for the RUF. It hadn't crossed their minds that a change of environment wouldn't immediately make us normal boys; we were dangerous, and brainwashed to kill." Laughing about the event afterward, Beah recalls, "We needed the violence to cheer us after a whole day of boring traveling and contemplation about why our superiors had let us go."[81]

Research has shown that child soldiers returning to their communities or attempting to make homes in new villages are not accepted easily. In Mozambique and Angola, Honwana states that those who have been exposed to war are considered polluted by contact with death and bloodshed and not easily accepted back into society. Child soldiers who return are considered to have a dangerous kind of disorder because of the violent acts they perpetuated. Home villages in these countries appear to see these youths as perpetrators rather than victims, but through culturally specific rituals and ceremonies that stress cleansing the soldier of his or her former actions and forgetting the past, varying levels of acceptance occur. These highly symbolic rituals might include the burning of clothing, the cleansing of the body, and the sacrificing of chickens. The particular method is not important, but the symbolic value is critical.[82] No doubt the child soldier is marked as a perpetrator in the community he or she returns to, but the symbolic ritual in some small way mitigates the wrongs committed, while still enforcing the acknowledgment that one must *own* one's actions. The ceremony permits a certain forgetting on the part of the community. But the life of the child soldier in this community will most probably continue to be one of hardship and loneliness, bereft not only of the family that bore him but also of the military group that became his community.

When reflecting on his experience now as a man, Beah's focus remains exclusively on his victimhood. He tells an interviewer what his state of mind was like when he participated in attacks against villages: "I was drugged. It became routine, something normal. I didn't think in terms of good or evil. We followed orders from our commander. Our faction was our family. We did absolutely everything we were asked to do. We didn't question anything. There was no more critical thought or morale. You had to kill or be killed. And if you didn't do it, you would be killed by your chief or your fellows because you had put their lives at risk. You become a killing machine because you don't have any other choice." Beah reiterates these sentiments when asked how he was received in Sierra Leone on a visit in 2006. "I think that people's perception has changed today. The majority of the inhabitants have accepted the fact that child soldiers were victims, even if there are still people who don't like us. I consider myself a victim. I was forced to take part into [*sic*] that war. I didn't have a choice. I had to kill or be killed."[83] We can only wonder whether Beah has come to terms with his own victimization of others.

"How I Found Myself in War"

Any cursory glance at the best-seller shelves will attest to the public fascination with soldiers as victims of circumstances. Autobiographical accounts of adult soldiers convey not only the misery of war—suffused with an ambivalent shift between glorifying and lamenting the work of killing for the state—but also its crippling effects on the men and women who become its pawns. The figure of the soldier still evokes heroism, but with the growing post–Vietnam War attention to PTSD, the soldier as victim of the state is becoming a more prominent image. Babchenko's *A Soldier's War* is a case in point. One interview with the author claims that he "didn't write about fighting in Chechnya to make his name as an author, nor to mount a political attack against Russia's rulers. He wrote to recover." Despite the thorny question of his voluntary participation the second time he went to fight against the Chechens, the article renders Babchenko a victim—not only of the Russian state that sent him to the front but of the humiliation that he would have experienced had he chosen otherwise. "I didn't want to defer," he says about his conscription while he was a university student. "I can't remember why ... youthful *romantika* maybe. Or maybe I'd read too much [Erich Paul] Remark. Of course I'd just as happily not have served. But at the end of the day it's humiliating to get out of it."[84] *To kill or to be humiliated?* Recall Arendt's disappointment with the fact that human history has proved Socrates wrong: we do not consider it better to suffer than to do wrong. How much humiliation is a life worth?

Babchenko relates that he and his fellow combatants were baffled by the senselessness of the war. When his comrade asks him one day, "Are Chechens citizens of Russia or enemies of Russia?' If they are citizens how can we fight against them?" Babchenko answers that no one, from the regimental commander to the rank-and-file soldier, understands the war or sees any sense in it. It is a war waged incompetently and all the mistakes are paid for with the lives of the soldiers: "For what purpose are these lives being laid down? The 'restoration of constitutional order,' the 'counter-terrorist operation' are nothing but meaningless words that are cited to justify the murder of thousands of people."[85] We can imagine the Chechen protesting to the Russian soldier with the same fury that Innocent Rwililiza expressed to the machete-wielding Hutus he surprised one day—*why are you killing us?*—and the response of the Russians would similarly be: Because we were ordered to kill you. *We were so busy killing we didn't think of you.*

Yet Babchenko remains focused on the unfairness of his comrades' own deaths. When one of the soldiers asks what an innocent girl had done to deserve death, he responds that the soldiers were themselves "herded into this war and killed by the hundred." They didn't even know how to shoot, he protests: "All that we were capable of was crying and dying." And die they did. Despite not having yet "seen life or even tasted its scent," they had already seen death. "We so wanted to live," Babchenko writes, "to die at the age of eighteen is a terrifying prospect. We were betrayed by everyone and we died in a manner befitting real cannon fodder—silently and unfairly."[86]

In words that echo Beah's, Babchenko defends his own acts of killing as "different," on a "lesser scale," and under his control: "The death I administered was not grotesque—just a small hole in the body and that was it. My kind of death was fair; it gave them a chance to hide from the bullet behind a wall, just as I had hidden from their bullets. But to hide from a large-caliber cannon was impossible. This caliber could reach you everywhere; it crushed walls and killed terribly, with a roar, tearing off heads, turning bodies inside out, blowing the flesh off a person and leaving bare bones inside their tunics." But the extent of this "different" killing stops there. "I did not feel any pity or twinges of conscience for the Chechens," Babchenko admits. "We were enemies. They had to be killed to the last man, and in any way possible. And the faster and technically easier it was to do this, the better."[87]

"How I Found Myself in War" is the title of a series of public forums featuring war veterans from Bosnia-Herzegovina, Croatia, Montenegro, and

Serbia that took place from 2002 to 2004, held by the Centre for Nonviolent Action, an NGO based in Sarajevo and Belgrade.[88] Note the double entendre. First, the passive perspective: I *found* myself in war; I did not choose it. Throughout the testimonies of veterans from all sides of the conflict, we hear the same ambivalence toward their own agency and responsibility as that of Babchenko and the child soldiers. Second, *finding oneself* in war could also allude to what Fanon and Sartre insist is the making of a man through violence. There is loss, then, and disillusionment at the end of a war.

Four veterans were asked if they and all other combatants had stood up and declared they didn't want this war, would war have occurred? "I believe the war would still take place," one veteran insisted; "there would always be someone who would initiate it, and then the devil's ring in which many have danced would start." Once the war begins, it is too late, another admitted. The time to resist was much earlier, as early as 1987. "The order to report to service was a pure formality then, because the line had already been overstepped. At that point the mere refusal of the gun is not enough, although that too can be a significant step."[89]

It is moving to read these personal accounts from veterans who speak in a setting that could easily put them at risk, exposed to the anger of the "enemy" group. The participants are full of regrets, many of them coming to view war as the worst possible response to conflict, yet they cling to the justifications they once needed to participate in war. As Nebojša Jovanović put it, it took strength to face the enemy, yet "I realized my responsibility" and never wanted another war to happen. In fact, he admitted, there would have been no war "if the draftees and the reservists had any say in this." He follows this with an expression of resentment toward those men who refused to go to war: "some guys still kept playing tennis." Jovanović appeared to be quite anxious about being used as cannon fodder in an incomprehensible war not of his making: "My participation in the war is a participation of a man who was lead [*sic*] not by his own will and who tried to understand the objective of that war, which I haven't been able to understand to this very day. My prevailing feeling about this war is an insult that war brings to an individual, taking his personal integrity away and turning him into a part of the multitude, a simple figure that one or the other general might need. I felt it as turning myself into a gun-carrying instrument."[90]

Saša Dujović similarly alluded to war being "forced" upon the Serbian people. He didn't want to become cannon fodder, but the media were feeding Serbia information about atrocities committed against Serbs, and he returned to the front voluntarily despite having left it a wounded soldier. Dujović admitted that he knew the difference between the media image and the reality, yet he returned to combat, explaining in terms reminiscent of Babchenko's that "war is a special kind of drug, a kind of opium."

> I was getting deeper and deeper into it. You start thinking you're big, strong, you have the uniform, the weapon.... All the time I was being bitten by a doubt, but opium is stronger than the doubt and it goes on until you see a dead friend and start asking yourself WHY? ... I often wonder if I'd been cheated, and if yes, by whom. Was it my dad who brought me up an orthodox Serbian, was it the society, history? I felt obliged and took the gun at that point. It was the worst possible way to choose. I'm not sorry for being in the war, because I thought I was doing the right thing, but I'm sorry this war ever happened."

Dujović's ambivalence is pronounced in these statements. He feels "cheated" by his circumstances—his socialization in a family, a religion, and society—and "obliged" to take up arms, and yet in the next breath he chastises himself for making this choice. Then he withdraws his claim—*I'm not sorry for being in the war*—because he thought at the time that it was the right thing to do.

These comments garner sympathy for the peculiar predicament of the soldier. We may feel outrage toward those who plan wars and pity for those who become cannon fodder, mere pawns in the power struggles of heads of state or rebel group commanders. We may be unwilling to judge these men—concluding that we would do the same under similar agonizing circumstances. Some of them, after all, are only a few years older than Ishmael Beah was when he was abducted and forced to kill. But this leaves us with the untenable position that killing in certain contexts is immune from moral judgment if it is carried out by victims, and that victims who become perpetrators do not need to be accountable for what they have done through fear or coercion. If excuses are made for soldiers' participation in the war, despite our insistence afterward that war should "never again" occur, what do we expect will happen when the conditions are once again ripe for violence? There may be no good reasons for taking up arms, but we manage to invent them anyway.

"The mere refusal of the gun" *is* enough. It is not only a significant step but the only step that will ultimately end the killing. The excuse that others will always be willing to take up arms and fill our place, should we refuse, is no

THE VIOLENCE OF VICTIMHOOD

reason to join an army and does not exonerate us. We are not responsible for others' choices, only our own. This is the refusal necessary for moral judgment, carried out in order to be able to live with ourselves. Remember Gwynne Dyer's story of the Forest Troop baboons. If we can be conditioned to accept war as part of the way we do politics, we can be conditioned to refuse it.

Tragedy

I have argued in this chapter that we must be wary of the public and humanitarian discourses on child soldiers that portray them as pure or absolute victims. This approach entails believing that "they know not what they do," that these children are without agency, without the resources necessary to make moral decisions or judgments. We have seen that this humanitarian rhetoric is based on particular beliefs about what constitutes childhood—on the fantasy of primal innocence—as well as on a universalized experience of soldiering, abstracted from the historical context of any conflict. My critique of this perspective is based on research that indicates that children do exercise moral agency and that many resist under very limited circumstances. They are victims, certainly, but they are also perpetrators—victims-as-killers—and if we do not acknowledge their agency, if we ignore their awful deeds, we fail to probe the process that renders them killers. Children are coerced but, like their adult counterparts, they are also ideologically primed to kill for revenge, survival, and empowerment. This is the process that must be investigated if we are to think and act preventively rather than punitively through a global justice system.

Child soldiers are not without moral agency, and the matter of their recruitment is not always a simple issue. They are responsible for their actions in the sense that they must bear the consequences of what they have done; the violence carried out by a victim is as reprehensible as any violent act, regardless of the tragic circumstances that led to it. I maintain with Arendt that one's responsibility does not cease simply because one becomes the victim of the world's injustice and cruelty.[92] But we have on our hands a monstrous tragedy that imposes limits on what seems reasonable in theory. This is the crux of the matter: that we are all forced to deal with the consequences of our actions, consequences we could not have anticipated of actions that were performed under extraordinary pressure, fear, and the threat of death. There is no comfort to offer here, no resolution. We must simply acknowledge that there are degrees of responsibility, of guilt and innocence, and that sometimes survival is more important than accountability.

There is no universally applicable antidote. For soldiers like Ongwen, the protection of others has to take precedence. We cannot deny that he made terrible choices; even if these were made under the most constricted circumstances, he has to take the consequences for the death and destruction committed by his hands. If we were to excuse his deeds on the basis of childhood indoctrination and violation, we would never be able to ask the adult sex offender whose childhood was marred by sexual molestation to take account of his or her offenses, and we would have no ground on which to protect other possible victims. For those who escape at a much younger age, the terrors of their childhood experiences, no doubt shadowing their adult lives, may be more than they can bear. There is no justice that can alleviate these tragedies, but there is mercy.

The demand for accountability is not so simple in the face of psychological trauma, and with the knowledge that individuals respond in different ways to victimhood. Defenses against psychic pain are what enable some victims to survive. This is the most difficult challenge of responding to victims of atrocity: how to walk that tenuous line between recognizing responsibility—requiring that we all own our actions—and recognizing when such a burden is too great to bear.

6

MERCY FOR THE MERCILESS

We must simply take up life again, since life has so decided.

Polish journalist Wojciech Tochman visited Bosnia and Herzegovina a few years after the war's end in 1995 to speak to survivors, especially widows.[1] He tells their stories in *Like Eating a Stone: Surviving the Past in Bosnia.* One widow he meets speaks of her dead husband's nightly visits. He sits silently on the edge of her bed, not listening when she tells him to go back to where he came from. When the sun rises, she gets up and is greeted by her son, who tells her: "Same thing again, Mama . . . . You were gnashing your teeth in the night . . . . As if you were eating a stone."[2] It is an apt metaphor for those who must face the colossal obstacles to a peaceful existence thrown up by war or genocide. The survivors must eat stones.

In Bosnia and Herzegovina, the project of ethnic cleansing succeeded. Although the general impression we are given is that the conflict from 1992 to 1995 was ethnopolitical in nature, caused by the crumbling of a socialist regime that held at bay the deep and very old animosities simmering beneath the surface of everyday life, many point out that ethnic hatred was the *effect* of the conflict, no matter how rooted it may have been in preexisting differences. Previously innocuous identifications in multiethnic communities were poisoned by ideologies that politicized difference. The region is now divided into cantons of ethnically cleansed villages and cities, many of whose former inhabitants fled and whose new inhabitants occupy homes that could be reclaimed by their rightful owners. Overcome by feelings of betrayal, living in towns not of their making, the Serbs ask, why did we fight this war? Where is this greater Serbia we were promised? Bosnian Muslim survivors of the massacre in Srebrenica applaud when the Bosnian Serb wartime leader Radovan Karadžić is indicted and sent to The Hague, and protest when their own commander, Naser Orić, must follow. That the scale of their crimes is incomparable is not the point; responsibility for one's contribution to conflict, however great or small, is difficult to acknowledge when reeling from victimization oneself. Meanwhile, the younger generation, many of whom spent several childhood years hiding in basements, focus on the enjoyment of life, generally indifferent to politics (and who could blame them?). Language, culture, religion, and identity appear more important than ever. Arbitrary divisions in a mixed society become the last word on where one lives, works, enjoys conversation. Politicians use these divisions to their advantage; sides must be taken.

How to deal with the mess left by violent conflict is the focus of this chapter. We have established that moral judgment is necessary in order for perpetrators to accept responsibility for their actions. If violence—often the most brutal—is frequently justified on the basis of prior victimization, it is imperative that we respond to victims in ways that do not imprison them in their own defense systems, excusing wrongs committed in the name of victimhood, and in the belief that they have no other recourse. The violence of victimhood is one in which suffering is inflicted to alleviate the pain of suffering endured and humanity is destroyed for the restoration of humanity. Whether we are considering an individual victim of discrimination or a community suffering the aftermath of genocide or war, this dynamic is similar. The humiliation of violation, occupation, enslavement, defeat, sexual assault, and the trauma of witnessing death or being forced to kill may be salved by the transformation of grief into grievance, fear into power, anger into violence. Fanon was right: man is re-created by violence, but re-created in the image of his enemy.

The need to acknowledge responsibility, however, must be balanced by the need to recognize the limitations that traumatic experiences may impose on the individual psyche or collective identity. We face what life throws at us with different resources, strengths, and weaknesses, developed through circumstances not always of our choosing.

Judgment is not only cognitive but affective, requiring empathy and compassion. There is always a risk, in maintaining this balance, that judgment may be too harsh or too lenient. At the level of international responses to atrocity, this risk manifests itself in an ongoing debate over justice and peace. A host of dichotomies springs up when we explore the global dimensions of this debate: on the one hand, we find a call for justice, the rule of law, retribution, punishment, and international human rights, and on the other, the demand for peace, reconciliation, conflict resolution, amnesty, and negotiation. Justice in this debate usually refers to criminal, retributive justice with a focus on accountability; peace is defined negatively, as the exclusion of violence, or positively, as the process in which communities build relationships of mutual trust and care.

While many have recognized the necessity of overcoming these dichotomies—arguing, for example, that we can work toward establishing justice *with* peace, or "justpeace"[3]—an increasing interest in a global justice system, served by an international court and backed by the criticism of impunity and an idealized reconciliation, keeps them in tension. In this chapter I explore the terms of this tension and attempt to divert attention from the often abstract debate over peace and justice to a more pragmatic discussion of "post-conflict reconstruction."[4] The work of "repair" can't be done without acknowledging the complexity and ambiguity of victimhood. Justice fails to do this. But victim-centered approaches to reconciliation that emphasize catharsis and empowerment, and justify resentment, often fail to note this ambiguity as well.

Implementing the very same strategies in *response* to violence that we would to *prevent* violence, with a focus on survival, is the recommendation of this chapter. I do not attempt to synthesize what is a vast and unwieldy field of inquiry fractured by a number of paradigms: conflict transformation, reconciliation, peacebuilding, transitional justice. My point is to demonstrate that the demand for accountability and the recognition of one's responsibility for wrongdoing—in an effort to "deal with the past"—provide only a narrow scope with which to view the challenges of rebuilding a life after atrocity. As we concluded in the previous chapter, sometimes we must give the gift of mercy, even when punishment may be deserved. This is not in the interest of any mystical notion of reconciliation or peace but for the pragmatic reason that life must go on, with or without the justice victims long for. Such survival—like eating a stone—requires diligent and rigorous attention to historical context and political process, and to the brute fact that while humans are radically foreign to one another, we are incapable of surviving without one another.[5]

The Hegemony of Justice

In recent decades scholarship debating the best methods for dealing with past atrocity has proliferated. This has led to a veritable "international justice industry" that often loses sight of historical particulars in its attempt to synthesize methods of response.[6] When reading Tochman's accounts, or talking to survivors themselves, I am struck by what appears to be an unbridgeable chasm between the chaotic, uncertain reality of daily life after a war ends, and the vast literature concerned with responses to this reality. Much of this work is by no means disconnected from actuality, but there is a tendency to assume the harmonious or consensual relations it wishes to bring about in communities torn apart by violence.

Reconciliation, forgiveness, justice—these are terms that may inspire appropriate practices after conflict that occurs among psychologically and politically healthy communities whose individual members can be persuaded to be reasonable and treat one another decently once again. But they must be scrutinized when extraordinary events have affected individuals to such an extent that being reasonable or decent seems impossible, at least for the time being, because fear, grief, or the desire to cause pain in return prevail over clear thinking and empathy for others. Recall Jean Améry's insistence that healing is "antimoral" because it threatens to forget wrongdoing. In any program of societal repair after violent conflict, we need to consider that there may be many who do not want to be "repaired," who fiercely resist letting go of their resentment, convinced of their moral entitlement to it, conditioned ideologically to believe that they are in the right. Furthermore, in some cases we may discover that a victim's very survival *depends* on this resistance, and on other defenses against pain. Multiply this by the hundreds or thousands of victims an intractable conflict may engender over time, and it is easy to imagine the immense obstacles to reconstructing a peaceful society after a period of violence.

In the relatively recent growth of interest in victim-centered approaches to justice and peace after conflict, this resistance and potential for violence on the part of the victim is often forgotten. Justice and peace are concepts conventionally premised on ideals of balance, equality, exchange, and harmonious reconciliation. Justice is aligned with the law, founded on a discernible division between perpetrator and victim and on the conviction that injustice can be rectified, the imbalance brought on by wrongdoing balanced through accountability, punishment, and reparation; peace is aligned with reconciliation, forgiveness, and, in the end, the triumph of harmonious relations with former enemies. Their respective goals are often thought to be at cross-purposes—working toward peace might mean forgoing justice if the peaceful existence of a population is threatened by bringing the masterminds of violent conflict to trial—but both ideals tend to assume that balance and harmony can be restored or achieved.

Peace can be as elusive an ideal as justice.[7] But understandings of peace have recently been elaborated beyond a utopian absence of violence, in the recognition that conflict is an essential part of human life and that peace is an ongoing process—we must *build* peace. Diana Francis, for example, argues for a definition of peacebuilding that would include a "caring approach to other species and to our planet." Her "agenda for positive peace" includes peaceful relationships and processes, economic well-being, environmental protection, and democracy.[8] This broader definition of peace is intended to reflect the growth of global militarism, evident even in practices that our global governance institutions call peacebuilding or peacekeeping. We discern a similar pragmatic approach in John Paul Lederach's definition of peacebuilding: "Building peace in today's conflicts calls for long-term commitment to establishing an infrastructure across the levels of a society, an infrastructure that empowers the resources for reconciliation from within that society and maximizes the contribution from outside. In short, constructing the house of peace relies on a foundation of multiple actors and activities aiming at achieving and sustaining reconciliation."[9]

This infrastructure is now extensive. There are good reasons to be impressed by the increasing international concern at the level of government and civil society with the prevention and management of violent conflict since the end of World War I. In addition to the work of the UN, there are thousands of NGOs working in the field of conflict transformation and peacebuilding. Yet there is also reason to be worried about the success of this field in meeting the challenges of current global politics. Simon Fisher and Lada Zimina have argued that what is missing from the peacebuilding community, which has lost "much of the raison d'etre which brought it into existence," is a "wholehearted engagement with power and politics."[10]

One of the central reasons for this state of affairs is that attempts to alleviate the tension between peace and justice in the field of postconflict reconstruction have erred on the side of justice. The association of justice with retribution—"the idea that for encroachment and pain inflicted a compensating pain and encroachment must be performed"—has been remarkably constant since the days of ancient Greece, argues Martha Nussbaum. Cosmologically speaking, she explains, if an encroachment takes place by one of the elements, an encroachment in the other direction must take place in order that "the doer should suffer."[11] Justice understood in this sense is proportional, founded on the premise that human life is a vulnerable thing that can be invaded, wounded, or violated by another's act. To respond appropriately, it seems that we need a counterinvasion, a retributive act that is precise in its proportion to the original invasion.[12] Certainly the examples in previous chapters bear this out.

Such an understanding of justice is quite pronounced in the rhetoric of the war on terror and the security politics it has fostered since 9/11, which is not surprising given the mass fear of terrorism and consequent desire for control over whatever we (often erroneously) believe we can control. The rule of law tends to give us a false sense of security. But a retributive sense of justice also underlies the current discourses informing global responses to atrocity, despite recent attempts to define an alternative kind of justice as restorative or reparative. I have argued that we live in an era when judgment has been abdicated in favor of cultural sensitivity or moral relativism; in this global context, judgment is exercised only in the form of a punitive justice that is selective, prey to political ends, and prohibitively expensive.

Seeking to repair the injustice rather than simply punish the wrongdoer, *restorative* justice methods focus on the needs of the victims, the responsibility of the perpetrators, and the relationship between them. It is thus considered a reparative approach, aiming to heal and empower victims and reconcile them with their victimizers, based on the recognition of the humanity of victims and perpetrators.[13] Both retributive and restorative concepts of justice have inspired practical measures to achieve the restoration of equality, harmony, or balance. A wrong committed must be accounted for, and rightful relations among humans restored to maintain equilibrium. Restorative justice, however, repudiates harsh punishment for the perpetrator motivated by a desire for revenge, and instead makes amends through a reconciliatory process.

The restorative approach attempts to bring strategies once considered to fall under the rubric of peacebuilding or reconciliation into the realm of justice. The ideal of justice has a powerful hold on our imaginations, and although abstract and nebulously defined, it is difficult to challenge. "How can one plausibly claim to be 'against' justice?" Trudy Govier asks. "How can one deny that 'justice must be done'?" She asks these questions in the context of a discussion of the International Criminal Court (ICC), noting that courts of law address only one aspect of justice under the difficult circumstances facing postconflict societies. This is a work of penal justice exclusively, she argues, subjecting only a few of those who are responsible for atrocity to a legal trial, thereby ignoring reparative or restorative justice, socioeconomic and distributive justice. While the focus on leaders makes sense, Govier adds, "leaders can lead only if there are others who follow them willingly." It is therefore "a considerable simplification to presume that 'justice' will have been 'done' when a select few of them are legally prosecuted."[14]

I agree with Govier's criticism, as will become clear in the next section, but I will go one step further: it isn't only penal justice we must scrutinize but justice *as the ideal of perfect balance*, whether we speak of distributive, restorative, or socioeconomic justice. In some circumstances balance, equality, and reciprocity will never be achieved. This is not to suggest that we must dispense with justice altogether. There are contexts in which striving toward an ideal of fairness or equal distribution of resources and opportunities at an institutional level, for example, is necessary, but in the aftermath of political violence, justice—as a term of exchange, balance, equality—may need to be neglected for the sake of a future without violence. This is not an easy road, of course; we have an overwhelming need for vindication when wronged, for the recognition of our innocence when falsely accused, and we can be outraged when others are treated unjustly. I can only imagine how these emotions are magnified by an egregious atrocity. Forgoing justice does not mean that we fail to consider the needs of victims and let perpetrators get away with murder, but that we focus on the survival of all those affected by violence through pragmatic measures at political, psychological, moral, and social levels. The law—tidy, definitive, appeasing our moral outrage—is ill equipped to deal with the ambiguous condition of victims who become perpetrators and the messy political and moral quandaries left in the wake of their violence. Acknowledging the limits of justice will prevent us from getting stuck in the debate over whether peace or justice should come first, based on which victims are perceived to need more. This has only led us to neglect political and ethical matters.

The "Juridicization" of Dealing with the Past

The International Center for Transitional Justice (ICTJ) opened the doors of its first office in March 2001 in New York City. Within six months it was operating in more than a dozen countries with the mandate of "helping societies to heal by accounting for and addressing past crimes after a period of repressive rule or armed conflict." The ICTJ claims that its main function is accountability. In order to promote justice, peace, and reconciliation, it helps countries develop "localized" approaches to transitional justice by "prosecuting perpetrators, documenting and acknowledging violations through nonjudicial means such as truth commissions, reforming abusive institutions, providing reparations to victims, and facilitating reconciliation processes."[15] The ICTJ literature highlights the use of local actors in building local capacity as well as the expertise of international organizations and individuals, and claims to prioritize the interests and perspectives of victims and survivors.

With the help of the ICTJ, "transitional justice" has become the new global paradigm for dealing with the aftermath of conflict. Proponents have been eager to promote it as a comprehensive approach, subsuming the kinds of practices typically identified with the fields of reconciliation or peacebuilding, in an attempt to acknowledge that there are limits to juridical approaches to dealing with the past, particularly in dealing with mass crimes such as genocide, ethnic cleansing, and crimes against humanity.[16] The ICTJ, for example, claims that transitional justice "seeks recognition for victims and to promote possibilities for peace, reconciliation and democracy."[17] Despite this attempt to extend its reach beyond the strictly juridical, the tenets and practices of transitional justice are still primarily founded in the language of law, generated by lawyers.[18] The dominance of the juridical is evident in the fact that the two primary sources informing transitional justice are the human rights movement—making it "self-consciously victimcentric," according to Louis Bickford—and international human rights and humanitarian law.[19]

Critics of the sweeping claims often made by transitional justice proponents are coming out of the woodwork. First, while its popular appeal has grown by leaps and bounds since the 1990s, transitional justice is poorly defined. The concept is said to have emerged in the late 1980s as a response to political change in Latin America, at that time referred to as the "transition to democracy." The origin of the term is thus tied to liberalization and the Western democratic tradition, but it highlights the role of law in the debates on political institutional transformation. In one of the first substantive books on the subject, Ruti Teitel defines transitional justice as "a concept of justice, intervening in a period of political change, characterized by a juridical answer to the wrong of past repressive regimes."[20] In a later work she amends this definition to "an increasing juridicization among diverse legal systems, international and national, and multiple paradigms of legitimacy in global order."[21]

Teitel believes that legal responses to periods of radical political transformation play "an extraordinary, constitutive role," particularly with respect to the matter of accountability for past wrongs and in reparative justice measures. Reparatory measures, she argues, attest to the liberalizing move, as they instantiate the recognition of individual rights and the establishment of the rule of law. Justice itself, however, is evasively defined by Teitel as constructivist, contextualized and partial: "What is deemed just is contingent and informed by prior injustice."[22] Unfortunately, this definition is characteristic of several decades of scholarship on the concept and practice of transitional justice.[23] Without any criteria for determining what is just or unjust, we are left with an international justice system vulnerable to political abuse, and to the accusation (frequently made, of late) that it is based on Western cultural ideals unfamiliar to the rest of the world.

Second, as previous chapters have shown, to be "victimcentric" may not be the unalloyed virtue we have come to believe it is. Responses that are increasingly victim-centered make assumptions about what is best for the victim based on what the victim desires—desires that should not simply be taken at face value. We have come to accept, for example, that recognition, acknowledgment, and the remembrance and memorializing of an injustice are absolutely necessary for a society to reconcile and move on in the aftermath of conflict. There are limits, however, to what Ian Buruma calls the "sentimental solidarity of remembered victimhood," and although this does not mean that memorials or accounts of suffering are insignificant, they can imprison victims within the ruins of their past.[24]

This solidarity also leads to the stubborn reticence of a victimized group to acknowledge its own war criminals and acts of violence. In their comprehensive study of the International Criminal Tribunal of the former Yugoslavia (ICTY) in Bosnia and Herzegovina, Laurel Fletcher and Harvey Weinstein show that proximity to a conflict determines how strong the desire is for criminal accountability for war crimes. Identification with victimhood thus colors an identity group's view of justice, rendering it vulnerable to political abuse. Bosnian judges and prosecutors in this study were asked if they believed that genocide occurred in Bosnia and Herzegovina, and if so, against whom. Responses were "remarkably similar" between members of the same national group. Bosniak (Bosnian Muslim) professionals were unequivocal in their statements that genocide had occurred against Bosniaks during the war, while Bosnian Serbs tended to state that genocide occurred against all three sides, that they had no knowledge of acts of genocide, or that it did not occur at all. Thus the professional identity of the participants was less important than group identity in determining who was considered the victim group with the right to demand the accountability of the perpetrator group. Fletcher and Weinstein conclude, "the need to identify one's national group as the principal victim of the conflict challenges the theory that criminal trials promote social healing by documenting and acknowledging the atrocities of the past . . . . If the need for acknowledgment of victimization overwhelms the ability to recognize and condemn the horrors perpetrated by one's national group, then criminal trials will achieve only partial success, at best."[25] We would do well to take note of this astute insight. Juridical processes must of necessity distinguish victims from perpetrators; a model that accomplishes this for the benefit of victims' empowerment and recognition will be especially unable to account for the ambiguous status of the victim-turned-perpetrator. It is particularly challenging in regions such as the Western Balkans, where a nation's or ethnic group's unwillingness to acknowledge its own war crimes becomes a serious detriment to any kind of reconciliation.

Fletcher and Weinstein continue to point out that criminal leaders are thought to be "purged" from public life through prosecution, fostering a new national narrative that stigmatizes only those leaders responsible for planning the atrocity, ritually purifying the public body and absolving the general population of collective responsibility.[26] The victim's thirst for revenge may be assuaged by criminal prosecutions, but there is no evidence to suggest that this leads to healing. The catharsis that comes from the process of retributive justice or from learning the truth about the past from a truth commission is short-lived and informed by cultural beliefs in therapeutic methods.

The close association of transitional justice with the ICC and international criminal tribunals is particularly coming under fire. Although "Never Again" is one of the most important slogans of the International Criminal Tribunal for Rwanda (ICTR), for example, the genocide there was followed by extreme violence and ethnic hostilities in Sierra Leone, Congo, Iraq, Chechnya, Liberia, and Sudan.[27] If one believes that one is unjustly accused, punishment does not seem to act as an effective deterrent. Nor do leaders believe they will be caught. Although deterrence is an oft-cited justification for international criminal trials, Fletcher and Weinstein state that there is no empirical evidence to suggest that trials deter war crimes or gross human rights violations.[28]

In theory, given the tenacious grip the ideal of justice has on our moral sensibilities, international law and tribunals may still hold immense appeal. But the practical reality of a tribunal is another story. Consider perhaps the most blatantly ineffective case of transitional justice in action: the ICTR that began in 1994 and is scheduled to end in 2013.[29] First and foremost, the costs of the ICTR have been astronomical, as the UN has flown in a community of witnesses, lawyers, and judges—all earning good UN salaries—to Arusha, a beautiful city in Tanzania close to Mount Kilimanjaro. The initial two-year budget was approved in 2002 at $256.9 million. By way of comparison, Stephanie Nolen tells us, $322 million was given in foreign aid to Rwanda in 2000, and many African countries in extreme need receive far less in foreign aid. Nolen points out the terrible irony: the world did nothing while nearly a million people were brutally hacked to death, then subsequently offered a UN criminal tribunal housed in a vast, air-conditioned building, "all blond wood and high tech gizmos." Twelve years and $1.2 billion later, twenty-five convictions had been made.[30] For 2010–11 the ICTR had a budget of roughly $245 million and a staff of 693.[31] Helena Cobban cynically describes the ICTR courtroom as a "citadel of boredom," as attorneys and judges—dressed in "capacious robes patterned on the gowns of medieval European clerics," some with British barristers' wigs perched atop headsets for interpretation— question victims and perpetrators about events that occurred too long ago for them to remember accurately. Arusha, she notes wryly, is a lovely place to live, with game parks, mountain hiking, and cheap household help.[32]

To criticize justice mechanisms does not mean we are indifferent to injustice or care little about the lives of victims. It means that we throw into question the effectiveness of the law in dealing with the aftermath of conflict. Prioritizing the victims' desire for justice should not be assumed to be a mor- ally pure act, for wants are not necessarily needs. We have already observed how resentment and identification with an ethnic group can affect victims. A justice that balances what has been rendered askew is thought to serve the needs of victims by helping to alleviate the pain they suffered at the hands of perpetrators; their innocence is validated by the state and their equality—in terms of humanity and empowerment—is thought to be restored to them. The punishment of perpetrators is then believed to be a deterrent by enforc- ing legal and moral norms and removing potential future threats to a regime.

Justice can certainly sabotage peace. But expanding the notion of justice to such an extent that it is rendered meaningless is not an effective response. Nolen claims that justice might mean "I want to forget" rather than punish the masterminds of war. In the words of Kadiatu Fofanah, who begs and sells candy to support her nine children after rebel soldiers cut off her legs during the civil war in Sierra Leone, "We amputees have been told to forgive and forget to sustain the peace. But what makes me forget is having something to eat and my kids going to school—so they can bring me something to survive. That's what would allow me to forget."[33] Why not call "I want to forget" the expression of a desire for a decent, meaningful life, and for relinquishing the need for retribution, rather than a cry for justice? This approach acknowledges the impossibility of ever balancing the scales of justice after such egregious events, and the corresponding belief that despite this impossibility, life can be better. There is no balance to be restored in a situation in which one's family members have been killed by those who now live and perhaps prosper in the house next door, or even in the victims' former home. Victims must look to a future that will come in any event, regardless of the perpetrator's punishment, and no matter how unfair their conditions.

To Forgive or to Resent

Whether we consider justice retributive or restorative, never before has the victim's desire for recognition and proportional justice occupied such a privileged position—at least in theory. Empowerment, recognition, vindication, healing for the victims of atrocity—these are the desired outcomes of an increasingly globalized mechanics of justice, whether reconciling with one's enemy or exercising a victim's "right" to retribution. It is worth noting that being victim-centered from a transitional justice approach means honoring the victim's desire for retribution—perceived as moral outrage—whereas from a reconciliation approach, it means freeing the victim from this very desire. This contradiction is most evident in debates on forgiveness and resentment, and it helps to explain further the stubbornness of the dichotomy between the ideal of justice and the ideal of peace. What both victim-centered approaches take for granted is the moral authority of the victim's perspective. But their antithetical positions—that on the one hand the victim is right to want to *forgive* her victimizer, while on the other the victim is right to *resent* her victimizer—demonstrate the difference that a juridicized view of postconflict reconstruction makes.

The daunting task of rebuilding trust when neighbors have harmed or killed neighbors tells us how necessary—if seemingly impossible—the work of reconciliation is after the death and destruction of war. Like transitional justice, reconciliation is a loosely defined paradigm that groups together practices of social reconstruction in the aftermath of violent conflict. David Bloomfield defines the term broadly as an overarching process "through which a society moves from a divided past to a shared future," a process that includes the search for truth, justice, forgiveness, and healing.[34] Like restorative justice, reconciliation is focused on repairing social relations between formerly antagonistic persons or groups. One can see here the attempt to incorporate juridical processes in order to broaden the understanding of reconciliation.[35]

The anti-apartheid struggle in South Africa, culminating in the Truth and Reconciliation Commission (TRC), has made an inestimable impact on the concept and practice of reconciliation. This is the case that celebrated the importance of knowing the truth about atrocities, forgiving perpetrators in the desire for reconciliation and peace, and the benefits of amnesty. The affirmation of forgiveness is one of the TRC's most prominent legacies, and it would be hard to overestimate the impact it has had on the postconflict reconstruction field. Thomas Brudholm goes so far as to say that forgiveness has achieved "near-hegemonic status" in the literature on transitional justice and reconciliation. Atrocity survivors who are ready to forgive are admired and appreciated, he writes; they "incarnate magnanimity, strength, and humanity—and they provide reasons to hope that recovery and reconciliation are possible even in the worst of cases."[36] Conversely, those unwilling to forgive are pathologized for harboring crippling negative emotions. While critical approaches are not difficult to find, they are drowned out by a Christian-inspired interpretation of the concept framed in popularized therapeutic language. What is remarkable about the discussion is the extent to which forgiveness is assumed without question to be a virtue of the highest caliber. We should be suspicious of the manner in which forgiveness is promoted—of the political uses to which it can be put—and aware of its limitations. With this caveat, I want to argue that what is useful about forgiveness is the element of forgetting.

To forgive is to pardon, to cancel the debt of another's wrongful actions against oneself, to release her from these actions and relinquish the demand for "payback." Forgiveness is thought to further the cause of peace and reconciliation and to be motivated either by compassion for the perpetrator or by the victim's need to "move on" by letting go of resentment. Critics would argue, however, that it brings peace at the expense of justice for the victim, that to forgive the perpetrator appears to let her off the hook, to grant impunity, to forget the wrongdoing and thus forgo judgment. Victims may be pressured to forgive for the sake of peace. But it is the demand for punishment and retribution that is relinquished, not judgment. This is an important distinction.

The conflation of punishment and judgment is evident in the criticisms of the amnesty granted to those responsible for apartheid in South Africa, forgiveness forming one of the central axes on which the transition to postapartheid democracy was organized. Dominated by the messianism of the South African leadership in the TRC, forgiveness was believed to free an individual or community from the desire for retributive justice, and in this case it was promoted as a conscious strategy to avoid reprisals by blacks against whites.[37]

Perpetrators who divulged the truth were granted amnesty; judgments were made regarding who was guilty and who was innocent, but no punishment was demanded.

Bishop Desmond Tutu, whose very name seems synonymous with the concept of forgiveness, is a proponent of the first view, that forgiveness is beneficial for the victim. He writes that it is "the best form of self-interest since anger, resentment, and revenge are corrosive of that *summum bonum*, that greatest good, communal harmony that enhances the humanity and personhood of all in the community."[38] Remaining in that state of resentment and anger can, he believes, "lock one in the state of victimhood," keeping the victim dependent on his or her perpetrator. The empowerment associated with the gesture is evident; the victim rises above the crippling emotions attached to his status as victim, becoming a better person than the victim who wallows in resentment.

Forgiveness is thus for Bishop Tutu the opposite of resentment and anger, which are assumed to lead to vengeance. Anger is dehumanizing, while forgiveness is profoundly humanizing, related to the African concept of *ubuntu*, which he defines as an openness to the humanity of others, and to the interrelatedness of persons: "I am human because I belong. I participate, I share." Tutu elaborates, "A person with ubuntu is open and available to others, affirming of others, does not feel threatened that others are able and good, for he or she has a proper self-assurance that comes from knowing that he or she belongs in a greater whole and is diminished when others are humiliated or diminished, when others are tortured or oppressed, or treated as if they were less than who they are."[39] Peace takes precedence over retributive justice, for Tutu. We are able to forgive because we allow ourselves to be vulnerable to others, presumably accepting their fallibility as we accept our own. This belonging to an idealized human community banishes negative emotions like anger and resentment. As Brudholm explains, "Forgiveness, on the one hand, restores relationships, social harmony, and thus also the sustenance that enables us—the victim no less than the perpetrator—to be truly human. Anger, resentment, and revenge, on the other hand, erode social harmony and thus also our possibility of being truly human."[40]

We may object here that anger and resentment are part of being human, but we could still maintain that they are damaging to the self. The belief that forgiveness can mitigate this damage is a common one. A cursory glance at popular titles tells us of the significant use made of forgiveness by the therapeutic and self-help industry for this reason: *Forgiveness Is a Choice; Forgiveness: How to Make Peace with Your Past and Get on with Your Life; Forgiveness: The*

Greatest Healer of All; Finding Forgiveness: A Seven Step Program for Letting Go of Anger and Bitterness. These books make liberal use of the language of psychological healing, premised on the assumption that if the victim does not relinquish resentment, she becomes stuck, unable to heal.[41] The expression of resentment and anger are considered from this perspective to be damaging to psychic health. Forgiveness is a form of therapy for the victim and not without its benefits for the perpetrators, who may be saved from being the victims of resentful acts of revenge.

Directly opposing this position, we find an affirmation of resentment as a *necessary* emotion in the demand for justice, inspired by the need for recognition and empowerment for victims. It conflates resentment with moral outrage, an emotional response to injustice, and assumes that judgment and justice (retributive, punitive) are one and the same. Margaret Urban Walker, for example, asserts that victims are "entitled" to the other's accounting for his or her actions. We have normative expectations about another's behavior toward us, expectations that embody a demand for the kind of behavior "we think we've a right to." Walker continues, "The expression of our sense of entitlement is our readiness to be aroused angrily at one whose noncompliant behavior threatens the authority of a norm by defying it. Resentment and indignation are this distinctive *accusing* and *rebuking* anger."[42]

This is a disturbing approbation of rage that can slip easily into a justification of violence. We may have expectations and hopes for another's behavior toward us, but it doesn't follow that this constitutes a "right." Once again, we observe the assumption of balance and reciprocity—that we can even the playing field by demanding that others meet our needs and norms. The moral purity of a desire for justice is assumed, the fine line between the demand for fairness and the cry for revenge unexamined. Significantly, the onus here is placed squarely on the other to meet my need to recover from victimization. It is his responsibility to me that is demanded, leaving me with a ready excuse to avoid mine.

Walker might appreciate the sentiment expressed by Innocent Rwililiza, survivor of the Rwandan genocide in 1994, who insists that forgiveness is *oppressive*. Who is talking about forgiveness, he asks—not the Tutsis or Hutus, not the freed prisoners or their families but the humanitarian organizations that are "importing" forgiveness to Rwanda wrapped in dollars. There is a publicly promoted "Forgiveness Plan" just as there is an "AIDS Plan," replete with "public awareness meetings, posters, petty local presidents, super-polite Whites in all-terrain turbo vehicles." Rwililiza admits that Rwandans speak of forgiveness to earn the good opinion—and the subsidies—of these foreigners, but when they talk among themselves, forgiveness has no place: "You see Adalbert return. He led the killings on Kibungo Hill, he was pardoned, he parades around Kigali, he wields his machete once more in his fields. You, you're from Kibungo, living five hundred meters from his house, and you lost your mama, papa, two sisters, wife, and little boy. You run into Adalbert downtown. He to you, you to him—who's going to say that word *forgiveness*? It's outside of nature."[43] The passage is suffused with resentment against those who would extort forgiveness from victims and against the perpetrators who do not suffer as the victims do and do not pay for their wrongful deeds. That this is an accusing or rebuking anger is immediately apparent, and although we may readily sympathize with Rwililiza—for indeed, this is an intolerable and unjust situation—this doesn't mean that the judgment is morally acceptable, or that it would bring about any kind of peaceful coexistence, as opposed to an equalization of suffering or benefits. Even if this equality were achieved, we should consider what kind of community would develop on the basis of resentment and retribution. Meeting the needs of the victims is a different matter from satisfying their desire for empowerment.

From Walker's and Brudholm's perspective, the act of forgiving represses rather than releases the very rage and resentment considered necessary to recognize injustice and maintain legitimate conflict and contestation in a society that strives toward pluralist, liberal democracy.[44] Victims are thought to deserve an apology and some recompense, in this view, and if an offense is ignored or an abusive relationship continued, victims become complicit in their own victimization.[45] For if we ask victims to forget their injuries, how will justice be achieved, and how will we prevent the exploitation of victims? But this query takes for granted that justice is unquestionably the right goal, one that can be met only by drawing a firm line between victims and perpetrators. It also equates moral outrage with resentment. Resentment and the desire for retribution, however, are not required to speak out against injustice. Resisting this impulse can help victims relegate horrific events to the past, and cut debilitating ties to the perpetrator.

A Duty to Forget?

To promote forgetting flies in the face of the current approbation of remembering and memorializing as necessary methods of dealing with the past. Memory can be used "too vigorously," writes Yadh Ben Achour, and ultimately aggravate suffering. "Sometimes the obligation to remember must cede to the imperatives of peace, order, and security." In fact, Achour believes that we have a *duty to forget* if we want to stop perpetuating the pain. Even a thorough knowledge of the truth can prevent this forgetting, and the necessary "quieting of emotions." In order to forget, "time needs silence."[46]

The debate over forgiveness and resentment hinges on the assumption that justice is a matter of distinguishing the victim from the perpetrator, and remembering—*memorializing*—this distinction. If we shift our focus from justice to the survival of communities—or victims *and* perpetrators—we come to see that forgetting is the essential part of forgiveness, for it allows the victim to refuse the identity and status of victimhood that keeps him tied to the past. Forgetting seems particularly necessary when faced with the *unforgivable*, and with an "enemy" whose behavior will not conform to our requirements or norms—in short, when we most need to find ways to coexist. Under these circumstances, to forget means that we let go of the need for perfect balance, social cohesion, and mutual understanding in the interests of managing conflict without violence.

Govier argues that coexistence is not enough and that lasting peace requires the kind of deep trust only possible through forgiveness. Peace without forgiveness may be an enormous achievement, she maintains, but remains minimal, defined only as an absence of overt physical violence. Nonviolent coexistence is thus only the first step toward a lasting peace, "unlikely to be sustainable if past wrongs are unexamined and feelings of hatred and alienation persist."[47] People must "work effectively together" in cooperation and trust, Govier states, defining trust as "an attitude of confident expectation that most others will act in a morally decent way most of the time. To trust other people in this sense is to believe—in the absence of certainty—that they will act in ways that are generally constructive and not harmful to us." It is this trust that empowers us to accept some degree of vulnerability, Govier concludes.[48] It doesn't follow, however, that such trust is impossible *without* forgiveness, for working effectively together can occur for reasons that don't include trusting that others will be morally decent toward us. We may work together because *we have to*, and trust may follow, eventually.

It is difficult to say what comes first in the long process of reconciling and building a peaceful civil society. It may be that the simple fact of coexistence and proximity—in other words, the necessity of living together—will eventually mean that former enemies will decide that they must work together and set aside their differences. While the motivating force might be something we call forgiveness, it could also be a practical determination to handle disputes in nonviolent ways. Most important would be a shared determination to move on. Working together effectively can only be achieved through practice, and with a common goal in mind that benefits everyone in a community, whether victim or perpetrator. But there will always be those, like Améry, who refuse to trust, fearing the risk of becoming once again vulnerable to another human being. The greater responsibility for creating a future must always be taken up by those with the most resources from which to draw.

At the end of her extraordinary account of the TRC in South Africa, Antjie Krog presents some conclusions that have probably surprised a number of readers. While the TRC created a forum for victims, opening a space for them in the national psyche and in South African history, its "biggest failure," writes Krog, lay in its approach to healing the trauma of these victims. The TRC succeeded fairly well in establishing the factual truth of apartheid, but it was far less successful in providing the moral truth of who was responsible. Few people believe that the TRC achieved reconciliation, at least reconciliation as "a mysterious Judaeo-Christian process."[49]

Yet the word reconciliation "still resounds in the land," Krog tells us. This is a demystified reconciliation—not appropriated by religion or ideology—the essence of which is survival and negotiation. This reconciliation "carries within it the full variety of survival strategies—among them choice, flight, amnesia, rituals, clemency, debate, negotiation, brinkmanship, and national consensus. The goal is not to avoid pain or reality, but to deal with the never-ending quest of self-definition and negotiation required to transform differences into assets. Reconciliation is not only a process. It is a cycle that will be repeated many times." Our ability to reconcile through negotiation for the sake of survival "is the reason why some of us are still around."[50]

Krog's understanding of reconciliation as a strategy of survival exercised through negotiation is reflected in the sentiments of Francine Niyitegeka, a survivor of the Rwandan genocide. She does not think that everything is forgivable, but she acknowledges the effects of time and the pragmatic needs of a community to survive. "You can forgive a man who has had one beer too many and beats his wife," she says, "but if he has worked at killing for a whole month, even on Sundays, how can he hope for pardon?" Whether offered or withheld, however, forgiveness does not detract life from its course:

> We must simply take up life again, since life has so decided. Thorn-bushes must not invade the farms; teachers must return to their school

blackboards; doctors must care for the sick in the health clinics. There must be strong new cattle, fabrics of all kinds, sacks of beans in the markets. In that case, many Hutus are necessary. One cannot line up all the killers in the same row. Those who were overwhelmed by events, they can come back from Congo and the prisons one day, and return to their farm plots. We will begin to draw water together again, to exchange neighborly words, to sell grain to one another. In twenty years, fifty years, there will perhaps be boys and girls who will learn about the genocide in books. For us, however, it is impossible to forgive.[51]

Forgetting a wrongful act—or at the very least the resentment attached to it—does not mean that judgment is abdicated. It is an act of mercy by the victim toward the perpetrator but also toward herself, understanding that human fallibility does not determine who we are, but neither does victimhood. In Arendt's brief discussion of forgiveness, we witness what I would call a merciful forgetfulness. Arendt defines the faculty of forgiving as "the possible redemption from the predicament of irreversibility—of being unable to undo what one has done though one did not, and could not, have known what he was doing."[52] Without this possibility of being released from the consequences of what we have done, our capacity to act would be confined to one single deed from which we could never recover; we would remain the victims of its consequences forever. This is an interesting departure from Arendt's assertion that we must take consequences for our actions, that we are never released from the "burden of irreversibility" (233). She elaborates, "But trespassing is an everyday occurrence which is in the very nature of action's constant establishment of new relationships within a web of relations, and it needs forgiving, dismissing, in order to make it possible for life to go on by constantly releasing men from what they have done unknowingly. Only through this constant mutual release from what they do can men remain free agents, only by constant willingness to change their minds and start again can they be trusted with so great a power as that to begin something new" (240). Forgiveness, from Arendt's point of view, is thus the opposite of vengeance, which keeps both the victim and perpetrator bound to the process. We are led to forgive by *respect*, by "a regard for the person from the distance which the space of the world puts between us, and this regard is independent of qualities which we may admire or of achievements which we may highly esteem" (243). Forgiveness constitutes a faculty of undoing what we have done, in order to control to a limited extent the consequences of our actions (246). But note that she is talking about releasing men from what they have done "unknow-ingly." Arendt had no qualms about Adolf Eichmann's death sentence; his crimes were unforgiveable.[53] There are limits to this "mutual release."

Mercy for the Merciless

To be released from the consequences of what we have done is to be treated with mercy. This could be the outcome of an act of forgiveness on the part of the victim or an act of judgment by a third party. Both acts could be motivated by compassion and empathy for the fallibility of another. Mercy is an atti-tude of compassion toward one who has committed a wrongful act, forbearing punishment "even when justice demands it." It derives from the French, *merci*, meaning reward, gift, kindness, but also to thank. The Latin root is *merced-*, *merces*, meaning "price paid," wages, merchandise. In the Middle Ages, mercy was related to forgiveness in its use of the term to mean "God's forgiveness of his creatures' offenses." There is thus an implied power relation in the practice of mercy, that of a benevolent god or judge granting clemency or leniency to a wrongdoer who deserves punishment but who is judged with compassion and given a lesser punishment. This is a power relation shared with that of forgive-ness, for both use the terms of financial transactions—a debt, payment, wages, and forgoing what is owed to one out of compassionate regard for the offender.

Unlike forgiveness, mercy is not necessarily granted by the victim of an injustice but by those considered qualified to make judgments and to demand accountability and reparations for the victim. We can judge a wrong to be wrong while cultivating the gentleness of mercy, Nussbaum asserts.[54] Her argument for the value of a merciful response to wrongdoing over a retribu-tive one rests on the idea that humans are capable of receiving another's life story into their imaginations and responding to that history with gentleness. This is particularly important now, she writes, given that "a simple form of retributivism has an increasing influence on our legal and political life" (125).

The roots of Nussbaum's view go back to Aristotle, who believes that legal judgments must be made with particular circumstances in mind. The moral term he uses is *epieikeia*, which, Nussbaum explains, intertwines two concepts: equity and mercy. The first concerns "the ability to judge in such a way as to respond with sensitivity to all the particulars of a person and situation," and the second involves "the 'inclination of the mind' toward leniency in punishing" (85–86). Thus, from the start, judgment is considered a flexible, particularized concept related to leniency in punishment—as the Greek orator Gorgias maintained, the "gentle equitable" rather than the "harshly stubborn just" (86).

In the archaic conception of justice as "an eye for an eye," the particulars of a case must be ignored. A parricide is a parricide. It matters not that Oedipus had extenuating circumstances. He committed incest without knowing it, but it was still incest. This is the retributive justice approach. *Epieikeia*, on the other hand, would acknowledge that "because the act that [Oedipus] intended and chose was not the act that we have judged him to have performed," we could judge him more gently (90). For Aristotle, the good judge is like a good architect who measures a complicated structure using a flexible strip of metal that bends to the shape of a stone, rather than a straight edge (93). This kind of judgment recognizes that the world is one

> of imperfect human efforts and of complex obstacles to doing well, a world in which humans sometimes deliberately do wrong, but sometimes also get tripped up by ignorance, passion, poverty, bad education, or circumstantial constraints of various sort[s]. It is a world in which bad things are sometimes simply bad, sometimes extremely bad, but sometimes—and more often, when one goes into them—somewhat less bad, given the obstacles the person faced on the way to acting properly. *Epieikeia* is a gentle art of particular perception, a temper of mind that refuses to demand retribution without understanding the whole story; it responds to Oedipus's demand to be seen for the person he is. (91–92)

This is the world of the child soldier, coerced to commit unthinkable atrocities. His circumstances are quite different from those of the adult soldier who believes he must fight or watch his family die, from the serial killer who commits premeditated murder, or from the state that exercises brutal preemptive strikes or acts of terror—these particular contexts need to be taken into account. But this does not mean that their actions are not all equally wrong and abhorrent, as Nussbaum claims. We can judge an act to be wrong no matter what the circumstances, yet recognize the unique context of individual wrongdoers. This fact prevents a merciful judgment from excusing the deed. We discern what is right and wrong and then decide how best to respond to the wrongdoer.

As Aristotle did not delve deeply enough into the concept of mercy, Nussbaum appeals to the Stoic philosopher Seneca for a full analysis. Stoic moral theory, like Aristotle's, is premised on the idea that rules and precepts should only function as guidelines when evaluating deeds (98). The Stoics were accordingly exact in their assessment of the offense and its punishment, judging from a vantage point of critical detachment. This is a tension, for Seneca, between good moral assessment and the detachment that "withholds psychological understanding, treating deep and complex predicaments as easily avoidable mistakes, simply refusing to see the obstacles to good action from the erring agent's own viewpoint" (99). Nussbaum sums up Seneca's approach: circumstances are the origins of vice rather than innate propensities; "and when the wise person looks at these circumstances clearly, he finds that they make it extremely difficult not to err. The world into which human beings are born is a rough place, one that confronts them with threats to their safety on every side" (100).

Nussbaum is anxious to convey that Seneca was not in favor of ignoring moral and legal responsibility for bad acts. Good judging does not ignore the facts or fail to declare that evil is evil but is exercised by those who remain capable of love and a merciful response (125). "Clementia"—clemency, or mercy—means that we should "cultivate humanity," which Seneca describes elsewhere as "to give pardon to the human species" (102). Mercy as "an inclination of the soul to mildness in exacting penalties" is the opposite of cruelty, which is often brought on by retributive anger (102). To punish a fault in full is, in fact, a fault itself, with negative effects. In Seneca's words, "A person who notes and reacts to every injustice, and who becomes preoccupied with assigning just punishments, becomes, in the end, oddly similar to the raging ungentle people against whom he reacts. Retributive anger hardens the spirit, turning it against the humanity it sees. And in turning against humanity, in evincing the rage and hardness of the angry, one then becomes perilously close to the callous wrongdoers who arouse rage in the first place" (101). The wrongs may be real, and accurately assessed to be unjust, but the reaction becomes, as Nussbaum puts it, "an engine of revenge, indifferent to the face of humanity" (101). Seneca's *De ira* provides an alternative to retributivism and to "cowardly denial and capitulation," Nussbaum concludes (124). It never denies that evil exists but assumes its pervasiveness, the immense difficulty of eradicating it, and the necessity of judging it. "Mercy is not acquittal," but privileges a self-scrutiny that leads to gentleness. Such "good judging" yields in mercy before the difficulty of life (125).

We are quite close here to Bishop Tutu's concept of *ubuntu*, an avowal of shared human vulnerability characterized by both empathic identification with the wrongdoer and understanding, rather than antagonism and condescension. In order to be a fair judge, one must recognize that none of us is without fault (103). When we see the complex history of our actions and acknowledge our own fallibility, we are able to understand and identify with others whose histories and circumstances are equally complex. As Seneca puts it, "A person will cease from retributive anger and be more moderate if he knows that every day he has to come before himself as judge" (104). This requires imagining what it is like for the perpetrator, acknowledging all the particularities of her obstacles, circumstances constrained or not, choices or lack thereof, and personal resources. We need empathy rather than impartiality.

But we have witnessed how this identification with the wrongdoer can sabotage moral judgment. There is a fine line between compassion that respects enough to judge and pity that paralyzes thinking and leads to a morally bankrupt tolerance. I am following Nussbaum in her preference for the term "compassion" over pity, sympathy, or empathy as the most important emotion in this cultivation of humanity. She defines compassion as "a painful emotion occasioned by the awareness of another person's undeserved misfortune."[55] Pity, with its connotations of condescension and superiority to the sufferer is less appropriate in this context. As Seneca put it, "Pity regards the plight, not the cause of it; mercy is combined with reason."[56] Furthermore, it presupposes that we cannot judge ourselves for wrongdoing—that in constrained circumstances we would fail to do the right thing, excusing ourselves owing to circumstances just as we excuse others. Compassion is not simply empathy, either, as empathy designates an imaginative reconstruction, without evaluation, of another person's experience.[57] One could therefore show empathy without compassion, according to Nussbaum, although compassion requires the capacity for empathy.

Compassion is not without judgment, Nussbaum insists, and requires a notion of responsibility and blame. We feel the emotion more readily when there are extenuating circumstances, for example. Even if we believe a person is at fault, most of us experience compassion if the circumstances are unfortunate. A compassionate person then accepts a certain picture of the world, "a picture according to which the valuable things are not always safely under a person's own control, but can in some ways be damaged by fortune."[58] We make judgments even as we experience compassion.

Essential to compassion is also the recognition of one's own related vulnerability—"the thing that makes the difference between viewing hungry peasants as beings whose sufferings matter and viewing them as distant objects whose experiences have nothing to do with one's own life."[59] When we share a common vulnerability to pain and suffering with others (humans or animals), we feel compassion, which explains the effectiveness of dehumanization—of rendering another utterly different from us—in the destruction of others. What ceases in this process is empathy; the dehumanized other is no longer one with whom we can imaginatively identify.

It is no doubt empathy that prompted my students to respond to Ishmael Beah's narrative with compassion. We "open our imagination and heart to admit the life story of someone else," and in doing so accept his deeds as though they were committed by us.[60] It is this sharing of vulnerability that leads us to treat others with mercy. But what happens when the mitigating circumstances are used as an excuse for wrongdoing, or when violence is justified on the basis of victimhood? Nussbaum does not address this potential risk in her discussion of mercy. Compassion risks encouraging irresponsibility, although it seems to be a risk we are frequently willing to take. We love our children but discipline them when they do wrong because they must learn to live peaceably with others and experience the consequences of their actions—they must learn to treat others with respect and dignity. Yet when there are mitigating circumstances, we lessen the punishment or consequences out of compassion, identifying with them in their predicament. In effect, we release them from the consequences of their actions.

There is always the risk that someone will take advantage of the merciful judge. But a merciful judgment based on a deep understanding of the humanity of the perpetrator is not the same as a "veneration of the other" that results when there is little or no respect for the object of our veneration, and perhaps a dose of condescension. Guilt and self-recrimination have no place in compassionate regard for others. They deny the other's agency or ability to account for his own deeds and take responsibility for the consequences. Compassion and judgment are therefore not mutually exclusive, but we must walk a fine line between them, mindful of the tragic circumstances within which an individual acts, while respectful of his agency and responsibility for survival.

Like Eating a Stone

Nenad Vukosavljević, a conscientious objector who has worked for many years with veterans of the Balkan wars, writes that the vast majority of veterans believed they were fighting for a just cause at the time. "I have never directly heard or sensed in a single person that they had gone to the war in order to commit crimes, to conquer territories and exile people," he declares, "even though after the war many have realized that they had been in the service of the machinery that was doing exactly that." The veterans had intended to defend their own people, their country, extended family, or the ideal of freedom. We should not condemn the actions of all people equally, Vukosavljević says. Those who are criminally responsible must be brought to justice; as for the vast majority of veterans, "let us leave people room to change. They carry the burden of responsibility that belongs to them and it would be good to support those who are ready to accept the responsibility and to act differently today in accordance with it." The influence of the veterans should not be underestimated; they have a great responsibility to act "in such a way as to prevent this evil from ever happening again."[61]

Vukosavljević seems worried about pronouncing judgment, warning against the self-righteousness that one may feel who knew that "evil . . . was about to happen and publicly stood to oppose it," and who condemns others for having been naïve and stupid. This is not helpful for the work of peacebuilding, he says. But he *is* making a moral judgment here—and a good one—assessing the motives of the veterans while he works with them, taking into account their circumstances, encouraging their acceptance of responsibility no matter which side they were on, and supporting them in the work of carrying the burden of change. In short, he judges with mercy, motivated by compassion for the human condition. In his rejection of the "grotesque" notion of a just war—for it "entails in itself the seed of the future war"—Vukosavljević never fails to declare that war is wrong through his own refusal to comply.[62] Working with veterans to nurture a culture of peace, against the hardened grain of a militarized culture, he is creating the conditions for a nonviolent future.

To act in such a way as to prevent evil from ever happening again is, of course, a tall order. The postconflict reconstruction industry deals with the *aftermath* of violence; it employs strategies to pick up the pieces after war and rebuild states and communities. Some of its fundamental concepts and practices are inadequate for dealing with the complexity and ambiguity of victimhood, as I have shown. If victims are not to remain mere victims, we need to rethink a global reliance on juridical measures as rigorously as we rethink our investment in victim empowerment and healing through memorializing and truth telling. Our responses to conflict should reflect an interest in preventing future violence. We must do more than concentrate all our efforts and resources on assigning guilt, punishing perpetrators, or even reconciling enemies, as crucial as these tasks are, for in the process we have failed to develop ideas, behaviors, and practices that might prevent violence.

Mercy is a gift that we bestow on those who may be merciless themselves; it risks erring on the side of compassion and neglecting the terms of justice—of establishing who is right in the eyes of the law, who suffers more, and who must be punished. Without mercy and compassion—and a certain willful forgetting—the task of rebuilding communities seems impossible. But the really hard work that survivors of war and genocide face is to reinvent a community that refuses violence. This is no doubt as unpalatable as eating a stone. Often missing in the new discourses on postconflict reconstruction is a sustained commitment to this work of reinventing politics and rebuilding civil society. On the one hand, empathy for suffering has taken precedence as the victim has been declared an authentic representative of history and truth. On the other, the certainty of the law's ability to judge and punish has been privileged as the conclusive way to deal with the past. Between these poles lies the mostly unexplored territory of politics at the level of community consensus, dissensus, and action, deliberating with one's avowed enemy under the threat of violence, without the promise of justice, with only an unknown future to bind former enemies.

7

LAY DOWN YOUR ARMS

It is precisely in [the] admission of one's own impotence that a last remnant of strength and even power can still be preserved even under desperate conditions.

We leap and there is grace. Acrobats know: do not look at the separation. Have eyes, have bodies, only for there, for the other.

An episode described by Erich Maria Remarque in *All Quiet on the Western Front* captures—with poignancy and cynicism—the contradictory human potential for kindness and cruelty.[1] The protagonist, a soldier named Paul Bäumer, finds himself in a shell hole in the midst of battle during World War I, unsure which direction is the safe way out. A body falls into the pit, and Paul reacts without thinking, stabbing the man in the neck but not killing him. The blood on his own hand nauseates him, and he shrinks from looking at the man he has knifed, who lies dying across from him. Eventually he looks, but he can't bear the "utter terror" in the wounded man's eyes when approached. Paul wants the stranger to know that he is trying to help him, by making his head more comfortable and giving him water from a puddle in the mud, but he knows the man cannot be saved and waits in agony for his death, without a revolver to hasten it. "I would shoot him," he says, but "stab him I cannot."[2] He explains that this is the first time he has killed with his own hands, and at close range. It is only after his victim dies that Paul examines him closely and speculates about the man's life. He feels he must talk to the dead soldier:

> Comrade, I did not want to kill you. If you jumped in here again, I would not do it, if you would be sensible too. But you were only an

idea to me before, an abstraction that lived in my mind and called forth its appropriate response. It was that abstraction I stabbed. But now, for the first time, I see you are a man like me. I thought of your hand-grenades, your bayonet, of your rifle; now I see your wife and your face and our fellowship. Forgive me, comrade. We always see it too late. Why do they never tell us that you are poor devils like us, that your mothers are just as anxious as ours, and that we have the same fear of death, and the same dying and the same agony—Forgive me, comrade; *how could you be my enemy?* (223, emphasis added)

Paul vows to write to the dead man's wife, imagining that he will help her and her child. But the final test of his endurance comes when he opens the man's pocketbook. "So long as I do not know his name perhaps I may still forget him," we read. "But his name, it is a nail that will be hammered into me and never come out again. It has the power to recall this forever, it will always come back and stand before me" (224). Paul finds letters in the pocketbook and, although not written in his language, each word that he is able to translate pierces him "like a stab in the chest" (225).

This remarkable account attests to how difficult it is to kill another human being at close range when the killer can gaze into his victim's face. Looking into his face and discovering the name of his victim destroys the abstract image Paul needs to be able to kill this stranger. He experiences empathy: *I see you are a man like me.* They share the same vulnerability, evidenced in their fear of death, the anxiety of their mothers, and the "utter terror" in the dying man's eyes.

If we stopped reading here, we might feel a warm flicker of hope in the belief that all we need is more empathy and understanding, to know one another's names, to feel our human commonality, in order to prevent violence. But Remarque's protagonist surprises us. Only a few hours later, still in the pit, Paul calms down and is no longer troubled by the name of his victim. By sundown he is out of the shell hole and has forgotten the dead man. Only the next day does he tell the story to his comrades, who console him. Paul decides that it was "mere driveling nonsense that I talked out there in the shell-hole" (229). His friend assures him that he need not lose any sleep over it, and with that Paul concludes that he hardly understands it himself anymore. "It was only because I had to lie there with him so long," he says. "After all, war is war" (229). Paul kills a man without thinking because he was trained to do so in a context within which it was the expected and correct thing to do. He is embarrassed by his sentimental overtures to a man whose death was his responsibility, because war sanctions death. Like Babchenko, he is anxious to avoid the humiliation of refusing the terms of war.

Had Paul gazed into the face of this man in other circumstances—encountered him simply as a stranger rather than an enemy—he might have treated him with compassion. Had someone else stabbed this man, he might have grieved the suffering of another. War, however, is founded on the distinction between friend and enemy. Once the killing begins, it creates its own moral universe, one in which an act of compassion by one soldier toward an enemy soldier would probably go unremembered. But the truth is out in Paul's agonized request for forgiveness: *how could you be my enemy?*

We could ask this question in the context of another story, this one unfortunately not fictional. The home of Dr. Izzeldin Abuelaish, a well-respected Palestinian obstetrician, was bombed during the Israeli attacks on Gaza in January 2009. At the time, Abuelaish lived in the Jabaliya camp in Gaza and specialized in treating infertility. He also worked part-time in Israel assisting Jewish women giving birth. At his Gaza clinic he trained medical students and arranged for the seriously ill to be transported to Israeli hospitals for treatment. The border officials and soldiers knew him well, we hear in a BBC documentary made of his life in 2001. We are told that he tolerated "the tedious and sometimes humiliating border checks with dignity and patience," and remained calm even when an angry Palestinian medical student chastised him for assisting in the birth of children who could be future soldiers of the occupation. A Gazan Palestinian at home among Israelis, Abuelaish describes himself as a bridge between the two worlds.[3]

Fluent in Hebrew, Abuelaish gave daily updates by phone as an unofficial correspondent to a Tel Aviv station during the military campaign against Gaza. He had been interviewed by the BBC World Service in the midst of the conflict and shared the information that the windows of his house were all blown out and that he was desperately worried about his eight children, whose mother died of leukemia in September 2008. Only one day before the ceasefire, just as Abuelaish left his daughters' bedroom with his small son on his shoulders, a shell blasted into the bedroom wall, killing three of his girls—twenty-year-old Bisan, fifteen-year-old Mayar, and thirteen-year-old Aya—and their seventeen-year-old cousin, Nur. "I rushed back to find their dead bodies," he tells the journalist, Lucy Ash, "—or rather parts of their bodies—strewn all over the room. One was still sitting in a chair but she had no legs. Tell me why did they have to die? Who gave the order to fire on my house?" He adds, "You know me, Lucy. You have been to my house, my hospital; you have seen my Israeli patients. I have tried so hard to bring people on both sides together and just look what I get in return."[4]

Minutes after the attack, Abuelaish called Shlomi Eldar, the anchorman on Israel's Channel 10, with whom he had been doing daily interviews. Eldar, who was doing the live newscast at the time, took Abuelaish's call on air. What followed can now be viewed by anyone in the world with access to the Internet. The raw anguish of Abuelaish and the unsuccessful attempt by the anchorman to control his emotions on public television as he relayed information testify to gross injustice and monstrous cruelty. Eldar could not cut Abuelaish off; visibly distraught, he called for an ambulance and requested that the Israeli Defense Forces go to his friend's aid.

The outpouring of sympathy on the part of the Israeli public for this Gazan doctor may not surprise those who are unfamiliar with the nearly impenetrable barriers between Israelis and Palestinians. But it was astonishing for this divided region. Abuelaish was a man with whom Israelis could identify, a public figure with a face and a name; his grief, therefore, was easily shared. As one Israeli woman from Sderot described it, "The Palestinian pain, which the majority of Israeli society doesn't want to see, had a voice and a face. The invisible became visible. For one moment it wasn't just the enemy—an enormous dark demon who is so easy and convenient to hate. There was one man, one story, one tragedy and so much pain."[5] It shouldn't take this much pain for one human being to express compassion for another. As in our fictional account of Paul, we should be wary of the effects of shared grief and the solidarity it may inspire when it is a short-lived aberration that occurs within a political context governed by normalized violence. There is an extraordinarily intimate element in the emotional response to another's pain, even when it is the pain of a stranger. But war is war, an occupation is an occupation; time has passed and the situation of Palestinians has not changed because of the compassionate response on the part of Israelis to a well-known, grief-stricken Palestinian doctor. What we do have—and this is certainly not nothing—is an exemplary human being who responded to one of the worst imaginable tragedies with these words: "Let my daughters be the last to die. . . . What we need is respect, and the inner strength to refuse to hate. Then we will achieve peace."[6] It is a truism to say that if everyone shared this sentiment, change would occur more quickly for Israelis and Palestinians.

How could you be my enemy? This question rocks the very foundations of a politics that has assumed violence as its modus operandi for so long that we believe there is no politics without an enemy. I turn to Israeli author David Grossman for an incisive description and analysis of what is at stake in this question. Like any Israeli, he says, "I myself have never known a life without an enemy . . . without the constant presence of an existential threat. Without the urge to fortify ourselves, to protect ourselves, and to act aggressively against those who threaten our homes and sometimes our lives."[7] To live without an enemy, he adds, requires meeting the enormous challenge of learning to live a life "not defined by hostility, anxiety, and violence"; its effects might include forgoing the "excessive admiration of power," the "obsessive" need for unity and internal consensus at any cost, and one-dimensional definitions of those who are for us or against us (91–93). In a passage that eloquently captures what Grossman calls "our most dubious talent" for being a victim (23), he writes:

> If we ever achieve a state in which we have no enemies, perhaps we will be able to break free from the all-too-familiar Israeli tendency to approach reality with the mind-set of a sworn survivor, who is practically programmed—*condemned*—to define the situations he encounters primarily in terms of threat, danger, and entrapment, or a daring rescue from all these. The survivor ignores anything that may complicate his worldview or delay his reactions, and so he tends to ignore the gray areas, the nuances, without truly facing the complex and contradictory nature of reality, with all the chances and promises it offers. He thereby all but dooms himself to exist forever within this partial, distorted, suspicious, and frightened picture of reality, and is therefore tragically fated to make his anxieties and nightmares come true time and time again. (93)

The political implications of a victim's worldview appear with stark clarity in the case of Israel, but also in the global war on terror and, as we have seen, in any number of other conflicts throughout the world. Grossman describes the distortion of reality that materializes when "fears consolidate ideals around themselves" (23)—a distortion that requires manipulation and justification, and that leads to the normalization of war and the dehumanization of the enemy. Israelis pay a high price for this distortion, for "one cannot truly adapt to such warped conditions," Grossman claims, without paying the highest price of all, "the price of living itself, the price of sensitivity, of humanity, of curiosity, and of liberty of thought" (47). In effect, after decades of fortifying and safeguarding, protecting and fighting, "we may be very close to becoming like a suit of armor that no longer contains a knight, no longer contains a *human*" (48).

I began this study with the question of how we might respond to victims in ways that will not imprison them in a victimhood identity that permits the justification of further violence. To answer this question we need to understand the condition and status of victimhood. Human responses to a violation of trust and the body's boundaries—to dehumanization—vary considerably, as manifested perhaps in the experience of a "shattered" self, melancholia, and the construction of a host of psychic defenses. Some defenses may lead to resentment, rage, or revenge, limiting a victim's ability to accept responsibility for these reactions, excusing retributive violence, escalating fear, sabotaging recovery and the rebuilding of trust. Our contemporary attentiveness to victims' needs and rights, while essential for broadening our understanding of the complexity of victimhood and for responding with greater empathy toward victims, has led to an increased reticence to judge, bestowing on victims a dangerous moral authority that keeps us imprisoned in the binary logic of victim versus perpetrator, friend versus enemy. I have argued that our response to past victimization and atrocity must be focused on the prevention of future acts of violence; that is, in dealing with the past, we invent a different kind of future. Moral judgment is necessary in order to cultivate a world in which we want to live, governed by respect for others rather than a moral code—for our agency and sense of responsibility to one another— a moral world in which conflict is negotiated and right distinguished from wrong for the safety and survival of all. It is a judgment exercised with mercy when the circumstances are extreme, when trauma debilitates. It is a judgment that *discerns*—requiring a rigorous attention to the historical and political context of an event or action, arising from thinking but also from empathy for one another. Bandaging wounds and applying the law are not enough to transform the conditions that lead to violent conflict.

Compassion and judgment won't get us very far if this larger context is governed by a politics the very essence of which is war, a politics dictated by the terms of violence, hostility, and the fear of real or imagined enemies. The empathy Paul Bäumer feels for the victim he murdered, the outpouring of sympathy for the Palestinian father of murdered daughters, will only be momentary aberrations consumed by an insidious war machine. Laying down one's arms—literally and figuratively—is a prerequisite for envisioning and practicing a moral and political life that will not lead us to mutual destruction. The idea is simple; acting on it can be extraordinarily difficult.

The Secret of Acrobatics

In a letter sent to the Parents Circle–Families Forum, an organization dedicated to bringing together bereaved families in Israel and Palestine, Bishop Desmond Tutu writes, "Peace is possible when we allow ourselves to be vulnerable."[8] The sentiment is poignant, but it ignores the fact that our vulnerability is also what makes violence possible, sometimes appealing, and always a risk. To be human is to be vulnerable; it is also to be capable of the utmost kindness *and* the worst cruelty. We are not *most* human when we are respectful and kind rather than vicious or murderous. We have no choice whether to "allow" ourselves to be vulnerable or not; we simply *are* vulnerable, and our choice lies in accepting or denying it, using or abusing it. Indeed, the cost of denying vulnerability may be greater than that of the violence that vulnerability may risk, as Grossman so eloquently demonstrates. In the attempt to ward off all that is bad in the human condition, we threaten to relinquish all that is good. There is no way to be vulnerable without at once accepting the risk of its violation.

We have seen throughout this book the destructive effects of violent acts on individuals and groups who are—or become in the moment of violation—vulnerable to the extreme. Victims of torture and rape have described the experience of being reduced to pain as though they were *only* wounded bodies. Children of war have always epitomized vulnerability, masked by the power they acquire when forced to kill or be killed. Adult soldiers attest to the fear that propels them to the front lines against their will, fear of death or injury, of having to kill, fear of the insecurity and uncertain future of their families, their villages and cities, their way of life. In war they are exposed to the worst unpredictability from one moment to the next, calculating which tactic will allow them to greet another dawn. An occupied people is maddeningly vulnerable to the whims of border guards and to a blind, indifferent international community. There is no safety for the occupied behind security fences that have been erected to protect everyone but them.

This does not sound like the kind of vulnerability we want to cherish. Of course we cannot do without safety—in the best of worlds we cultivate it for our children, ease our youth into the world of risk with caution, guard against injury as well as we can, create certainty within the limits of an unpredictable, contingent world. Those who lack security in infancy and childhood often carry the effects with them like clumsy baggage throughout their adult lives; ambivalent attachments render the weight difficult to unload. We have witnessed the elaborate psychological and political defense systems erected to mitigate the damage done by a vulnerability abused, and in the wish to become invulnerable. Victims naturally crave protection from the possibility of further suffering. "Never again!" means for them that the cost of future security—even death and destruction—will never again be too great to bear. The fantasy of a guarantee that one can become invulnerable to attack is a powerful, driving force that may stop at nothing. We experience the need for security so absolutely that we forget to question the wisdom of giving up civil rights in its name. Fear propels us, eliminating all checks and balances in its path. We quietly accept censure, xenophobia, and strip searches from arrogant border guards, and we are comforted by a concrete wall where once an orchard of lemon trees grew.[9] No watch tower can be too high, no wall too thick—no mistrust, suspicion, and resentment too great to bear. At the extreme, we accept not only murder but suicide.[10]

That peace is possible if we allow ourselves to be vulnerable means that we can be deeply affected by another's vulnerability, particularly as it is exposed when grieving and suffering, and this affective connection can overcome the hostility and fear fostered by war. We can be in the midst of an argument with our most beloved, wielding words that we know will hurt, when the defenses of the other suddenly give way and we are face to face with raw emotion, expressive of a psyche's history, old wounds, and reactions, in short, with vulnerability. The angry person we protect ourselves from becomes the beloved again, and we let him back in because we have seen him from the inside, fragile, ambivalent, afraid, hurt. From this defenselessness—not without its own power—there must be an acceptance of the risk of letting the other in. It is not then even a question of knowing the truth but of giving up the need to be right, being the first to lay down one's arms and relegate the past to the past. In any loving relationship, being right must sometimes give way to being kind.

Hélène Cixous captures the risk of vulnerability in a lovely analogy: "So is love the secret of acrobatics? It is trust, yes: the desire to cross over into the other. The acrobat's body is his soul. Is the crossing vertiginous? Like every crossing. Useless to contemplate or fathom what separates: the abyss is always invented by our fear. We leap and there is grace. Acrobats know: do not look at the separation. Have eyes, have bodies, only for there, for the other."[11] For Grossman, a writer is like this acrobat, desiring to know the other from within him, to feel what it means to be that other, "to be able to touch, if only for a moment, the blaze that burns within another human being."[12] The writer's desire is not to project oneself onto another, a fictional character, but to cast off the "shackles" of his own self and experience the core of the other as an other. He can then glimpse and linger in that place that is otherwise rare and difficult to know. In other words, we both let the other in and experience ourselves in the other, refusing to be reduced to the one-dimensional, faceless creatures that war turns us into. In this one-dimensional space people are turned into masses, and discernment, the flexibility of thought, and the courage to understand and change are all sabotaged.[13]

In a passage evocative of the interest Paul Bäumer takes in his dying victim, of Tutu's notion of *ubuntu*, of Cixous's acrobatic secrets, of Seneca's "cultivation of humanity," Grossman concludes, "When we know the Other from within him—even if that Other is our enemy—we can never again be completely indifferent to him. Something inside us becomes committed to him, or at least to his complexities. It becomes difficult for us to completely deny him or cancel him out as 'not human.' We can no longer employ our usual ease and expertise to avoid his suffering, his justice, his *story*. Perhaps we can even be a little more tolerant of his mistakes. For we then see these mistakes as part of his tragedy."[14] The leap required here is one that exposes oneself to another and, in the process, permits the possibility of communication, intimacy, understanding, and compassion. It is when we are open or exposed to others that they let down their guard as well, and we discover within this opening our fundamental commonality. We also find difference, of course, but there is always a point of commonality, if it is only the emotions we share, our responses to joy or suffering, our fallibility, and our will to survive. Negotiating this tension—between commonality and difference, and their corollaries, consensus and dissensus—is at the heart of politics and the moral life.

The Politics of the Vulnerable

These ideas are not new. The affirmation of empathy for, and vulnerability to, others is behind every dialogue group that seeks to bring current or former enemies together to bridge the divides caused by conflict, break the chains of hate, and heal the wounds of war. We find the same call from some philosophical quarters, especially phenomenology, concerned with empathy and intersubjectivity.[15] But the celebration of difference in a range of disciplines has rendered these ideas rather out of fashion in recent decades, and in both academic discourses and postconflict reconstruction practice we find a tendency to relegate such approaches to an ethical, interpersonal realm, where love and friendship abide in a kind of prepolitical sphere.

This appears to be changing with recent interest in the political resistance of vulnerable populations who experience what Judith Butler calls "precarious life." The concern might be traced to Arendt's discussion of "mere existence" in her famous essay "The Decline of the Nation-State and the End of the Rights of Man." In a critique of the necessary relation between the fact of birth and human rights, she describes the condition of a person who has been stripped of his political existence, the refugee or stateless person, whose disconnection from his place of birth renders him without the right to have rights. Those reduced to "mere existence" are beyond the pale of the law, not merely unequal before the law but completely outside it, not merely oppressed, as nobody wants even to oppress them. Without a political community to which they belong, through which their needs will be met, their rights cannot be protected, and their voices will not count. Thus "a man who is nothing but a man has lost the very qualities which make it possible for other people to treat him as a fellow-man."[16] And yet, he is still *merely* human.

The irony, then, is that those who need human rights the most are disqualified for being only human. Arendt describes the predicament of the refugee as one who cries out, "Nobody knows who I am!" It is not that the refugee laments being recognized as this or that kind of being but that he is not considered *worthy of being* a this or that. Dignity, respect, equality—these are terms that all point to something fundamental in human existence We don't want to be invisible to others. We want to count, to matter; we want our selves to be worthy in someone else's eyes. The inherent worthiness of a life is what the torturer takes from the tortured, the colonizer from the colonized, the medical practitioner from the patient when she sees him as a body without a name or face, without desires and the power to make decisions about his life. It is this worthiness that makes the difference between being killed with impunity or allowing to live. It is also fundamental to political inclusion.

This is what we mean by "dehumanization," described throughout this book as essential to overcoming the psychological obstacles to killing another human being. The abstraction of a life, the erasure of particularity and the human "in-common"—that bond we share as a species—permits killing, as we saw in Remarque's story (and as any soldier must know). Giorgio Agamben writes of *homo sacer*, or sacred man, "an obscure figure of archaic Roman law" who was judged for committing a crime and thereafter could not be sacrificed. In fact, if one designated *homo sacer* were killed, the act was not considered a homicide. The victim was reduced to a nameless, rightless mere existence—to what Agamben calls "bare life."[17] Significantly, bare life is not outside of politics but remains a kind of absent presence within it, included only by way of its exclusion—somewhat like the excommunicated or banned member of society whose phantom presence lingers at the table. War produces *homo sacer*, or bare life, in abundance.

Agamben's examples of bare life indicate that he is intent on refuting any association of the condition with an impotent frailty. From the Muselmann— the figure of bare life par excellence—who languishes on the threshold of death and life in the Nazi concentration camp, to the protesters of Tiananmen Square, whose obscure power arises from their lack of a "representable identity," Agamben alludes to a *refusal of powerlessness*. The Muselmann, for example, "no longer belongs to the world of men in any way. . . . Mute and absolutely alone, he has passed into another world without memory and without grief." As a result, the guard is suddenly powerless before him, "as if struck by the thought that the Muselmann's behavior—which does not register any difference between an order and the cold—might perhaps be a silent form of resistance."[18] In the case of the Tiananmen protesters, Agamben implies that it is the very fact that they were not an identity group struggling for control of the state but individual singularities "peacefully [demonstrating] their being in common" that rendered them a threat to the state.[19] As such, bare life has become for Agamben (as it did for Foucault) both the subject and the object of the conflicts of the political order, "the one place for both the organization of State power and emancipation from it."[20] We are prone to forgetting the latter part.

I want to highlight this peaceful demonstration of "being in common," for it is "nonviolent" political action that is often neglected, or at least unnamed, in the current interest in mere existence or bare life.[21] Agamben's perhaps offhand remark is significant for a consideration of the relevance and function of vulnerability in politics. As we have seen, the wish to be invulnerable by fighting fire with fire can set off a destructive chain of events. Butler, for example, insists that vulnerability—or precarity, as she prefers to call it—does have political implications, but she isn't entirely clear on what a precarious politics might entail other than providing solidarity. She claims that precarity can form the basis of a renewed political life, one that *could have* resulted from the unbearable vulnerability Americans were exposed to in the 2001 terrorist attacks. The conditions for this political life, Butler maintains, are vulnerability to violence and shared loss, features of human existence that expose the incontrovertible fact that we are "undone" by others, that our lives are inextricably entangled. All lives should be "grievable," she writes, critical of the fact that the war on terror has designated some deaths as worthy of grief and others unmemorable.

While human life is by definition precarious or vulnerable, certain populations become exposed to injury and violence in greater degrees, vulnerable before the very state to which they need to appeal for protection. We could list any number of categories here: migrants, refugees, the "untouchables," trafficked children and adults, slaves, victims of war, and so on. Precarity is thus "politically induced" in an operation that separates the human from the unhuman, those whose lives have been rendered worthless. Butler doesn't stop here, however, insisting that vulnerability could also be the basis of our political strength, the ground of an alliance in opposition to state violence and exploitation. Something needs to be made of grief besides a cry for war if we want to stop cycles of violence.[22]

Unfortunately, it is doubtful whether Butler's proposal for this "something" would prevent any grievous cries for war.[23] Nonviolence can't be a universal principle, she remarks, given that we are formed through norms that are by definition violent;[24] it is merely "an address or an appeal" that we must decide when to answer. This is not a call to a peaceful state but a struggle to "make rage articulate and effective—the carefully crafted 'fuck you.'"[25] Butler is not alone in making this kind of defiant statement—a disappointing approbation of rage and resentment—as the terms of nonviolence or peace are met with indifference or even ridicule, while violence is defined so broadly or opaquely as to become meaningless and ubiquitous. Slavoj Žižek ends his book on violence with the assertion that we are threatened today not by passivity but by too much activity, intervention, and meaningless discussion, propelled by the need to do something. It is more of a challenge to withdraw, he insists. Defining violence as "a radical upheaval of the basic social relations," Žižek quips, "crazy and tasteless as it may sound, the problem with historical monsters who slaughtered millions was that they were not violent enough."[26] There seems to be little point, aside from being tasteless, to defining violence thus. Unfortunately, we can't always tell from mortar fire or bombs whose rage is the "good" and effective rage Butler condones. But surely we can tell the difference between a radical upheaval of social relations and slaughter, and can understand the importance of maintaining the distinction.

More inspiring discussions of political engagement by vulnerable populations can be found. Partha Chatterjee writes of the politics of "the governed"—the teeming human life that hums around the train tracks of Calcutta's slums, for example, a community of impoverished noncitizens. This is not the politics of "civil" society, then—which would require legitimate citizenship—but of what he calls "political society," which includes those groups who may live and act illegally (and highly creatively) in a number of ways for the sake of survival but who "make a claim to a habitation and a livelihood as a matter of right."[27] They act as if they have a right to such a life. They have acquired a political existence where none was provided, although it may thrive in unexpected places. Sandro Mezzadra writes similarly of the political potential of migrants in Europe, those living in limbo across or between borders, without status, rights, or political voice.[28] These are vulnerable populations excluded from politics, reduced to a condition of mere existence, but they are busy enacting a refusal of this exclusion by acting *as if* they occupied a place at the table. For Jacques Rancière, this refusal *is* politics, as opposed to *policing:* those "who have no part," those who have no place at the political table, *assume* their fundamental equality and contest the forces that seek to take it away.[29] I would argue that it is not equality that is assumed here but responsibility for a better future and a shared commitment to working toward it.

In these examples we find the promise of a politics that interrupts the world-view of victimhood. The power of the refusal of powerlessness does not derive from the victim's moral authority, which depends on the guilt of the bystander, but from "humanity's revolt against an enforced position . . . an attempt to regain control over one's own sense of responsibility," as Václav Havel put it.[30] This is the "power of the powerless," of those living within the truth in a context of lies. Those who are not allowed a political voice, who live in circumstances marked by poverty, violence, or other forms of injustice must struggle to exercise their own agency and responsibility, sometimes against all odds.

Havel writes in the context of posttotalitarian politics, but I am appealing to a pragmatic approach to politics at the level of civil society—or political society, if we favor Chatterjee's distinction—which is certainly relevant now:

> The real sphere of potential politics in the post-totalitarian system is elsewhere: in the continuing and cruel tension between the complex

demands of that system and the aims of life, that is, the elementary need of human beings to live, to a certain extent at least, in harmony with themselves, that is, *to live in a bearable way,* not to be humiliated by their superiors and officials, not to be continually watched by the police, to be able to express themselves freely, to find an outlet for their creativity, to enjoy legal security. . . . to live like a human being. (emphasis added)[31]

This is not a call for perfect peace but for a life lived with enough harmony to make life worth living, and with the freedom to contest those forces that threaten to make life unbearable.

Lay Down Your Arms

Thinking about politics is rather like writing in the dark.[32] Although we would like to, we can't come up with political theories or programs that will resolve the dilemmas that any and every particular community or state encounters. Political relations and their historical contexts are always particular. But we can point to examples of how things work and trust that there are always parallels and extrapolations to be made. More important, we can think about the conditions required for effective politics to occur. Agamben urges us to formulate alternative approaches to political thought and engagement that "work towards the prevention of disorder and catastrophe, and not merely towards their control." It is the logic of security that stymies this effort, leading to "a gradual neutralisation of politics."[33]

The question for politics is how *to live in a bearable way* in what Étienne Balibar, following Herman van Gunsteren, calls "communities of fate." These are formed wherever one happens to live and work: "They are communities that already include difference and conflict, where heterogeneous people and groups have been 'thrown together' by history and economy, in situations where their interests or cultural ideals cannot spontaneously converge, but also cannot completely diverge without risking *mutual destruction* (or *common elimination* by external forces)."[34] It is the simple fact of residence, the necessity of surviving intolerable conditions *with one's neighbors* that matters. We might think of this as "survivor's politics," amending Mamdani's "survivor's justice," which transcends the victim/perpetrator binary by designating both as survivors of war and forging a new community on that basis.

The condition, he stipulates, is that one must relinquish one's weapons and accept the exposure to risk.[35]

In the case of Rwanda, for example, Mamdani argues that the Tutsis will sooner or later have to consider that power is *not* the precondition for survival; rather, "the prerequisite to cohabitation, to reconciliation, and a common political future may indeed be to give up the monopoly of power. . . . Giving up political power may be a surer guarantee of survival than holding on to it." The only exclusions to be made are against those who would refuse to lay down their arms as a precondition to sitting down at the negotiating table. But he is mindful of the nightmare on the minds of Tutsi survivors, the fact that they are an imperiled minority afraid of once again coming under the thumb of a guilty majority. This risk is the *almost* unbearable burden for victims, and if we did not have any examples of individuals who carried it, we might not believe it possible. Mamdani concludes from this that there can be no sustained reconciliation between Hutu and Tutsi without the recognition that "neither the tragedy of Rwanda nor its possible salvation can be exclusively, or even mainly, a Rwandan responsibility."[36] We outsiders or bystanders cannot stand idly by, indifferent to this nightmare. Our responsibility—those of us with resources, those of us with the strength and power to effect change—is to mitigate the terrible risk taken by those who lay down their arms.

We can't stress this point enough. There will always be those who remain shattered beyond repair, whose fragile hold on life or normalcy is founded on a defense system always readied for attack, who perceive threat all around them and believe they must fight to exist. If there are no real enemies to attack, they will invent them. These could be terrorists, crazed dictators, warlords, or leaders of liberal democracies whose sense of justice has become distorted. In all but the most severe cases—for there will also always be sadists and sociopaths with whom there may be no possibility of coexistence—there is still negotiation. We must return to the table again and again, *without arms*, and with the help of others.

We have already noted the necessity of thinking and judging, and of a compassionate regard that respects another's agency, in the task of preventing the conditions that lead to violence. Resentment and revenge, as I have indicated, are not the only ways that individuals and communities respond to violation. Rami Elhanan, mourning the murder of his daughter by a terrorist, speaks of the way of understanding, the more difficult path to take when you or someone you love has become a victim. Susan Brison grapples with the necessity of coming to terms with the vulnerability and uncertainty of life when all a victim craves is a permanent guarantee against harm. Her recourse is to create a narrative, to relegate an act of violation to the past despite its relentless lingering psychological and physical effects. The veterans of wars in the Western Balkans struggle to *rehumanize* their former enemies, acknowledge the suffering their own hands caused, and take responsibility for building a more peaceful future. In Israel and Palestine bereaved families who join together to share in the grief of those living just on the other side of the Green Line (yet worlds apart) believe they can prevent the use of grief as a means to expand enmity between their peoples through collaborative action. The Israeli Committee Against House Demolitions engages in illegal acts of friendship, blocking bulldozers and rebuilding homes for those without the right to stop the destruction.

These are responses to suffering that may at the same time prevent the conditions that lead to further suffering, opening possibilities rather than burning bridges, crossing over to the other, like the acrobat refusing to look at "the separation." These individuals and groups reject the worldview of the victim, literally or figuratively *laying down their arms*. This is not a passive refusal but an act of political will, ignited by the very pragmatic need for a bearable life. To lay down our arms means to refuse the dictated terms of the fight, exit the ring, reject the means of defense provided. While this appears to leave us powerless or defenseless—the other cheek turned in a display of utter passivity—it only does so if we haven't rejected the binary terms on which the power struggle is waged. It is not the power of the sword that the victimized need, or the power of a moral authority granted to the victim, but the power of political will—a power that can arise spontaneously out of shared vulnerability. It may be an act of civil disobedience, dissent, or the slow, patient work of changing attitudes—of "reviving the person inside the suit of armor"[37]—in any case, the operative principle is a refusal to march blindly to the drummer's beat without reflection, collective deliberation, or judgment. This is the political work that we must never "neutralize": the cultivation of civil coexistence—of communities of fate—that refuse violent solutions to conflict.

To prevent the conditions that lead to war—and the normalization of politics as violence—we need to elaborate alternatives that embrace neither consensus and unity as utopian peace nor dissensus and conflict as violence. As Balibar puts it, we have to defend politics against "the twin enemies of extreme violence and consensus."[38]

Obedience could be worse than intolerance in situations of rising political unrest, and disobedience more important than reconciliation.[39] In a discussion of what peoples of the former Yugoslavia need, for example, Boris Buden states unequivocally that it isn't truth commissions or reconciliation programs. The region has undergone a "depoliticization" that no truth of the past will eradicate. To *repoliticize* would mean to "invent a new form of political solidarity" that transcends their national, ethnic, and religious identities—a public life that includes political argument and contestation,[40] not merely, as Buruma puts it, "the soothing rhetoric of healing."[41] Disagreement, disobedience, conflict—these are indispensable ingredients in the practical work of politics *and* its necessary conditions. This claim does not contradict the demand to lay down one's arms. Conflict need not lead to violence.

But to be vigilant against the incursion of a politics defined by the terms of war requires above all a vigilance against becoming immune to empathy and its effects. For Remarque's Paul Bäumer, restoring his enemy to humanity occurs too late. We need to ward off the process of dehumanizing one's enemy before it begins. We are already too late when identities are formed on the basis of political ideologies and when victims are granted an unquestioned moral authority. To prevent the conditions of war, we must learn to see ourselves through the eyes of others.

Although Arendt insists that the potentially affirmative conditions of "mere life" are outside of politics, related to love and friendship, her description of these conditions is precisely what politics requires: "This mere existence, that is, all that which is mysteriously given us by birth and which includes the shape of our bodies and the talents of our minds, can be adequately dealt with only by the unpredictable hazards of friendship and sympathy, or by the great and incalculable grace of love, which says with Augustine, '*Volo ut sis* (I want you to be),' without being able to give any particular reason for such supreme and unsurpassable affirmation."[42] The "incalculable grace of love"—like Cixous's acrobatic leap of grace—can motivate us to forget the unforgivable and to judge the merciless with mercy. Friendship in the solidarity of suffering need not lead to an abdication of responsibility for the world. And while almost all of the world's inhabitants are strangers to us, we can give them, without any particular reason, the affirmation of "I want you to be." To modify a famous line from Derrida, to be capable of friendship and to be able to honor in the enemy the friend he can become, is a sign of freedom.[43] Empathy can be developed and nurtured; we can become habituated to thinking, deliberating, and judging, motivated by a compassionate regard for others. *It takes practice* to manage conflict without violence, and the slow, steady nurturing of the right conditions for such practice. When we cultivate this side of our humanity, our ambivalence about victims becomes necessary in the work of moral judgment and political engagement, rather than paralyzing.

Havel asks whether "the brighter future is really always so distant. What if, on the contrary, it has been here for a long time already, and only our own blindness and weakness has prevented us from seeing it around us and within us, and kept us from developing it?"[44] We have our work cut out for us.

NOTES

INTRODUCTION

1. For studies of victimhood, see Erica Bouris, *Complex Political Victims* (Bloomfield, Conn.: Kumarian Press, 2007); Jean-Michel Chaumont, *La concurrence des victimes: Génocide, identité, reconnaissance* (Paris: La Découverte, 2002); Alyson M. Cole, *The Cult of True Victimhood: From the War on Welfare to the War on Terror* (Stanford: Stanford University Press, 2007); Fatima Naqvi, *The Literary and Cultural Rhetoric of Victimhood: Western Europe, 1970–2005* (New York: Palgrave Macmillan, 2007); and Charles Sykes, *A Nation of Victims. The Decay of the American Character* (New York: St. Martin's Press, 1992).

2. Eva Illouz, *Oprah Winfrey and the Glamour of Misery: An Essay on Popular Culture* (New York: Columbia University Press, 2003), 5.

3. Slavoj Žižek, "A Soft Focus on War: How Hollywood Hides the Horrors of War," *In These Times,* April 21, 2010, http://www.inthesetimes.com/article/5864/a_soft_focus_on_war/ (accessed May 15, 2010).

4. Sykes, *Nation of Victims,* 10, 5–6, 11.

5. Cole, *Cult of True Victimhood,* 3, 2.

6. Cole is defensive regarding the charge against feminism, but she fails to offer counterarguments that would provide insight into why the daughters of the 1960s generation of feminists would criticize 1990s feminism for nurturing a generation of victim-identified women. Even Betty Friedan complained in 1998 that it was "all too tempting … to cast men as monsters and women as victims," and warned that feminists should not simply "wallow in victimhood" when what really matters is that "we [empower] ourselves out of the victim state." See Friedan, *"It Changed My Life": Writings on the Women's Movement* (Cambridge: Harvard University Press, 1998), xii, quoted in Cole, *Cult of True Victimhood,* 195n50.

7. Cole, *Cult of True Victimhood,* 7.

8. See Diane Enns, *Speaking of Freedom: Philosophy, Politics, and the Struggle for Liberation* (Stanford: Stanford University Press, 2007).

9. For Derrida's major political works, see *Negotiations: Interventions and Interviews, 1971–2001,* ed. and trans. Elizabeth G. Rottenberg (Stanford: Stanford University Press, 2002); *Politics of Friendship,* trans. George Collins (London: Verso, 1997); *Rogues: Two Essays on Reason,* trans. Pascale-Anne Brault and Michael Naas (Stanford: Stanford University Press, 2004); *Specters of Marx: The State of the Debt, the Work of Mourning, and the New International,* trans. Peggy Kamuf (New York: Routledge, 1994); and Derrida and Elisabeth Roudinesco, *For What Tomorrow …: A Dialogue,* trans. Jeff Fort (Stanford: Stanford University Press, 2004).

10. For further discussion of this argument, see my "Beyond Derrida: The Autoimmunity of Deconstruction," *Symposium: Canadian Journal of Continental Philosophy* 11, no. 1 (2007): 121–40.

11. Todd May, *The Political Thought of Jacques Rancière: Creating Equality* (University Park: Pennsylvania State University Press, 2008), 102.

12. For more on not speaking for others, see Gilles Deleuze and Michel Foucault, "Intellectuals and Power," in Foucault, *Language, Counter-Memory, Practice: Selected Essays and Interviews*, ed. Donald F. Bouchard, trans. Donald F. Bouchard and Sherry Simon (Ithaca: Cornell University Press, 1977), 209, quoted in ibid., 139n2. On "universality," see Foucault, "Truth, Power, Self: An Interview with Michel Foucault," by Martin Rue, in *Technologies of the Self*, ed. Luther H. Martin, Huck Gutman, and Patrick Hutton (Amherst: University of Massachusetts Press, 1988) (interview conducted in 1982), 11, quoted in ibid., 139n3.

13. Derrida, *Negotiations*, 295.

14. Derrida himself frequently alludes to the paralysis to which deconstruction in the realm of politics can lead. No one, however, including Derrida, has satisfactorily addressed the question of why we need deconstruction in politics. What does it do for us, politically speaking? We have heard repeatedly that the nature of undecidability motivates us to act in the name of justice, but no one has actually been able to demonstrate this. Undecidability's greatest benefit to political and ethical thought is also the source of its profound problematic: that we can see any situation or concept from multiple viewpoints, that there are no simple binary oppositions, that one element bleeds into its opposite—these features are absolutely necessary for deliberation, but they fail to show us how to move from that kind of slow deliberation to action. Ultimately, I find deconstruction a useful kind of critical analysis. It is a method, and any pretension to something "beyond" ("deconstruction is justice," for example) is rather exaggerated. Derrida was not the first to deconstruct ideas and events, although he did develop the process into a formula or logic.

15. We certainly find this pragmatic approach in the work of some thinkers who are considered part of this tradition—Étienne Balibar and Antonio Negri, for example.

16. Hannah Arendt, *The Human Condition* (Chicago: University of Chicago Press, 1989), 178.

17. For Jacques Rancière, politics happens rarely, only when "those who have no part," those whose political voice is not heard or doesn't matter, disturb the status quo. Politics is thus disagreement. See Rancière, *Disagreement: Politics and Philosophy*, trans. Julie Rose (Minneapolis: University of Minnesota Press, 1999).

18. Ibid., 9.

19. For a discussion of politics as policing, see ibid., especially chapter 2. For a similar notion in the context of feminism, see Wendy Brown, "The Impossibility of Women's Studies," in Brown, *Edgework: Critical Essays on Knowledge and Politics* (Princeton: Princeton University Press, 2005), 116–36.

20. The International Criminal Court spent half a billion Euros (roughly $655 million) in its first six years of existence. See Guénaël Mettraux, "The Cost of Justice—Is the ICC Living Beyond Its Means?" (2009), http://www.internationallawbureau.com/blog/?p=503 (accessed September 16, 2010).

CHAPTER 1

1. Brown, "Impossibility of Women's Studies," 122. Brown's comment arises in the somewhat different context of a discussion of the policing of intellectual boundaries in the creation of women's studies curricula, but in both cases, feminists (whether students or faculty) effectively police the discussion of what is permitted in the classroom. See also Rancière on the notion of politics as policing in *Disagreement*.

2. G. W. F. Hegel, *The Phenomenology of Spirit*, trans. A. V. Miller (Oxford: Oxford University Press, 1977), 92.

3. See Enns, *Speaking of Freedom*, chapter 1.

4. Todd May, *Reconsidering Difference: Nancy, Derrida, Levinas, Deleuze* (University Park: Pennsylvania State University Press, 1997), 4.

5. Michel Foucault, preface to *Anti-Oedipus: Capitalism and Schizophrenia*, by Gilles Deleuze and Félix Guattari, trans. Robert Hurley, Mark Seem, and Helen R. Lane (New York: Viking Press, 1977), xxiii.

6. Luce Irigaray, *This Sex Which Is Not One*, trans. Catherine Porter (Ithaca: Cornell University Press, 1985), 28–30.

7. I am not suggesting here a direct, causal connection between works of philosophy and historical events. Derrida's or Foucault's emphasis on difference is obviously not responsible for ethnic conflict or genocide. But the relationship between shifts in ideas and movements in history is a fascinating one, however direct or tenuous.

8. Simone de Beauvoir, *The Second Sex*, trans. Constance Borde and Sheila Malovany-Chevallier (New York: Knopf, 2009), 6.

9. Ibid., 6n3.

10. Feminists have recently begun addressing this gap. See, for example, Susan L. Miller, *Victims as Offenders: The Paradox of Women's Violence in Relationships* (New Brunswick: Rutgers University Press, 2005).

11. Himani Bannerji, *The Dark Side of the Nation: Essays on Multiculturalism, Nationalism, and Gender* (Toronto: Canadian Scholars' Press, 2000), 81.

12. I have come to dislike the term "women of color" and its associates, "student of color," "people of color," and so on, and I actively avoid using these terms. I have heard numerous complaints by women who arrive in Canada and wonder why they suddenly become "women of color" within our borders. In this section, however, I use the term because it is the favored one in the feminist discourses of women's studies.

13. Chandra Talpade Mohanty, *Feminism Without Borders: Decolonizing Theory, Practicing Solidarity* (Durham: Duke University Press, 2003), 22. For a refreshing look at this period of feminism, see Benita Roth, who demonstrates that feminism in America has never been simply "white, liberal and middle-class," in *Separate Roads to Feminism: Black, Chicana, and White Feminist Movements in America's Second Wave* (Cambridge: Cambridge University Press, 2004).

14. See bell hooks, *Outlaw Culture* (New York: Routledge, 1994), 14–15.

15. Mohanty's use of "Two-Thirds World" and "One-Third World" is an attempt to alleviate the misleading geographical and ideological opposition between the terms "First World" and "Third World" by focusing on social minorities and majorities on the basis of the quality of life in the North and the South. She borrows these classifications from Gustavo Esteva and Madhu Suri Prakash in *Grassroots Post-Modernism: Remaking the Soil of Cultures* (London: Zed Books, 1998). See Mohanty, *Feminism Without Borders*, 227n11.

16. Gayatri Chakravorty Spivak, *The Postcolonial Critic: Interviews, Strategies, Dialogues*, ed. Sarah Harasym (New York: Routledge, 1990), 61.

17. Ibid., 66.

18. Sara Suleri, "Woman Skin Deep: Feminism and the Postcolonial Condition," *Critical Inquiry* 18 (1992): 758.

19. Friedrich Nietzsche, *On the Genealogy of Morals and Ecce Homo*, trans. Walter Kaufmann and R. J. Hollingdale (New York: Random House, 1967), 36.

20. Ibid., 127.

21. Wendy Brown, *States of Injury: Power and Freedom in Late Modernity* (Princeton: Princeton University Press, 1995), 27.

22. Ibid., 46, 70.

23. Ranjana Khanna, *Dark Continents: Psychoanalysis and Colonialism* (Durham: Duke University Press, 2003), 209.

24. Kelly Oliver, *The Colonization of Psychic Space: A Psychoanalytic Social Theory of Oppression* (Minneapolis: University of Minnesota Press, 2004), xxiii.

25. See Rudi Visker, "Is Ethics Fundamental? Questioning Levinas on Irresponsibility," *Continental Philosophy Review* 36, no. 3 (2003): 264.

26. Visker provides a provocative response to these questions when he asks whether it might be more soothing "to live with the conviction that we are perpetually falling short of our infinite responsibility before the other, than to entertain the thought that irresponsibility could have to do with something within us which not only doesn't respond to the other, but not even to ourselves." The comfort, according to Visker, is derived from a fundamental intersubjectivity that ignores the unbearable "metaphysical loneliness" of human existence. Ibid., 268.

27. Emmanuel Levinas, "Substitution," in Levinas, *Otherwise Than Being: Or Beyond Essence*, trans. Alphonso Lingis (Pittsburgh: Duquesne University Press, 1981), 114.

28. Ibid., 1.

29. Enrique Dussel, *Filosofiá de la liberación*, 3d ed. (Buenos Aires: Ediciones La Aurora, 1985), 24, quoted in Elina Vuola, "Thinking Otherwise: Dussel, Liberation Theology, and Feminism," in *Thinking from the Underside of History: Enrique Dussel's Philosophy of Liberation*, ed. Linda Martín Alcoff and Eduardo Mendieta (New York: Rowman & Littlefield, 2000), 151n12.

30. Ofelia Schutte, *Cultural Identity and Social Liberation in Latin American Thought* (New York: SUNY Press, 1993), 179.

31. Oliver, *Colonization of Psychic Space*, xvi.

32. Ibid., xxiii.

33. I am not, of course, suggesting that the U.S. government (and other Western governments) are not at fault for "killing in the name of justice, democracy, and freedom." I am objecting, rather, to a certain tone here that contributes to the polarization of us versus them, guilty versus innocent.

34. Oliver, *Colonization of Psychic Space*, xxiii, xxiv.

35. Emmanuel Levinas, "Substitution," in Levinas, *Basic Philosophical Writings*, trans. Adrian T. Peperzak, Simon Critchley, and Robert Bernasconi (Bloomington: Indiana University Press, 1996), 90.

36. Levinas, *Otherwise Than Being*, 94.

37. Any reader familiar with Levinas will note that what has happened here is a loss of the incommensurable alterity of the other. Dussel asks who the other is in relation to the self, that is, who the impoverished Latin American other is in relation to the European imperialist. Oliver, although she relies on a Levinasian notion of responsibility and alterity, constructs a simple binary opposition in reverse that fails to convince us that we are responsible for what we do not and cannot know. Both authors thus fundamentally misinterpret Levinas.

38. Oliver, *Colonization of Psychic Space*, xxiv.

CHAPTER 2

1. The first epigraph to this chapter is a statement by Arnon Sofer, a professor of geology at Haifa University, made during an interview published in the *Jerusalem Post*, May 21, 2004, quoted in Jeff Halper, *Obstacles to Peace: A Re-framing of the Palestinian-Israeli Conflict* (Jerusalem: ICAHD, 2009), 47. The second comes from the title of Philip C. Winslow's book *Victory for Us Is to See You Suffer: In the West Bank with the Palestinians and the Israelis* (Boston: Beacon Press, 2007).

2. Mahmood Mamdani, *When Victims Become Killers: Colonialism, Nativism, and the Genocide in Rwanda* (Princeton: Princeton University Press, 2001), 14.

3. Mahmood Mamdani, "Making Sense of Political Violence in Postcolonial Africa," in *Experiments with Truth: Transitional Justice and the Processes of Truth and Reconciliation, Documenta11_Platform2*, ed. Okwui Enwezor et al. (Ostfildern-Ruit, Germany: Hatje Cantz, 2002), 37.

4. Ibid., 36–37.

5. NGOs estimated Palestinian deaths between 1,387 and 1,417; Gaza authorities put the number at 1,444 and the Israeli government at 1,166. See the UN report on Gaza, "Human Rights in Palestine and Other Occupied Arab Territories: Report of the United Nations Fact Finding Mission on the Gaza Conflict," September 12, 2009, 10, http://www2.ohchr.org/english/bodies/hrcouncil/specialsession/9/factfindingmission.htm (accessed February 11, 2011).

6. Canada was a member of the UN Human Rights Council from 2006 to 2009. The United States was not a member at the time of this motion. For current and past lists of the forty-seven member nations, see http://www2.ohchr.org/english/bodies/hrcouncil/membership.htm.

7. Bruce Campion-Smith and Les Whittington, "Canada Votes Alone for Israel," *Toronto Star*, January 13, 2009, http://www.thestar.com/article/569872 (accessed February 1, 2009).

8. Quoted in Diane Enns, "A Conversation with Étienne Balibar," *Symposium* 9, no. 2 (2005): 390.

9. "Israel Hits Hamas Targets in Gaza," BBC News, February 1, 2009, http://news.bbc.co.uk/2/hi/middle_east/7863500.stm (accessed February 10, 2009). Speaking at the weekly Israeli cabinet meeting, Mr. Olmert warned that Israel would respond forcefully to renewed rocket fire. "We've said that if there is rocket fire against the south of the country, there will be a disproportionate Israeli response to the fire on the citizens of Israel and its security forces," he said. "The response will come at the time, the place and the manner that we choose."

10. Ghassan Hage, "'Comes a time we are all enthusiasm': Understanding Palestinian Suicide Bombers in Times of Exighophobia," *Public Culture* 15, no. 1 (2003): 68.

11. Frantz Fanon, *The Wretched of the Earth*, trans. Richard Philcox (New York: Grove Press, 2004), 1.

12. Jean-Paul Sartre, preface to ibid., li.

13. Ibid., lxii.

14. Hannah Arendt, *On Violence* (New York: Harcourt Brace, 1969), 21–22.

15. See Étienne Balibar, "Outline of a Topography of Cruelty: Citizenship and Civility in the Era of Global Violence," in *We, the People of Europe? Reflections on Transnational Citizenship*, trans. James Swenson (Princeton: Princeton University Press, 2004), 115–32; Walter Benjamin, "Critique of Violence," trans. Edmund Jephcott, in Benjamin, *Selected Writings*, vol. 1, *1913–1926* (Cambridge: Belknap Press of Harvard University Press, 1996), 236–52; Jacques Derrida, "Violence and Metaphysics: An Essay on the Thought of Emmanuel Levinas," in Derrida, *Writing and Difference*, trans. Alan Bass (Chicago: University of Chicago Press, 1978), 79–153; Emmanuel Levinas, *Totality and Infinity: An Essay on Exteriority*, trans. Alphonso Lingis (Pittsburgh: Duquesne University Press, 1969).

16. Slavoj Žižek, *Violence* (London: Picador, 2008), 213, 217.

17. See Michael Ignatieff, *The Lesser Evil: Political Ethics in an Age of Terror* (Princeton: Princeton University Press, 2004).

18. Balibar, *We, the People of Europe*, 131.

19. Hannah Arendt, "Personal Responsibility Under Dictatorship," in Arendt, *Responsibility and Judgment*, ed. Jerome Kohn (New York: Schocken Books, 2003), 36.

20. Jacqueline Rose, *The Last Resistance* (London: Verso, 2007), 113.

21. Faisal Darraj, "Ethics of Resistance," an open letter to Étienne Balibar, *Al-Ahram Weekly*, May 2–8, 2002, http://weekly.ahram.org.eg/2002/584/op2.htm (accessed February 10, 2011).

22. Quoted in Wendy Pearlman, *Occupied Voices: Stories of Everyday Life from the Second Intifada* (New York: Thunder's Mouth Press/Nation Books, 2003), 88.

23. Eyad El-Sarraj, "Suicide Bombers: Dignity, Despair, and the Need for Hope," *Journal of Palestine Studies* 31, no. 4 (2002): 72.

24. Ted Honderich, "Terrorism for Humanity" (lecture given at the International Social Philosophy Conference at Northeastern University, Boston, revised March 4, 2004), 5, 6, http://www.ucl.ac.uk/~uctytho/terrforhum.html (accessed February 9, 2010).

25. Ibid., 7.

26. Ted Honderich, "Obligations to the Future: Palestinian Terrorism, Morality, and Germany," *Counterpunch*, October 25–26, 2003, http://www.counterpunch.com/honderich 10252003.html (accessed January 6, 2009).

27. Hage, "'Comes a time we are all enthusiasm,'" 75.

28. "Il est de toute façon catastrophique pour la lutte du peuple palestinien. . . . Il est donc profondément autodestructeur." Étienne Balibar, "Universalité de la cause palestinienne," *Le Monde Diplomatique*, May 2004, 26–27.

29. For an excellent discussion of the bystander's responsibility, see Erwin Staub, *The Psychology of Good and Evil: Why Children, Adults, and Groups Help and Harm Others* (Cambridge: Cambridge University Press, 2003).

30. Simon R. Cottee, "Excusing Terror," *Journal of Human Rights* 5 (2006): 152, 153, 158.

31. Ibid., 158.

32. Avraham Burg, *The Holocaust Is Over; We Must Rise from Its Ashes* (New York: Palgrave Macmillan, 2008), 13, 23, 24.

33. Yael Zerubavel, *Recovered Roots: Collective Memory and the Making of Israeli National Tradition* (Chicago: University of Chicago Press, 1995), 193.

34. Apparently, Israeli soldiers take an oath there: "Masada Shall Not Fall Again." It is one of the most important symbols for Jews, epitomized in the idea that it is better to die than be a slave. One can even buy a T-shirt with the oath. See http://www.zahal.org/products/ massada-shall-not-fall-again-shirt (accessed September 16, 2010).

35. Zerubavel, *Recovered Roots*, 194.

36. Idith Zertal, *Israel's Holocaust and the Politics of Nationhood*, trans. Chaya Galai (New York: Cambridge University Press, 2005), 4.

37. Mamdani, *When Victims Become Killers*, 270–72.

38. Burg, *Holocaust Is Over*, 24.

39. Giorgio Agamben, "Security and Terror," trans. Carolin Emcke, *Theory and Event* 5, no. 4 (2001), http://muse.jhu.edu/login?uri=/journals/theory_and_event/v005/5.4agamben. html (accessed February 12, 2011).

40. See the daily blogs on *Ha'aretz* at http://www.haaretz.com/.

41. Seamus Milne, "Israel and the West Will Pay a Price for Gaza's Bloodbath," *Guardian*, January 8, 2009, http://www.guardian.co.uk/commentisfree/2009/jan/08/gaza-israel-hamas-us (accessed January 22, 2009).

42. Baruch Kimmerling, "Israel's Culture of Martyrdom," *Nation*, December 22, 2004, 7, http://www.thenation.com/doc/20050110/kimmerling/print (accessed February 26, 2009).

43. Gwynne Dyer, *War* (Toronto: Vintage Canada, 2005), 419. See also Natalie Angier, "No Time for Bullies: Baboons Retool their Culture," *New York Times*, April 13, 2004, http:// www.primates.com/baboons/culture.html; and "Emergence of a Peaceful Culture in Wild Baboons," http://www.ncbi.nlm.nih.gov/pmc/articles/PMC387823.

44. See Angier, "No Time for Bullies."

45. Ibid., quoted in Dyer, *War*, 420.

46. Ibid.

47. Hannah Arendt, *Eichmann in Jerusalem: A Report on the Banality of Evil*, rev. and enl. ed. (New York: Penguin Books, 1977), 233.

48. From the documentary *ScaredSacred*, directed by Velcrow Ripper (Toronto: ScaredSacred Films, Inc./Mongrel Media, 2006).

49. See Elhanan's personal story at http://www.theparentscircle.com/stories.asp.

50. See http://www.theparentscircle.com/ (accessed February 17, 2010).

51. For an extensive list of such organizations, see the Palestinian-Israeli Peace NGO Forum at http://www.peacengo.org/.

52. Mamdani, *When Victims Become Killers*, 279. For a provocative discussion of survivor's justice, see 272–82.

53. Ibid., 279.

54. Halper, *Obstacles to Peace*, 35, 40, 41.

55. Jeff Halper, *An Israeli in Palestine: Resisting Dispossession, Redeeming Israel* (London: Pluto Press, 2008), 5–6 (quotation on p. 5).

56. Halper, *Obstacles to Peace*, 42.

57. Ibid., 5.

58. Jeff Halper, "Reframing the Israel/Palestine Conflict" (lecture, McMaster University, Hamilton, Ontario, January 21, 2009).

59. Halper, *Israeli in Palestine*, 11.

CHAPTER 3

1. The first epigraph is from Jean Améry, *At the Mind's Limits: Contemplations by a Survivor on Auschwitz and Its Realities*, trans. Sidney Rosenfeld and Stella P. Rosenfeld (Bloomington: Indiana University Press, 1980), 36. The second comes from Susan J. Brison, *Aftermath: Violence and the Remaking of a Self* (Princeton: Princeton University Press, 2003), 21.

2. Mari Ruti, *A World of Fragile Things: Psychoanalysis and the Art of Living* (Albany: SUNY Press, 2009), 10.

3. Fanon, *Wretched of the Earth*, 181. Hereafter cited parenthetically in the text.

4. Frantz Fanon, *Black Skin, White Masks*, trans. Charles L. Markmann (New York: Grove Press, 1967), 113, 112.

5. Ibid., 14.

6. Ibid., 230–31, 235, 239, 238.

7. Ibid., 14, 231, 228–29. Fanon does not focus exclusively on the "suffering, pain, depression, shame, anger, or alienation" of the colonized, nor does he suggest that violence is the only or best recourse available to the colonized, although he has been interpreted in these ways (Oliver, *Colonization of Psychic Space*, 88). Oliver argues that the lack of positive self-images and social acceptance, and the ability to create meaning—all necessary for psychic life—are responsible for the condition of the oppressed. She suggests that "it could be that violence is necessary to redirect the colonizer's affects, particularly anger, outward" (59). Neither of these arguments reflects either hindsight or foresight. To claim that victims lack the resources to create meaning ignores the tremendously productive and creative responses to victimhood that have occurred throughout history. Such a move merely repeats the initial victimization, imprisoning the victim in an agentless condition.

8. Sigmund Freud, "Mourning and Melancholia," in *The Standard Edition of the Complete Psychological Works of Sigmund Freud*, vol. 14, *1914–1916: On the History of the Psycho-analytic Movement, Papers on Metapsychology, and Other Works*, trans. James Strachey (London: Hogarth Press, 1957), 244–45.

9. Anne Anlin Cheng, *The Melancholy of Race: Psychoanalysis, Assimilation, and Hidden Grief* (Oxford: Oxford University Press, 2001), 7.

10. Khanna, *Dark Continents*, 21.

11. Freud, "Mourning and Melancholia," 244, 246, 22.

12. See Cheng, *Melancholy of Race*; W. E. B. Du Bois, *The Souls of Black Folk* (New York: New American Library, 1969); Fanon, *Black Skin, White Masks*; Paul Gilroy, *The Black Atlantic: Modernity and Double Consciousness* (Cambridge: Harvard University Press, 1993); and Paul Gilroy, *Postcolonial Melancholia* (New York: Columbia University Press, 2005).

13. Du Bois, *Souls of Black Folk*, 45–51.

14. Cheng, *Melancholy of Race*, xi.

15. Ibid., xi, 12, 7, 14.

16. Ralph Ellison, *Invisible Man* (New York: Vintage Books, 1990), 4–5, quoted in ibid., 15–16.

17. Ibid., 16–17.

18. Didier Fassin and Richard Rechtman, *The Empire of Trauma: An Inquiry into the Condition of Victimhood*, trans. Rachel Gomme (Princeton: Princeton University Press, 2009), 6.

19. Ibid., xi.

20. Ruth Leys, *Trauma: A Genealogy* (Chicago: University of Chicago Press, 2000), 2.

21. Ibid., 31, 32, 34.

22. Fassin and Rechtman discuss the importance of this shift in thinking about trauma. The concept of trauma that emerged in the 1960s reversed Freud's own shift from seeing the cause of trauma as an external event to positing it as an internal force universally experienced. Beginning in the 1960s, the blame for trauma neuroses shifted from "a traumatic sexuality from which everyone suffers to a traumatized sexuality, the cause of which lies squarely on the shoulders of an external abuser." *Empire of Trauma*, 34.

23. For discussion of this shift, see in particular ibid.; Leys, *Trauma: A Genealogy*; and Judith Lewis Herman, *Trauma and Recovery* (New York: Basic Books, 1992).

24. Herman, *Trauma and Recovery*, 32.

25. Fassin and Rechtman, *Empire of Trauma*, 42–43.

26. In this they depart from other historians of psychoanalysis, such as Elisabeth Roudinesco, and military doctors such as Claude Barrois and Louis Crocq, who believe that World War II inaugurated a radical shift in thinking about trauma due to the influence of psychoanalysis. Fassin and Rechtman claim that this argument is inaccurate, pointing out that the psychiatric concepts these scholars ascribe to that historical time frame were unknown until after the liberation of the Nazi camps. Ibid., 66–67n11. The discussion and quotations in this and the following paragraph are from ibid., 69–70.

27. Herman, *Trauma and Recovery*, 26–27.

28. Fassin and Rechtman, *Empire of Trauma*, 18.

29. Cathy Caruth, "Introduction," *Trauma: Explorations in Memory*, ed. Cathy Caruth (Baltimore: Johns Hopkins University Press, 1995), 11, quoted in ibid., 19. The discussion and quotations in the remainder of this section are from Fassin and Rechtman, *Empire of Trauma*, cited parenthetically in the text.

30. Améry, *At the Mind's Limits*, xiii. Hereafter cited parenthetically in the text.

31. Jean Améry, *On Suicide: A Discourse on Voluntary Death*, trans. John D. Barlow (Bloomington: Indiana University Press, 1999), 101.

32. Fassin and Rechtman, *Empire of Trauma*, 80–81.

33. Betty Friedan, *The Feminine Mystique* (New York: W. W. Norton, 1963), 306.

34. Herman, *Trauma and Recovery*, 29.

35. Quoted in ibid., 30. Hereafter cited parenthetically in the text.

36. Kristin Bumiller, *In an Abusive State: How Neoliberalism Appropriated the Feminist Movement Against Sexual Violence* (Durham: Duke University Press, 2008), 160. Hereafter cited parenthetically in the text.

37. Brison, *Aftermath*, xii. Hereafter cited parenthetically in the text.

38. For an excellent discussion of agency in the context of psychoanalysis, see Ruti, *World of Fragile Things.*

CHAPTER 4

1. The first epigraph to this chapter is taken from Jean Hatzfeld, *Life Laid Bare: The Survivors in Rwanda Speak*, trans. Linda Coverdale (New York: Other Press, 2007), 103; the second is from Hannah Arendt, *The Origins of Totalitarianism*, new ed. (New York: Harcourt Brace, 1973), 6.

2. Arendt, "Personal Responsibility Under Dictatorship," 19, 18.

3. Quoted in Hannah Arendt, *The Jew as Pariah: Jewish Identity and Politics in the Modern Age*, ed. Ron Feldman (New York: Grove Press, 1978), 243.

4. Quoted in Geoffrey York, "Rwanda's Blood-Soaked History Becomes a Tool for Repression," *Globe and Mail* (Toronto), March 2, 2010, http://www.theglobeandmail.com/news/world/rwandas-blood-soaked-history-becomes-a-tool-for-repression/article1487568/ (accessed March 5, 2010). On Ingabire's arrest, see "Kagame Rival Arrested in Rwanda," http://news.bbc.co.uk/2/hi/africa/8635890.stm (accessed April 22, 2010).

5. Of course, it should be noted that this attitude is a product of decades of hard work to change a culture that did tend to blame women for rape, and sometimes still does.

6. Arendt, *Origins of Totalitarianism*, 5. Hereafter cited parenthetically in the text.

7. For more on this point, see Raluca Munteanu Eddon, "Gershom Scholem, Hannah Arendt, and the Paradox of 'Non-Nationalist' Nationalism," *Journal of Jewish Thought and Philosophy* 2, no. 1 (2003): 59.

8. Richard J. Bernstein, *Hannah Arendt and the Jewish Question* (Cambridge MIT Press, 1996), 56.

9. Hatzfeld, *Life Laid Bare*, 103.

10. Arendt, "Personal Responsibility Under Dictatorship," 18.

11. Arendt, *Jew as Pariah*, 248.

12. Richard J. Bernstein, *Radical Evil: A Philosophical Interrogation* (Cambridge: Polity Press, 2002), 217.

13. Hannah Arendt, *The Life of the Mind* (London: Harcourt, 1978), 4.

14. Arendt, *Eichmann in Jerusalem*, 288.

15. Améry, *At the Mind's Limits*, 25.

16. For an overview of the controversy and a bibliography of relevant sources see Michael Ezra, "The Eichmann Polemics: Hannah Arendt and Her Critics," *Democratiya* 9 (Summer 2007): 141–65 (now *Dissent*), http://dissentmagazine.org/. See also Steven E. Aschheim, *Hannah Arendt in Jerusalem* (Berkeley and Los Angeles: University of California Press, 2001); and Bernstein, *Hannah Arendt and the Jewish Question*.

17. Arendt, *Eichmann in Jerusalem*, 118, 134, 117.

18. Ibid., 124, 125.

19. Hannah Arendt, "Answers to Questions Submitted by Samuel Grafton," in Arendt, *The Jewish Writings*, ed. Jerome Kohn and Ron Feldman (New York: Schocken Books, 2007), 481.

20. Arendt, *Eichmann in Jerusalem*, 231–32.

21. Arne Johan Vetlesen, *Evil and Human Agency: Understanding Collective Evildoing* (Cambridge: Cambridge University Press, 2005), 146–47.

22. Hannah Arendt, *Human Condition*, 233–34.

23. I should mention that the students in my classrooms are often predominantly of leftist political persuasion, given the programs in which I teach (peace studies, globalization,

women's studies) and the topics on which I focus (violence, self-determination, victimhood, politics and ethics, human rights, etc.).

24. Žižek, *Violence*, 107, 115.

25. Ibid., 139.

26. Spivak, *Post-Colonial Critic*, 62–63.

27. For interesting discussions of Arendt's unfinished work on judging, see Ronald Beiner, "Hannah Arendt on Judging," in Arendt, *Lectures on Kant's Political Philosophy*, ed. Ronald Beiner (Chicago: University of Chicago Press, 1992), 89–156; Max Deutscher, *Judgment After Arendt* (Burlington, Vt.: Ashgate, 2007); Leah Bradshaw, *Acting and Thinking: The Political Thought of Hannah Arendt* (Toronto: University of Toronto Press, 1989); and Jerome Kohn's introduction to Arendt's *Responsibility and Judgment*, vii–xxix.

28. Beiner, "Hannah Arendt on Judging," 91, 92.

29. Peter J. Steinberger, "Hannah Arendt on Judgment," *American Journal of Political Science* 34, no. 3 (1990): 804.

30. Deutscher, *Judgment After Arendt*, 69.

31. Arendt, "Personal Responsibility Under Dictatorship," 45.

32. Arendt, *Life of the Mind*, 5.

33. Quoted in Arendt, "Sixth Session," in *Lectures on Kant's Political Philosophy*, 40n92.

34. Quoted in ibid., 41n94.

35. Ibid., 40.

36. Quoted in ibid., 42n96.

37. Ibid., 42.

38. Quoted in ibid., 42n97.

39. Hannah Arendt, "Truth and Politics," in Arendt, *Between Past and Future: Eight Exercises in Political Thought* (New York: Penguin Books, 1993), 241, 242.

40. Arendt, *Life of the Mind*, 5.

41. Deutscher, *Judgment After Arendt*, 129.

42. Bradshaw, *Acting and Thinking*, 97.

43. Arendt, "Personal Responsibility Under Dictatorship," 44.

44. Arendt, "Some Questions of Moral Philosophy," in *Responsibility and Judgment*, 97.

45. Arendt, "Personal Responsibility Under Dictatorship," 45, 47.

46. Steinberger, "Hannah Arendt on Judgment," 816.

47. Arendt, *Life of the Mind*, 215–16.

48. Deutscher, *Judgment After Arendt*, 135.

49. Hannah Arendt, *Men in Dark Times*, trans. Clara Winston and Richard Winston (New York: Harcourt Brace, 1968), 75–79.

50. Kathleen Taylor, *Cruelty: Human Evil and the Human Brain* (Oxford: Oxford University Press, 2009), 117.

51. Arendt, "Twelfth Session," in *Lectures on Kant's Political Philosophy*, 68–69.

52. Arendt, "Truth and Politics," 242, 243.

53. Vetlesen, *Evil and Human Agency*, 224, 226, 246.

54. Arendt, *Eichmann in Jerusalem*, 295–96.

55. Quoted in Arendt, *Jew as Pariah*, 242–43.

56. Quoted in ibid., 278.

57. Ibid., 246.

58. Arendt, *Jewish Writings*, 483.

59. Ibid., 186.

60. Arendt, "On Humanity in Dark Times: Thoughts About Lessing," in *Men in Dark Times*, 13.

61. Ibid., 13, 16–17.

62. Mark Greif, "Arendt's Judgment," *Dissent* (Spring 2004), http://www.dissentmaga-zine.org/article/?article=388 (accessed February 10, 2011).

63. Arendt, "Some Questions of Moral Philosophy," 111, 145–46.

64. Ibid., 111, 112.

65. Eyal Sivan, "Archive Images: Truth or Memory? The Case of Adolf Eichmann's Trial," in Enwezor et al., *Experiments with Truth*, 284.

66. Ibid., 285.

67. Rony Brauman and Eyal Sivan, *Éloge de la désobéissance* (Paris: Le Pommier, 1999), quoted in ibid., 286n18.

68. Arendt, "Personal Responsibility Under Dictatorship," 37, 26–27.

CHAPTER 5

1. The first epigraph to this chapter is from Ishmael Beal, "Ishmael Beah: A Long Way from a Kalashnikov to a Pen," interview by Damien Roustel, trans. Jonathan Pier-rel, *L'Humanité*, http://humaniteinenglish.com/spip.php?article840 (accessed February 11, 2011). The second is from Arkady Babchenko, *One Soldier's War*, trans. Nick Allen (New York: Grove Press, 2006), x.

2. Virginia Rounding, "A Touch of Tolstoy in Russia's Vietnam," review of *One Soldier's War*, by Arkady Babchenko, trans. Nick Allen, *Independent*, November 9, 2007. http://www.independent.co.uk/arts-entertainment/books/reviews/one-soldiers-war-in-chechnya-by-arkady-babchenko-trans-nick-allen-399565.html (accessed May 18, 2009).

3. Babchenko, *One Soldier's War*, x.

4. This report led to the opening of the Office of the Special Representative of the Secretary General for Children and Armed Conflict in 1997. See Alcinda Honwana, *Child Soldiers in Africa* (Philadelphia: University of Pennsylvania Press, 2006), 2. For the 1996 UN report by Graça Machel, see *Impact of Armed Conflict on Children*, http://www.unicef.org/graca; for a ten-year review, see http://www.un.org/children/conflict/english/themachelstudy.html (accessed March 19, 2010).

5. Vera Achvarina and Simon F. Reich, "No Place to Hide: Refugees, Displaced Persons, and the Recruitment of Child Soldiers," *International Security* 31, no. 1 (2006): 128. Rough estimates in 2005 placed the number of child insurgents in the Taliban alone at eight thousand. See the UN Office for the Coordination of Humanitarian Affairs, "Afghanistan: Eight Thousand Children Under Arms Look for a Future," http://www.irinnews.org/InDepth-Main.aspx?InDepthId=24&ReportId=66989&Country=Yes (accessed February 11, 2011).

6. See Unicef, "Adult Wars, Child Soldiers: Voices of Children Involved in Armed Conflict in the East Asia and Pacific Region," October 2002, quoted in Achvarina and Reich, "No Place to Hide," 129.

7. "The number of governments that deployed children in combat or other frontline duties in their armed forces has not significantly decreased since 2004. Children have been used in armed conflict by government forces in nine situations compared with 10 in the previous four-year period. The most notable offender remains Myanmar, whose armed forces, engaged in long-running counter-insurgency operations against a range of ethnic armed groups, are believed to contain thousands of children. Children were also reported to have been used in hostilities in Chad, the DRC, Somalia, Sudan and Uganda. Additionally, Palestinian children were used on several occasions by defence forces in Israel as human shields. There were reports of child soldier use by Yemeni armed forces in fighting in 2007. A few under-18s in the UK armed forces were sent to Iraq." Coalition to Stop the Use of Child Soldiers, *Child Soldiers Global Report 2008*, http://www.childsoldiersglobalreport.org/ (accessed June 4, 2009).

8. Ibid. The "Optional Protocol" regarding the use of child soldiers in armed combat was adopted in May 2000 and specifies that "States Parties shall take all feasible measures to ensure that members of their armed forces who have not attained the age of 18 years do not take a direct part in hostilities." Furthermore, they "shall ensure that persons who have not attained the age of 18 years are not compulsorily recruited into their armed forces." Voluntary recruitment under the age of eighteen must be "genuinely" voluntary and made with the informed consent of parents, and recruitments must be informed of the military duties required. The Optional Protocol also specifies that "each State Party shall take all necessary legal, administrative and other measures to ensure the effective implementation and enforcement of the provisions of the present Protocol within its jurisdiction." See http://www2 .ohchr.org/english/law/crc-conflict.htm (accessed March 27, 2010). For the most up-to-date signatories, see http://treaties.un.org/Pages/ViewDetails.aspx?src=TREATY&mtdsg_ no=IV-11-b&chapter=4&lang=en (accessed February 7, 2011).

9. See Coalition to Stop the Use of Child Soldiers, *Child Soldiers Global Report 2008*.

10. Ibid. The list includes Afghanistan, Burundi, Central African Republic, Chad, Colombia, Cote d'Ivoire, the Democratic Republic of Congo, India, Indonesia, Iraq, Israel and the Occupied Palestinian Territories, Myanmar, Nepal, the Philippines, Somalia, Sri Lanka, Sudan, Thailand, and Uganda.

11. Michael Wessells, *Child Soldiers: From Violence to Protection* (Cambridge: Harvard University Press, 2006), 9–11.

12. David M. Rosen, *Armies of the Young: Child Soldiers in War and Terrorism* (New Brunswick: Rutgers University Press, 2005), 5.

13. Ibid., 8, 6, 7. See also Charles London, *One Day the Soldiers Came: Voices of Children in War* (New York: HarperCollins, 2007). He writes that in the Middle Ages, there was no great effort to protect children from the adult world. For example, "childhood sexuality was not taboo, but a source of great amusement" (18), and "the idea of childhood was a luxury for the wealthy and the safe" (19).

14. Wessells, *Child Soldiers*, 5.

15. Honwana writes that in Angola, the Tchokwè people name children according to their occupation or roles. For example, *tchitutas* are girls and boys around five to seven years of age whose role is to fetch water and tobacco for elders, and *kambumbu* are children who participate in household chores at around seven to thirteen years of age. *Child Soldiers in Africa*, 41–42.

16. Rosen, *Armies of the Young*, 3.

17. David M. Rosen, "Child Soldiers, International Humanitarian Law, and the Globalization of Childhood," *American Anthropologist* 109, no. 2 (2007): 296. These humanitarian groups include Amnesty International, Human Rights Watch, the Quaker United Nations Office, the International Save the Children Alliance, and the International Committee of the Red Cross. Several of these also serve on the steering committee for the Coalition to Stop the Use of Child Soldiers.

18. Stephen Kabera Karanja, "Child Soldiers in Peace Agreements: The Peace and Justice Dilemma!" *Global Jurist* 8, no. 3 (2008): 3.

19. Unicef, "Cape Town Principles and Best Practices," adopted at the Symposium on the Prevention of the Recruitment of Children into the Armed Forces and on Demobilization and Social Reintegration of Child Soldiers in Africa, Cape Town, April 27–30, 1997, http://www.unicef.org/emerg/index_childsoldiers.html (accessed May 21, 2010). See also Unicef, "Fact Sheet: Child Soldiers," http://www.unicef.org/emerg/index_childsoldiers.html (accessed May 21, 2010).

20. Victoria Forbes Adam (then the director of the Coalition to Stop the Use of Child Soldiers), "Coalition Letter to United Nations Security Council Members in Advance of the

Debate on Children and Armed Conflict," April 20, 2009, 4, http://www.child-soldiers.org/home (accessed May 11, 2009).

21. Rosen, "Child Soldiers," 297.

22. Rosen, *Armies of the Young*, 1.

23. It is worth reflecting on why Palestinian youth who become suicide bombers are not typically referred to as child soldiers, and why little thought is given to whether they are victims in any sense. It may be in part because the child soldier must be perceived as unambiguously innocent in order to gain the world's sympathies, and the Palestinian—adult, youth, or child—has unfortunately come to symbolize terrorism.

24. Rosen, *Armies of the Young*, 21, 23, 56.

25. Daniel Williams, "Young Bombers Nurtured by Despair Among Palestinians, a Growing Attitude of Little to Live For," *Washington Post*, March 23, 2002.

26. Joshua Hammer, *A Season in Bethlehem* (New York: Free Press, 2003), 160, quoted in Rosen, *Armies of the Young*, 91.

27. Of these 169 children and youth, 92.9 percent had witnessed shooting, 89.9 percent had witnessed wounding, and 84 percent had been seriously beaten. See Christophe Pierre Bayer, Fionna Klasen, and Hubertus Adam, "Association of Trauma and PTSD Symptoms with Openness to Reconciliation and Feelings of Revenge Among Former Ugandan and Congolese Child Soldiers," *Journal of the American Medical Association* 298, no. 5 (2007): 557, http://www.ncbi.nlm.nih.gov/pubmed/17666676 (accessed February 11, 2011).

28. In this study, 77.5 percent of the boys had shot someone; 67 percent had lost family members or close friends in the war; 76 percent had witnessed killing; and 61 percent said they had been in life-or-death situations. The average time spent in an armed group for these boys was 3.8 years. See Wessells, *Child Soldiers*, 131.

29. Honwana, *Child Soldiers in Africa*, 84–85.

30. Wessells, *Child Soldiers*, 128.

31. Ibid., 133–34.

32. Ibid., 23.

33. Ibid., 3.

34. Honwana, *Child Soldiers in Africa*, 65, 68, 69.

35. Ibid., 71.

36. Ibid.

37. London, *One Day the Soldiers Came*, 38.

38. See http://www.alongwaygone.com/long_way_gone.html (accessed February 7, 2011).

39. Ishmael Beah, *A Long Way Gone: Memoirs of a Boy Soldier* (New York: Farrar, Straus and Giroux, 2007), 61.

40. Ibid., 199.

41. Marc Lacey puts the figure at twenty thousand; see his article "Atrocity Victims in Uganda Choose to Forgive," *New York Times*, April 18, 2005, http://www.nytimes.com/2005/04/18/international/africa/18uganda.html?_r=1 (accessed May 20, 2009). See also "The Abduction and Return Experiences of Youth," *Survey of War Affected Youth* (April 2006), quoted in Erin Baines, "Complicating Victims and Perpetrators in Uganda: On Dominic Ongwen," *Field Note* 7 (July 2008): 6n12, http://www.justiceandreconciliation.com/ (accessed April 5, 2010). This defines youth as between the ages of thirteen and thirty. The Justice and Reconciliation Project is a joint project of the Gulu District NGO Forum and the Liu Institute for Global Issues.

42. Alice Lakwena was originally Alice Auma, who changed her name after she claimed that a spirit named Lakwena, meaning "messenger" in the Acholi language, came to visit her. Her army practiced bizarre warfare tactics, influenced by Lakwena's spiritual beliefs. See Peter Eichstaedt, *First Kill Your Family: Child Soldiers of Uganda and the Lord's Resistance Army* (Chicago: Lawrence Hill Books, 2009), 14–17.

43. Baines, "Complicating Victims and Perpetrators in Uganda," 8.

44. Ongwen is accused of seven counts of individual criminal responsibility, including three counts of crimes against humanity (murder, enslavement, and inhuman acts of inflicting serious bodily injury and suffering) and four counts of war crimes (murder, cruel treatment of civilians, intentionally directing an attack against civilians, and pillaging). Ibid., 12. See also http://ongwen.blogspot.com/; and http://www.trial-ch.org/en/.

45. Baines, "Complicating Victims and Perpetrators in Uganda," 10, 12.

46. Bouris argues in *Complex Political Victims* that transitional justice scholarship reproduces the categories of victim and perpetrator as though they were discrete categories and homogeneous groups. To call victims "complex" recognizes that victims hold some degree of responsibility and provides a more nuanced understanding of the victim that has significant policy implications.

47. Baines, "Complicating Victims and Perpetrators in Uganda," 1, 2.

48. For accounts of these claims, see Gabriel Sherman, "The Fog of Memoir: The Feud over the Truthfulness of Ishmael Beah's *A Long Way Gone*," *Slate*, March 6, 2008, http://www.slate.com/id/2185928 (accessed March 28, 2010). For Bryan Appleyard's article on Beah's book and on his interview with Beah, see "Bryan Appleyard's Full Account of His Interview with Ishmael Beah," *Sunday Times* (London), February 3, 2008, http://www.timesonline.co.uk/tol/news/world/africa/article3294474.ece (accessed February 11, 2011).

49. For a few sample blogs, see http://www.radioopensource.org/ishmael-beah-boy-soldier/; http://trentito.blogspot.com/2007/05/ishmael-beah-long-way-gone.html (accessed September 21, 2010).

50. See Leon Neyfakh, "Ishmael Beah Defends Himself and His Memoirs Against Accusations of Misrepresentation," *New York Observer*, January 22, 2008, http://www.observer.com/ (accessed May 18, 2009).

51. Unicef calculates the number of Lost Boys ("mostly boys") at twenty thousand. See "The Lost Boys of the Sudan," http://www.unicef.org/sowc96/closboys.htm (accessed February 8, 2011).

52. See Emmanuel Jal's website at http://www.emmanueljal.org/ (accessed May 25, 2009).

53. Sarah Hampson, "A Child Soldier Trades Rifles for the Rap Game," *Globe and Mail* (Toronto), March 2, 2009.

54. "Jallaba" literally means "long, loose garment," but it is also used to mean Arab and/or slave trader.

55. See the Introduction to this book.

56. There is now an Ishmael Beah Foundation, a private, independent institution dedicated to helping former child soldiers reintegrate into society and improve their lives. "The Foundation aims at creating and financing educational and vocational opportunities for children and youth who have been affected by war, so that they can be empowered to choose a life free of conflict. The Foundation will focus its efforts in closely monitoring children during and after the rehabilitation phase to prevent them from re-entering the cycle of conflict and violence." See http://www.beahfound.org/ (accessed May 18, 2009).

57. The fascination with violence makes these narratives more sensational than David Eggers's work of fiction, *What Is the What: The Autobiography of Valentino Achak Deng* (Toronto: Vintage Canada, 2006), based on the life story of Achak Deng, one of the "Lost Boys" of Sudan who did not enter combat. See the Valentino Achak Deng Foundation website at http://www.valentinoachakdeng.org/.

58. Rosen, *Armies of the Young*, 157–58.

59. Alcinda Honwana, "Reintegration of Youth into Society in the Aftermath of War," 21, www.un.org/esa/socdev/unyin/documents/namibia_honwana.pdf (accessed August 10, 2011).

60. Machel, *Impact of Armed Conflict on Children*, 5.

61. Hugh Miall, Oliver Ramsbotham, and Tom Woodhouse, eds., *Contemporary Conflict Resolution* (Cambridge: Polity Press, 1999), 28.

62. See Peter Wallensteen and Margareta Sollenberg, "Armed Conflict, 1989–99," *Journal of Peace Research* 37, no. 5 (2000): 635–46.

63. Christian Scherrer, *Ethno-nationalismus als globales Phänomen: Zur Krise der Staaten in der Dritten Welt und der früheren UDSSR* (Duisburg, Germany: Gerhard-Mercator-Universität, 1994), 74, quoted in Andreas Wimmer, "Introduction: Facing Ethnic Conflicts," in *Facing Ethnic Conflict: Toward a New Realism*, ed. Andreas Wimmer, Richard J. Goldstone, and Donald L. Horowitz (Toronto: Rowman & Littlefield, 2004), 1.

64. Wimmer, "Introduction," 1.

65. Hugh Miall, *The Peacemakers: Peaceful Settlement of Disputes Since 1945* (London: Macmillan, 1992), quoted in Jay Rothman and Marie L. Olson, "From Interests to Identities: Towards a New Emphasis in Interactive Conflict Resolution," *Journal of Peace Research* 38, no. 3 (2001): 290.

66. Lieutenant Colonel Dave Grossman argues for "the existence of a powerful, innate human resistance toward killing one's own species and the psychological mechanisms that have been developed by armies over the centuries to overcome that resistance." Grossman, *On Killing: The Psychological Cost of Learning to Kill in War and Society* (Boston: Little, Brown, 1996), xxix.

67. Vetlesen, *Evil and Human Agency*, 150–51.

68. Grossman, *On Killing*, 4, xxix. Grossman claims that 80 to 85 percent of World War II soldiers did not fire at the enemy (24).

69. Baines, "Complicating Victims and Perpetrators in Uganda," 18.

70. Quoted in Eichstaedt, *First Kill Your Family*, 1–2.

71. Wessells, *Child Soldiers*, 79–80.

72. For more on this subject, see Joanna Bourke, *An Intimate History of Killing: Face-to-Face Killing in Twentieth-Century Warfare* (London: Granta Books, 1999).

73. Honwana, *Child Soldiers in Africa*, 58.

74. Wessells, *Child Soldiers*, 81.

75. Ibid. The Philippine boy soldier is quoted in Unicef, "Adult Wars, Child Soldiers," quoted in ibid., 81.

76. Beah, *Long Way Gone*, 108. Hereafter cited parenthetically in the text.

77. Emmanuel Jal, with Megan Lloyd Davies, *War Child: A Child Soldier's Story* (New York: St. Martin's Press, 2009), 73, 74, 75.

78. Ibid., 90, 141.

79. Wessells, *Child Soldiers*, 141.

80. The staff at Benin House deny that this fight took place.

81. Beah, *Long Way Gone*, 135, 136.

82. Honwana, *Child Soldiers in Africa*, 105, 9–11.

83. Beah, "Ishmael Beah: A Long Way from a Kalashnikov to a Pen."

84. Quoted in Meg Clothier, "No Quiet on the Chechen Front," review of *One Soldier's War in Chechnya*, by Arkady Babchenko, Guardian.co.uk, November 21, 2007, http://www.guardian.co.uk/books/2007/nov/21/biography (accessed May 11, 2009).

85. Babchenko, *One Soldier's War*, 94.

86. Ibid., 108–9.

87. Ibid., 230.

88. The Centre for Nonviolent Action (CNA) is a nongovernmental organization devoted to promoting "cultures of nonviolence and dialogue" in Bosnia-Herzegovina, Croatia, and Serbia. Operating out of offices in Sarajevo and Belgrade, the CNA's projects focus on developing critical thought, encouraging responsibility for society and community, reassessing

attitudes, and accepting diversity. Dealing with the past, the CNA's website explains, necessitates deconstructing enemy images and establishing a "culture of remembrance." Particularly interesting is the organization's work with former combatants in the Balkan conflicts. For further information, see http://www.nenasilje.org/.

89. Centre for Nonviolent Action, "Four Views: How I Found Myself in War; How to Reach Sustainable Peace," Public Forums in Serbia, June 2002, *Vreme*, July 4, 2002, http://www.nenasilje.org/publikacije/4pogleda_e.html, 18 (accessed September 21, 2010).

90. Ibid., 12.

91. Ibid., 13, 14.

92. Arendt, *Origins of Totalitarianism*, 6.

CHAPTER 6

1. The epigraph to this chapter is taken from Hatzfeld, *Life Laid Bare*, 42.

2. Wojciech Tochman, *Like Eating a Stone: Surviving the Past in Bosnia*, trans. Antonia Lloyd-Jones (London: Portobello Books, 2009), 120.

3. See Véronique Dudouet and Beatrix Schmelzle, eds., *Human Rights and Conflict Transformation: The Challenges of Just Peace*, Berghof Handbook Dialogue Series no. 9 (Berlin: Berghof Conflict Research, 2010), http://www.berfhof-handbook.net/dialogue-series/no.-9-human-rights-and-conflict-transformation/.

4. I agree with David Bloomfield that this term is problematic. Bloomfield correctly points out that "conflict issues do not disappear when the fighting ends," but his alternative, "post-violence," is problematic for the same reason. The violence of war or genocide often gives way to other forms of violence after the *worst* violence is over. I use the term "postconflict," fully aware that conflict issues never end and, when dealt with in nonviolent ways, are necessary for politics, to signal the point at which the worst may be over and negotiation and reconstruction become feasible. See David Bloomfield, *On Good Terms: Clarifying Reconciliation*, Berghof Report no. 14 (Berlin: Berghof Conflict Research, 2006), http://www.berghof-conflictresearch.org/en/publications/berghof-reports/ (accessed July 11, 2011).

5. Étienne Balibar, "What is Political Philosophy? Contextual Notes," trans. Catherine Porter and Philip E. Lewis, in *Jacques Rancière: History, Politics, Aesthetics*, ed. Gabriel Rockhill and Philip Watts (Durham: Duke University Press, 2009), 104.

6. For recent scholarship in this field, see Mohammed Abu-Nimer, *Reconciliation, Justice, and Coexistence* (Lanham, Md.: Lexington Books, 2001); David Bloomfield, Teresa Barnes, and Luc Huyse, eds., *Reconciliation After Violent Conflict: A Handbook* (Stockholm: International Institute for Democracy and Electoral Assistance, 2003); Mark Gibney et al., *The Age of Apology: Facing Up to the Past* (University Park: Pennsylvania State University Press, 2008); Trudy Govier, *Taking Wrongs Seriously: Acknowledgment, Reconciliation, and the Politics of Sustainable Peace* (Amherst, N.Y.: Humanity Books, 2006); Martha Minow, *Breaking the Cycles of Hatred: Memory, Law, and Repair* (Princeton: Princeton University Press, 2002); Martha Minow, *Between Vengeance and Forgiveness: Facing History After Genocide and Mass Violence* (Boston: Beacon Press, 1998); Ruti G. Teitel, *Transitional Justice* (Oxford: Oxford University Press, 2000); Eric Stover and Harvey M. Weinstein, eds., *My Neighbor, My Enemy: Justice and Community in the Aftermath of Mass Atrocity* (Cambridge: Cambridge University Press, 2004); and Margaret Urban Walker, *Moral Repair: Reconstructing Moral Relations After Wrongdoing* (Cambridge: Cambridge University Press, 2006).

7. For an excellent discussion of the current problems facing peace and peacebuilding, see Beatrix Schmelzle and Martina Fischer, eds., *Peacebuilding at a Crossroads? Dilemmas and Paths for Another Generation*, Berghof Handbook Dialogue Series no. 7 (Berlin: Berghof

Research Center for Constructive Conflict Management, 2009), http://www.berghof-hand-book.net/dialogue-series/no.-7-peacebuilding-at-a-crossroads (accessed February 10, 2011).

8. Diana Francis, *From Pacification to Peacebuilding: A Call to Global Transformation* (London: Pluto Press, 2010), 76, 168.

9. John Paul Lederach, *Building Peace: Sustainable Reconciliation in Divided Societies* (Washington, D.C.: United States Institute of Peace, 1997), xvi.

10. Simon Fisher and Lada Zimina, "Just Wasting Our Time? Provocative Thoughts for Peacebuilders," in Schmelzle and Fischer, *Peacebuilding at a Crossroads*, 33.

11. Martha Nussbaum, "Equity and Mercy," *Philosophy and Public Affairs* 22, no. 2 (1993): 89n13 (Nussbaum is quoting Aeschylus here, from *Choephoroi* 1.313).

12. Ibid., 89.

13. See Minow, *Between Vengeance and Forgiveness*, 91–92.

14. Govier, *Taking Wrongs Seriously*, 144.

15. See the ICTJ's website at http://ictj.org/.

16. Alex Boraine, "Transitional Justice as an Emerging Field" (paper presented at the "Repairing the Past: Reparations and Transitions to Democracy" symposium, Ottawa, March 2004), http://www.idrc.ca/uploads/user-S/10829975041revised-boraine-ottawa-2004 .pdf (accessed April 27, 2010).

17. See http://ictj.org/.

18. Marie Breen Smyth writes, "Much of the literature on transitional justice, whether located within the field of law or international relations, adopts a legal, retributive justice focus, and is often generated by lawyers." Smyth, *Truth, Recovery, and Justice After Conflict* (New York: Routledge, 2007), 1.

19. Louis Bickford, "Transitional Justice," in *Encyclopedia of Genocide and Crimes Against Humanity*, vol. 3, ed. Dinah Shelton (Macmillan Reference USA, 2004), 1045.

20. Teitel, *Transitional Justice*, 69.

21. Ruti G. Teitel, "The Law and Politics of Contemporary Transitional Justice," *Cornell International Law Journal* 38 (2005): 837, http://papers.ssrn.com/so13/papers.cfm?abstract_ id=943069#%23 (accessed February 14, 2011).

22. Teitel, *Transitional Justice*, 4, 8, 6 (quotation).

23. Like Teitel, the ICTJ understands transitional justice as "a response to systematic or wide-spread violations of human rights"—it is not a "special form of justice but justice adapted to societies transforming themselves after a period of pervasive human rights abuse" (http://ictj .org/). The UN has followed suit, defining transitional justice as "the full range of processes and mechanisms associated with a society's attempts to come to terms with a legacy of large-scale past abuses, in order to ensure accountability, serve justice and achieve reconciliation." See Governance and Social Development Resource Centre, "Transitional Justice," http://www.gsdrc .org/index.cfm?objectid=D1CA8E73-0838-7B7B-AC85F9607F70703D (accessed April 27, 2010).

24. Ian Buruma, "The Joys and Perils of Victimhood," *New York Review of Books*, April 8, 1999, http://www.nybooks.com/articles/archives/1999/apr/08/the-joys-and-perils-of-victimhood/ (accessed February 14, 2011).

25. Laurel E. Fletcher and Harvey M. Weinstein, "Violence and Social Repair: Rethinking the Contribution of Justice to Reconciliation," *Human Rights Quarterly* 24, no. 3 (2002): 588–89, 602, 603 (quotation).

26. Ibid., 589–600.

27. Martha Minow makes a similar point about the Nuremberg trials, which were supposed to act as a deterrent to further mass violence. She argues that the failure of international bodies to craft a legal response to the mass murders in Cambodia, South Africa, and Kurdistan, among many others, casts doubt on the long-term effects of the trials. *Between Vengeance and Forgiveness*, 27–28.

28. Fletcher and Weinstein, "Violence and Social Repair," 591.

29. See http://liveunictr.altmansolutions.com/.

30. Stephanie Nolen, "Africa's Unjust Deserts," *Globe and Mail* (Toronto), June 14, 2008, http://www.theglobeandmail.com/news/world/article690940.ece (accessed August 17, 2010).

31. See the website of the International Criminal Tribunal for Rwanda, at http://www.unictr.org/tabid/101/default.aspx (accessed May 8, 2010).

32. Helena Cobban, "Healing Rwanda: Can an International Court Deliver Justice?" *Boston Review*, December 2003–January 2004, 1–5, http://bostonreview.net/BR28.6/cobban.html (accessed May 8, 2010).

33. Quoted in Nolen, "Africa's Unjust Deserts."

34. David Bloomfield, "Reconciliation: An Introduction," in Bloomfield, Barnes, and Huyse, *Reconciliation After Violent Conflict*, 12.

35. Lederach, *Building Peace*, xvi.

36. Thomas Brudholm, *Resentment's Virtue: Jean Améry and the Refusal to Forgive* (Philadelphia: Temple University Press, 2008), 3.

37. Mahmood Mamdani writes that Wynand Malan's minority report blamed the dehistoricization and decontextualization of apartheid on "the religious messianism of the leadership in the Commission." See Mamdani, "Amnesty or Impunity? A Preliminary Critique of the Report of the Truth and Reconciliation Commission of South Africa (TRC)" *Diacritics* 32, nos. 3–4 (2002): 57.

38. Desmond Tutu, *No Future Without Forgiveness* (New York: Doubleday, 1999), 35.

39. Ibid., 31.

40. Brudholm, *Resentment's Virtue*, 48.

41. Sharon Lamb and Jeffrie G. Murphy, "Introduction: Reasons to Be Cautious About the Use of Forgiveness in Psychotherapy," in *Before Forgiving: Cautionary Views of Forgiveness in Psychotherapy*, ed. Sharon Lamb and Jeffrie G. Murphy (Oxford: Oxford University Press, 2002), 3–9.

42. Walker, *Moral Repair*, 24, 25.

43. Quoted in Jean Hatzfeld, *The Antelope's Strategy: Living in Rwanda After the Genocide*, trans. Linda Coverdale (New York: Farrar, Straus and Giroux, 2009), 18.

44. Brudholm, *Resentment's Virtue*, 48.

45. Bill Puka, "Forgoing Forgiveness," in Lamb and Murphy, *Before Forgiving*, 139–40.

46. Yadh Ben Achour, "The Order of Truth and the Order of Society," in Enwezor et al., *Experiments with Truth*, 130.

47. Trudy Govier, *Forgiveness and Revenge* (New York: Routledge, 2002), 143.

48. Govier, *Taking Wrongs Seriously*, 17–19.

49. Antjie Krog, *Country of My Skull: Guilt, Sorrow, and the Limits of Forgiveness in the New South Africa* (New York: Three Rivers Press, 2000), 385.

50. Ibid., 386.

51. Quoted in Hatzfeld, *Life Laid Bare*, 42–43.

52. Arendt, *Human Condition*, 237. Hereafter cited parenthetically in the text.

53. In the epilogue to *Eichmann in Jerusalem*, Arendt writes, "Because he had been implicated and had played a central role in an enterprise whose open purpose was to eliminate forever certain 'races' from the surface of the earth, he had to be eliminated" (277).

54. Nussbaum, "Equity and Mercy," 125. Hereafter cited parenthetically in the text.

55. Martha Nussbaum, *Upheavals of Thought: The Intelligence of Emotions* (Cambridge: Cambridge University Press, 2001), 301.

56. Seneca *On Mercy* 2.4.4–5.4, in *Seneca: Moral Essays*, trans. John W. Basore, 3 vols. (London: William Heinemann, 1928–35), 1:439.

57. Nussbaum, *Upheavals of Thought*, 302.

58. Ibid., 314–15.

59. Ibid., 319.

60. Nussbaum, "Equity and Mercy," 125.

61. Nenad Vukosavljević, "One Injustice Cannot Be Made by Causing a New One," in *Twenty Pieces of Encouragement for Awakening and Change: Peacebuilding in the Region of the Former Yugoslavia*, ed. Helena Rill, Tamara Smidling, and Ana Bitoljanu (Belgrade-Sarajevo: Centre for Nonviolent Action, 2007), 160, 161.

62. Ibid., 160–61, 155.

CHAPTER 7

1. The first epigraph to this chapter is from Arendt, "Personal Responsibility Under Dictatorship," 45; the second is from Hélène Cixous, "Tancredi Continues," in *Coming to Writing and Other Essays*, ed. Deborah Jenson (Cambridge: Harvard University Press, 1991), 79.

2. Erich Maria Remarque, *All Quiet on the Western Front*, trans. A. W. Wheen (New York: Ballantine Books, 1956), 221. Hereafter cited parenthetically in the text.

3. Dina Kraft, "Gazan Doctor and Peace Advocate Loses Three Daughters to Israeli Fire and Asks Why," http://www.nytimes.com/2009/01/18/world/middleeast/18doctor.html (accessed February 18, 2011).

4. Lucy Ash, "Gaza Doctor's Loss Grips Israelis," BBC World Service, http://news.bbc .co.uk/2/hi/middle_east/7838465.stm (accessed February 18, 2011).

5. Quoted in Izzeldin Abuelaish, *I Shall Not Hate: A Gaza Doctor's Journey* (Toronto: Random House Canada, 2010), 16.

6. Ibid., 189.

7. David Grossman, *Writing in the Dark: Essays on Literature and Politics*, trans. Jessica Cohen (New York: Farrar, Straus and Giroux, 2008), 91. Hereafter cited parenthetically in the text.

8. Archbishop Desmond Tutu to Parents Circle–Families Forum, April 2004, http://www.theparentscircle.com/about.asp (accessed February 18, 2011).

9. This is a reference to *The Lemon Tree*, a film directed by Eran Riklis that tells the story of Salma, a forty-five-year-old widow who lives a simple life alone in a tiny Palestinian village on the West Bank, supported by a small orchard of lemon trees planted by her family generations ago. Her life changes irrevocably when the Israeli minister of defense moves in on the other side of the Green Line, a stone's throw from her orchard, and demands increased security. The lemon trees could hide terrorists, the Israelis insist. A legal battle ensues, and Salma is forced her to cut her lemon trees to a height that kills them. In the end, a "security fence" is built between the properties to protect the defense minister, rendering the death of the lemon trees a senseless display of power. They could have been left to grow and sustain Salma's humble, challenging, but not unpleasant existence. She loses all, but the defense minister also loses. Fear is his prison.

10. Grossman, *Writing in the Dark*, 25–26.

11. Cixous, "Tancredi Continues," 79.

12. Grossman, *Writing in the Dark*, 36.

13. Ibid., 37, 51.

14. Ibid., 52.

15. We could refer in particular to Jürgen Habermas, Edmund Husserl, Maurice Merleau-Ponty, and Edith Stein.

16. Arendt, *Origins of Totalitarianism*, 300; see also 295–96.

17. Giorgio Agamben, *Homo Sacer: Sovereign Power and Bare Life*, trans. Daniel Heller-Roazen (Stanford: Stanford University Press, 1998), 71ff.

18. Ibid., 185.

19. Giorgio Agamben, *The Coming Community*, trans. Michael Hardt (Minneapolis: University of Minnesota Press, 1993), 85–87.

20. Agamben, *Homo Sacer*, 9.

21. The general reluctance to consider nonviolence seriously these days is no doubt the consequence of an increasingly militarized culture, but it may also have something to do with the utopian connotations of the word *peace*. In some academic quarters this may stem from concerns over consensus and unity that dogged European thinkers who witnessed the totalitarianism and fascism of the twentieth century. I prefer the term nonviolence over peace, with the caveat that nonviolence does not mean the absence of conflict. To be nonviolent is to refuse to engage in actions of physical force that cause harm to others.

22. Judith Butler, *Frames of War: When Is Life Grievable?* (London: Verso, 2009), 25–26, 32.

23. I have addressed this further in a review essay of *Frames of War*. See Diane Enns, "When Is a Book Grievable?" *Postmodern Culture* 20, no. 2 (January 2010), http://www.muse.jhu.edu/login?uri=/journals/postmodern_culture/v020/20.2.enns.html.

24. Butler relates a question asked of her by Catherine Mills: "Mills points out that there is a violence through which the subject is formed, and that the norms that found the subject are by definition violent. She asks how, then, if this is the case, I can make a call for nonviolence." Quoted in *Frames of War*, 167.

25. Ibid., 165, 182.

26. Žižek, *Violence*, 217.

27. Partha Chatterjee, *The Politics of the Governed: Reflections on Popular Politics in Most of the World* (New York: Columbia University Press, 2004), 40.

28. See Sandro Mezzadra, "Citizenship in Motion," http://www.makeworlds.org/node/83 (accessed February 17, 2011).

29. Rancière, *Disagreement*.

30. Václav Havel, "The Power of the Powerless," in Havel, *Open Letters: Selected Writings, 1965–1990*, ed. and trans. Paul Wilson (New York: Vintage Books, 1992), 153.

31. Ibid., 161.

32. *Writing in the Dark* is the title of David Grossman's collection of essays on literature and politics.

33. Agamben, "Security and Terror."

34. Balibar, *We, the People of Europe*, 132.

35. Mamdani, *When Victims Become Killers*, 271–72. I refer to survivor's justice in chapter 2.

36. Ibid., 279, 280.

37. Grossman, *Writing in the Dark*, 50.

38. Étienne Balibar and Sandro Mezzadra, "Borders, Citizenship, War, Class: A Discussion with Étienne Balibar and Sandro Mezzadra," by Manuela Bojadžijev and Isabelle Saint-Saëns, *New Formations* 58, no. 1 (2006): 27.

39. These are the words of Goran Božičević, who has been active in peace work in Croatia since 1993 and who participated in a peacebuilding workshop on the relationship between international and local peacebuilding efforts in Sarajevo in June 2010. There is a similar need in Rwanda. Consider an anecdote related to me by a Canadian who spent from 2005 to 2008 teaching in a Rwandan elementary school. In an essay that explores how to teach history and critical thinking after genocide, Catherine Twizere writes of the confusion her students experienced when asked questions that required more than mere reading comprehension. In one case, students had read about Ruby Bridges, the first African American child to attend an all-white school in the American South. It was a straightforward story with familiar vocabulary, Twizere tells us, yet when asked on an exam "why was the crowd shouting at Ruby?" only a handful out of about 180 students ventured an opinion. Most answered by quoting a line

from the text: "The crowd shouted at Ruby as they pushed and shoved." Twizere concludes, "I came to understand that the students had hardly ever been asked questions that demanded simple interpretation before." Twizere, "Thinking About History: Adopting Critical Thinking Methods in Post-Conflict History Classrooms" (research paper, Institute on Globalization and the Human Condition, McMaster University, Hamilton, Ontario, 201c).

40. Boris Buden, "Truth and Reconciliation Are Not What We Really Need," in Enwezor et al., *Experiments with Truth*, 78.

41. Buruma, "Joys and Perils of Victimhood."

42. Arendt, *Origins of Totalitarianism*, 301.

43. The original line is: "To be capable of friendship, to be able to honor in the friend the enemy he can become, is a sign of freedom." Derrida, *Politics of Friendship*, 282.

44. Havel, "Power of the Powerless," 214.

BIBLIOGRAPHY

Abuelaish, Izzeldin. *I Shall Not Hate: A Gaza Doctor's Journey.* Toronto: Random House Canada, 2010.

Abu-Nimer, Mohammed. *Reconciliation, Justice, and Coexistence.* Lanham, Md.: Lexington Books, 2001.

Achvarina, Vera, and Simon F. Reich. "No Place to Hide: Refugees, Displaced Persons, and the Recruitment of Child Soldiers." *International Security* 31, no. 1 (2006): 127–64.

Agamben, Giorgio. *The Coming Community.* Translated by Michael Hardt. Minneapolis: University of Minnesota Press, 1993.

———. *Homo Sacer: Sovereign Power and Bare Life.* Translated by Daniel Heller-Roazen. Stanford: Stanford University Press, 1998.

———. "Security and Terror." Translated by Carolin Emcke. *Theory and Event* 5, no. 4 (2001). http://muse.jhu.edu/login?uri=/journals/theory_and_event/v005/5.4agamben.html (accessed February 12, 2011).

Améry, Jean. *At the Mind's Limits: Contemplations by a Survivor on Auschwitz and Its Realities.* Translated by Sidney Rosenfeld and Stella P. Rosenfeld. Bloomington: Indiana University Press, 1980.

———. *On Suicide: A Discourse on Voluntary Death.* Translated by John D. Barlow. Bloomington: Indiana University Press, 1999.

Arendt, Hannah. *Between Past and Future: Eight Exercises in Political Thought.* New York: Penguin Books, 1993.

———. *Eichmann in Jerusalem: A Report on the Banality of Evil.* New York: Penguin Books, 1977.

———. *The Human Condition.* Chicago: University of Chicago Press, 1989.

———. *The Jew as Pariah: Jewish Identity and Politics in the Modern Age.* Edited by Ron Feldman. New York: Grove Press, 1978.

———. *The Jewish Writings.* Edited by Jerome Kohn and Ron Feldman. New York: Schocken Books, 2007.

———. *Lectures on Kant's Political Philosophy.* Edited and with an interpretive essay by Ronald Beiner. Chicago: University of Chicago Press, 1992.

———. *The Life of the Mind.* London: Harcourt, 1978.

———. *Men in Dark Times.* Translated by Clara Winston and Richard Winston. New York: Harcourt Brace, 1968.

———. *On Violence.* New York: Harcourt Brace, 1969.

———. *The Origins of Totalitarianism.* New ed. New York: Harcourt Brace, 1973.

———. *Responsibility and Judgment.* Edited by Jerome Kohn. New York: Schocken Books, 2003.

Aristotle. *The Nicomachean Ethics.* Translated by David Ross. Oxford: Oxford University Press, 1998.

Aschheim, Steven E. *Hannah Arendt in Jerusalem.* Berkeley and Los Angeles: University of California Press, 2001.

Babchenko, Arkady. *One Soldier's War.* Translated by Nick Allen. New York: Grove Press, 2006.

Baines, Erin. "Complicating Victims and Perpetrators in Uganda: On Dominic Ongwen." *Field Note 7* (July 2008). http://www.justiceandreconciliation.com/#/publications/4540226079 (accessed April 5, 2010).

Balibar, Étienne. "Universalité de la cause palestinienne." *Le Monde Diplomatique* (Paris), May 2004. http://www.monde-diplomatique.fr/2004/05/BALIBAR/11174 (accessed February 12, 2011).

———. *We, the People of Europe? Reflections on Transnational Citizenship.* Translated by James Swenson. Princeton: Princeton University Press, 2004.

———. "What Is Political Philosophy? Contextual Notes." Translated by Catherine Porter and Philip E. Lewis. In *Jacques Rancière: History, Politics, Aesthetics,* ed. Gabriel Rockhill and Philip Watts, 95–105. Durham: Duke University Press, 2009.

Balibar, Étienne, and Sandro Mezzadra. "Borders, Citizenship, War, Class: A Discussion with Étienne Balibar and Sandro Mezzadra." By Manuela Bojadžijev and Isabelle Saint-Saëns. *New Formations* 58, no. 1 (2006): 10–30.

Bannerji, Himani. *The Dark Side of the Nation: Essays on Multiculturalism, Nationalism, and Gender.* Toronto: Canadian Scholars' Press, 2000.

Bayer, Christophe Pierre, Fionna Klasen, and Hubertus Adam. "Association of Trauma and PTSD Symptoms with Openness to Reconciliation and Feelings of Revenge Among Former Ugandan and Congolese Child Soldiers." *Journal of the American Medical Association* 298, no. 5 (2007): 555–59. http://www.ncbi.nlm.nih.gov/pubmed/17666676 (accessed February 11, 2011).

Beah, Ishmael. "Ishmael Beah: A Long Way from a Kalashnikov to a Pen." Interview by Damien Roustel. Translated by Jonathan Pierrel. *L'Humanité* (Saint-Denis, France), February 22, 2008. http://humaniteinenglish.com/spip.php?article840 (accessed February 11, 2011).

———. *A Long Way Gone: Memoirs of a Boy Soldier.* New York: Farrar, Straus and Giroux, 2007.

Beauvoir, Simone de. *The Second Sex.* Translated by Constance Borde and Sheila Malovany-Chevallier. New York: Knopf, 2009.

Beiner, Ronald. "Hannah Arendt on Judging." In Hannah Arendt, *Lectures on Kant's Political Philosophy,* ed. Ronald Beiner, 89–156. Chicago: University of Chicago Press, 1992.

Ben Achour, Yadh. "The Order of Truth and the Order of Society." In *Experiments with Truth: Transitional Justice and the Processes of Truth and Reconciliation, Documenta11_Platform2,* ed. Okwui Enwezor, Carlos Basualdo, Ute Meta Bauer, Susanne Ghez, Sarat Maharaj, Mark Nash, and Octavio Zaya, 123–34. Ostfildern-Ruit, Germany: Hatje Cantz, 2002.

Benjamin, Walter. "Critique of Violence." Translated by Edmund Jephcott. In Benjamin, *Selected Writings,* vol. 1, *1913–1926,* 236–52. Cambridge: Belknap Press of Harvard University Press, 1996.

Bernstein, Richard J. *Hannah Arendt and the Jewish Question.* Cambridge: MIT Press, 1996.

———. *Radical Evil: A Philosophical Interrogation.* Cambridge: Polity Press, 2002.

Bickford, Louis. "Transitional Justice." In *Encyclopedia of Genocide and Crimes Against Humanity,* vol. 3, ed. Dinah Shelton, 1045–47. Macmillan Reference USA, 2004.

Bloomfield, David. *On Good Terms: Clarifying Reconciliation.* Berghof Report no. 14. Berlin: Berghof Conflict Research, 2006. http://www.berghof-conflictresearch.org/en/publications/berghof-reports/ (accessed July 11, 2011).

Bloomfield, David, Teresa Barnes, and Luc Huyse, eds. *Reconciliation After Violent Conflict: A Handbook.* Stockholm: International Institute for Democracy and Electoral Assistance, 2003.

Boraine, Alex. "Transitional Justice as an Emerging Field." Paper presented at the "Repairing the Past: Reparations and Transitions to Democracy" symposium, Ottawa, March 2004. http://www.idrc.ca/uploads/user-S/10829975041revised-boraine-ottawa-2004.pdf (accessed April 27, 2010).

Bouris, Erica. *Complex Political Victims.* Bloomfield, Conn.: Kumarian Press, 2007.

Bourke, Joanna. *An Intimate History of Killing: Face-to-Face Killing in Twentieth-Century Warfare.* London: Granta Books, 1999.

Bradshaw, Leah. *Acting and Thinking: The Political Thought of Hannah Arendt.* Toronto: University of Toronto Press, 1989.

Brauman, Rony, and Eyal Sivan. *Eloge de la désobéissance.* Paris: Le Pommier, 1999.

Brison, Susan J. *Aftermath: Violence and the Remaking of a Self.* Princeton: Princeton University Press, 2003.

Brown, Wendy. "The Impossibility of Women's Studies." In Brown, *Edgework: Critical Essays on Knowledge and Politics,* 116–36. Princeton: Princeton University Press, 2005.

———. *States of Injury: Power and Freedom in Late Modernity.* Princeton: Princeton University Press, 1995.

Brownmiller, Susan. *Against Our Will.* New York: Ballantine Books, 1971.

Brudholm, Thomas. *Resentment's Virtue: Jean Améry and the Refusal to Forgive.* Philadelphia: Temple University Press, 2008.

Buden, Boris. "Truth and Reconciliation Are Not What We Really Need." In *Experiments with Truth: Transitional Justice and the Processes of Truth and Reconciliation, Documenta11_Platform2,* ed. Okwui Enwezor, Carlos Basualdo, Ute Meta Bauer, Susanne Ghez, Sarat Maharaj, Mark Nash, and Octavio Zaya, 65–78. Ostfildern-Ruit, Germany: Hatje Cantz, 2002.

Bumiller, Kristin. *In an Abusive State: How Neoliberalism Appropriated the Feminist Movement Against Sexual Violence.* Durham: Duke University Press, 2008.

Burg, Avraham. *The Holocaust Is Over; We Must Rise from Its Ashes.* New York: Palgrave Macmillan, 2008.

Buruma, Ian. "The Joys and Perils of Victimhood." *New York Review of Books,* April 8, 1999. http://www.nybooks.com/articles/archives/1999/apr/08/the-joys-and-perils-of-victimhood/ (accessed February 14, 2011).

Butler, Judith. *Frames of War: When Is Life Grievable?* London: Verso, 2009.

Caruth, Cathy, ed. *Trauma: Explorations in Memory.* Baltimore: Johns Hopkins University Press, 1995.

Centre for Nonviolent Action. "Four Views: How I Found Myself in War; How to Reach Sustainable Peace." Public Forums in Serbia, June 2002. *Vreme,* July 4, 2002. http://www.nenasilje.org/publikacije/4pogleda (accessed September 21, 2010).

Chatterjee, Partha. *The Politics of the Governed: Reflections on Popular Politics in Most of the World.* New York: Columbia University Press, 2004.

Chaumont, Jean-Michel. *La concurrence des victimes: Génocide, identité, reconnaissance.* Paris: La Découverte, 2002.

Cheng, Anne Anlin. *The Melancholy of Race: Psychoanalysis, Assimilation, and Hidden Grief.* Oxford: Oxford University Press, 2001.

Cixous, Hélène. "Tancredi Continues." In Cixous, *Coming to Writing and Other Essays,* ed. Deborah Jenson, 78–103. Cambridge: Harvard University Press, 1991.

Clothier, Meg. "No Quiet on the Chechen Front." Review of *One Soldier's War in Chechnya,* by Arkady Babchenko. Guardian.co.uk, November 21, 2007. http://www.guardian.co.uk/books/2007/nov/21/biography (accessed May 11, 2009).

Coalition to Stop the Use of Child Soldiers. *Child Soldiers Global Report 2008.* http://www.childsoldiersglobalreport.org/ (accessed February 7, 2011).

Cobban, Helena. "Healing Rwanda: Can an International Court Deliver Justice?" *Boston Review*, December 2003–January 2004, 1–5. http://bostonreview.net/BR28.6/cobban .html (accessed May 8, 2010).

Cole, Alyson M. *The Cult of True Victimhood: From the War on Welfare to the War on Terror*. Stanford: Stanford University Press, 2007.

Cottee, Simon R. "Excusing Terror." *Journal of Human Rights* 5 (2006): 149–62.

Darraj, Faisal. "Ethics of Resistance." Open letter to Étienne Balibar. *Al-Ahram Weekly*, May 2–8, 2002. http://weekly.ahram.org.eg/2002/584/op2.htm (accessed February 10, 2011).

Deleuze, Gilles, and Michel Foucault. "Intellectuals and Power." In Michel Foucault, *Language, Counter-Memory, Practice: Selected Essays and Interviews*, ed. Donald F. Bouchard, trans. Donald F. Bouchard and Sherry Simon, 205–17. Ithaca: Cornell University Press, 1977.

Derrida, Jacques. *Negotiations: Interventions and Interviews, 1971–2001*. Edited and translated by Elizabeth G. Rottenberg. Stanford: Stanford University Press, 2002.

———. *Politics of Friendship*. Translated by George Collins. London: Verso, 1997.

———. *Rogues: Two Essays on Reason*. Translated by Pascale-Anne Brault and Michael Naas. Stanford: Stanford University Press, 2004.

———. *Specters of Marx: The State of the Debt, the Work of Mourning, and the New International*. Translated by Peggy Kamuf. New York: Routledge, 1994.

———. "Violence and Metaphysics: An Essay on the Thought of Emmanuel Levinas." In Derrida, *Writing and Difference*, trans. Alan Bass, 79–153. Chicago: University of Chicago Press, 1978.

Derrida, Jacques, and Elisabeth Roudinesco. *For What Tomorrow . . . : A Dialogue*. Translated by Jeff Fort. Stanford: Stanford University Press, 2004.

Deutscher, Max. *Judgment After Arendt*. Burlington, Vt.: Ashgate, 2007.

Du Bois, W. E. B. *The Souls of Black Folk*. New York: New American Library, 1969.

Dudouet, Véronique, and Beatrix Schmelzle, eds. *Human Rights and Conflict Transformation: The Challenges of Just Peace*. Berghof Handbook Dialogue Series no. 9. Berlin: Berghof Conflict Research, 2010. http://www.berfhof-handbook.net/dialogue-series/ no.-9-human-rights-and-conflict-transformation/.

Dussel, Enrique. *Filosofiá de la liberación*. 3d ed. Buenos Aires: Ediciones La Aurora, 1985.

Dyer, Gwynne. *War*. Toronto: Vintage Canada, 2005.

Eddon, Raluca Munteanu. "Gershom Scholem, Hannah Arendt, and the Paradox of 'Non-Nationalist' Nationalism." *Journal of Jewish Thought and Philosophy* 2, no. 1 (2003): 55–68.

Eggers, Dave. *What Is the What: The Autobiography of Valentino Achak Deng*. Toronto: Vintage Canada, 2006.

Eichstaedt, Peter. *First Kill Your Family: Child Soldiers of Uganda and the Lord's Resistance Army*. Chicago: Lawrence Hill Books, 2009.

Ellison, Ralph. *Invisible Man*. New York: Vintage, 1990.

El-Sarraj, Eyad. "Suicide Bombers: Dignity, Despair, and the Need for Hope." *Journal of Palestine Studies* 31, no. 4 (2002): 71–76.

Enns, Diane. "Beyond Derrida: The Autoimmunity of Deconstruction." *Symposium: Canadian Journal of Continental Philosophy* 11, no. 1 (2007): 121–40.

———. "A Conversation with Étienne Balibar." *Symposium: Canadian Journal of Continental Philosophy* 9, no. 2 (2005): 375–99.

———. *Speaking of Freedom: Philosophy, Politics, and the Struggle for Liberation*. Stanford: Stanford University Press, 2007.

———. "When Is a Book Grievable?" Review of *Frames of War*, by Judith Butler. *Postmodern Culture* 20, no. 2 (2010). http://www.muse.jhu.edu/login?uri=/journals/postmodern_ culture/v020/20.2.enns.html.

Enwezor, Okwui, Carlos Basualdo, Ute Meta Bauer, Susanne Ghez, Sarat Maharaj, Mark Nash, and Octavio Zaya, eds. *Experiments with Truth: Transitional Justice and the Processes of Truth and Reconciliation, Documenta 11_Platform 2.* Ostfildern-Ruit, Germany: Hatje Cantz, 2002.

Esteva, Gustavo, and Madhu Suri Prakash. *Grassroots Post-Modernism: Remaking the Soil of Cultures.* London: Zed Books, 1998.

Ezra, Michael. "The Eichmann Polemics: Hannah Arendt and Her Critics." *Democratiya* 9 (Summer 2007): 141–65.

Fanon, Frantz. *Black Skin, White Masks.* Translated by Charles L. Markmann. New York: Grove Press, 1967.

———. *The Wretched of the Earth.* Translated by Richard Philcox. New York: Grove Press, 2004.

Fassin, Didier, and Richard Rechtman. *The Empire of Trauma: An Inquiry into the Condition of Victimhood.* Translated by Rachel Gomme. Princeton: Princeton University Press, 2009.

Fisher, Simon, and Lada Zimina. "Just Wasting Our Time? Provocative Thoughts for Peacebuilders." In *Peacebuilding at a Crossroads? Dilemmas and Paths for Another Generation*, ed. Beatrix Schmelzle and Martina Fischer, 11–35. Berghof Handbook Dialogue Series no. 7. Berlin: Berghof Research Center for Constructive Conflict Management, 2009. http://www.berghof-handbook.net/dialogue-series/no.-7-peacebuilding-at-a-crossroads (accessed February 10, 2011).

Fletcher, Laurel E., and Harvey M. Weinstein. "Violence and Social Repair: Rethinking the Contribution of Justice to Reconciliation." *Human Rights Quarterly* 24, no. 3 (2002): 573–639.

Foucault, Michel. Preface to *Anti-Oedipus: Capitalism and Schizophrenia*, by Gilles Deleuze and Félix Guattari, trans. Robert Hurley, Mark Seem, and Helen R. Lane, xiii–xvi. New York: Viking Press, 1977.

———. "Truth, Power, Self: An Interview with Michel Foucault." By Martin Rue. In *Technologies of the Self*, ed. Luther H. Martin, Huck Gutman, and Patrick Hutton, 9–15. Amherst: University of Massachusetts Press, 1988.

Francis, Diana. *From Pacification to Peacebuilding: A Call to Global Transformation.* London: Pluto Press, 2010.

Freud, Sigmund. "Mourning and Melancholia." In *The Standard Edition of the Complete Psychological Works of Sigmund Freud*, vol. 14, *1914–1916: On the History of the Psychoanalytic Movement, Papers on Metapsychology, and Other Works*, trans. James Strachey, 237–58. London: Hogarth Press, 1957.

Friedan, Betty. *The Feminine Mystique.* New York: W. W. Norton, 1963.

———. *"It Changed My Life": Writings on the Women's Movement.* Cambridge: Harvard University Press, 1998.

Gibney, Mark, Rhoda E. Howard-Hassmann, Jean-Marc Coicaud, and Niklaus Steiner. *The Age of Apology: Facing Up to the Past.* University Park: Pennsylvania State University Press, 2008.

Gilroy, Paul. *The Black Atlantic: Modernity and Double Consciousness.* Cambridge: Harvard University Press, 1993.

———. *Postcolonial Melancholia.* New York: Columbia University Press, 2005.

Governance and Social Development Resource Centre. "Transitional Justice." http://www.gsdrc.org/index.cfm?objectid=D1CA8E73-0838-7B7B-AC85F96C7F70703D (accessed April 27, 2010).

Govier, Trudy. *Forgiveness and Revenge.* New York: Routledge, 2002.

———. *Taking Wrongs Seriously: Acknowledgment, Reconciliation, and the Politics of Sustainable Peace.* Amherst, N.Y.: Humanity Books, 2006.

Greif, Mark. "Arendt's Judgment." *Dissent* (Spring 2004). http://www.dissentmagazine.org/article/?article=388 (accessed February 10, 2011).

Grossman, Dave. *On Killing: The Psychological Cost of Learning to Kill in War and Society.* Boston: Little, Brown, 1996.

Grossman, David. *Writing in the Dark: Essays on Literature and Politics.* Translated by Jessica Cohen. New York: Farrar, Straus and Giroux, 2008.

Hage, Ghassan. "'Comes a time we are all enthusiasm': Understanding Palestinian Suicide Bombers in Times of Exighophobia." *Public Culture* 15, no. 1 (2003): 65–89.

Halper, Jeff. *An Israeli in Palestine: Resisting Dispossession, Redeeming Israel.* London: Pluto Press, 2008.

———. *Obstacles to Peace: A Re-framing of the Palestinian-Israeli Conflict.* Jerusalem: Israeli Committee Against House Demolitions, 2009.

———. "Reframing the Israel/Palestine Conflict." Lecture, McMaster University, Hamilton, Ontario, January 21, 2009.

Hammer, Joshua. *A Season in Bethlehem.* New York: Free Press, 2003.

Hatzfeld, Jean. *The Antelope's Strategy: Living in Rwanda After the Genocide.* Translated by Linda Coverdale. New York: Farrar, Straus and Giroux, 2009.

———. *Life Laid Bare: The Survivors in Rwanda Speak.* Translated by Linda Coverdale. New York: Other Press, 2007.

Havel, Václav. "The Power of the Powerless." In Havel, *Open Letters: Selected Writings, 1965–1990,* ed. and trans. Paul Wilson, 125–214. New York: Vintage Books, 1992.

Hegel, G. W. F. *The Phenomenology of Spirit.* Translated by A. V. Miller. Oxford: Oxford University Press, 1977.

Herman, Judith Lewis. *Trauma and Recovery.* New York: Basic Books, 1992.

Honderich, Ted. "Obligations to the Future: Palestinian Terrorism, Morality, and Germany." *Counterpunch,* October 25, 2003. http://www.counterpunch.com/honderich10252003.html (accessed October 19, 2008).

———. "Terrorism for Humanity." Lecture given at the International Social Philosophy Conference at Northeastern University, Boston, revised March 4, 2004. http://www.ucl.ac.uk/~uctytho/terrforhum.html (accessed September 12, 2010).

Honwana, Alcinda. *Child Soldiers in Africa.* Philadelphia: University of Pennsylvania Press, 2006.

hooks, bell. *Outlaw Culture.* New York: Routledge, 1994.

Ignatieff, Michael. *The Lesser Evil: Political Ethics in an Age of Terror.* Princeton: Princeton University Press, 2004.

Illouz, Eva. *Oprah Winfrey and the Glamour of Misery: An Essay on Popular Culture.* New York: Columbia University Press, 2003.

Irigaray, Luce. *This Sex Which Is Not One.* Translated by Catherine Porter. Ithaca: Cornell University Press, 1985.

Jal, Emmanuel, with Megan Lloyd Davies. *War Child: A Child Soldier's Story.* New York: St. Martin's Press, 2009.

Karanja, Stephen Kabera. "Child Soldiers in Peace Agreements: The Peace and Justice Dilemma!" *Global Jurist* 8, no. 3 (2008): 1–39.

Khanna, Ranjana. *Dark Continents: Psychoanalysis and Colonialism.* Durham: Duke University Press, 2003.

Kimmerling, Baruch. "Israel's Culture of Martyrdom." *Nation,* December 22, 2004. http://www.thenation.com/doc/20050110/kimmerling/print (accessed February 26, 2009).

Krog, Antjie. *Country of My Skull: Guilt, Sorrow, and the Limits of Forgiveness in the New South Africa.* New York: Three Rivers Press, 2000.

Lamb, Sharon, and Jeffrie G. Murphy, eds. *Before Forgiving: Cautionary Views of Forgiveness in Psychotherapy.* Oxford: Oxford University Press, 2002.

Lederach, John Paul. *Building Peace: Sustainable Reconciliation in Divided Societies.* Washington, D.C.: United States Institute of Peace, 1997.

Levinas, Emmanuel. *Otherwise Than Being: Or Beyond Essence.* Translated by Alphonso Lingis. Pittsburgh: Duquesne University Press, 1981.

———. "Substitution." In Levinas, *Basic Philosophical Writings*, trans. Adrian T. Peperzak, Simon Critchley, and Robert Bernasconi, 79–96. Bloomington: Indiana University Press, 1996.

———. *Totality and Infinity: An Essay on Exteriority.* Translated by Alphonso Lingis. Pittsburgh: Duquesne University Press, 1969.

Leys, Ruth. *Trauma: A Genealogy.* Chicago: University of Chicago Press, 2000.

London, Charles. *One Day the Soldiers Came: Voices of Children in War.* New York: HarperCollins, 2007.

Machel, Graça. *Impact of Armed Conflict on Children.* http://www.unicef.org/graca (accessed February 11, 2011).

Mamdani, Mahmood. "Amnesty or Impunity? A Preliminary Critique of the Report of the Truth and Reconciliation Commission of South Africa (TRC)." *Diacritics* 32, nos. 3–4 (2002): 33–59.

———. "Making Sense of Political Violence in Postcolonial Africa." In *Experiments with Truth: Transitional Justice and the Processes of Truth and Reconciliation, Documenta11_Platform2*, ed. Okwui Enwezor, Carlos Basualdo, Ute Meta Bauer, Susanne Ghez, Sarat Maharaj, Mark Nash, and Octavio Zaya, 21–42. Ostfildern-Ruit. Germany: Hatje Cantz, 2002.

———. *When Victims Become Killers: Colonialism, Nativism, and the Genocide in Rwanda.* Princeton: Princeton University Press, 2001.

May, Todd. *The Political Thought of Jacques Rancière: Creating Equality.* University Park: Pennsylvania State University Press, 2008.

———. *Reconsidering Difference: Nancy, Derrida, Levinas, Deleuze.* University Park: Pennsylvania State University Press, 1997.

Mezzadra, Sandro. "Citizenship in Motion." http://www.makeworlds.org/node/83 (accessed February 17, 2011).

Miall, Hugh. *The Peacemakers: Peaceful Settlement of Disputes Since 1945.* London: Macmillan, 1992.

Miall, Hugh, Oliver Ramsbotham, and Tom Woodhouse, eds. *Contemporary Conflict Resolution.* Cambridge: Polity Press, 1999.

Miller, Susan L. *Victims as Offenders: The Paradox of Women's Violence in Relationships.* New Brunswick: Rutgers University Press, 2005.

Minow, Martha. *Between Vengeance and Forgiveness: Facing History After Genocide and Mass Violence.* Boston: Beacon Press, 1998.

———. *Breaking the Cycles of Hatred: Memory, Law, and Repair.* Princeton: Princeton University Press, 2002.

Mohanty, Chandra Talpade. *Feminism Without Borders: Decolonizing Theory, Practicing Solidarity.* Durham: Duke University Press, 2003.

Naqvi, Fatima. *The Literary and Cultural Rhetoric of Victimhood: Western Europe, 1970–2005.* New York: Palgrave Macmillan, 2007.

Nietzsche, Friedrich. *Beyond Good and Evil: Prelude to a Philosophy of the Future.* Translated by Walter Kaufmann. New York: Vintage Books, 1989.

———. *On the Genealogy of Morals and Ecce Homo.* Translated by Walter Kaufmann and R. J. Hollingdale. New York: Random House, 1967.

Nussbaum, Martha. "Equity and Mercy." *Philosophy and Public Affairs* 22, no. 2 (1993): 83–125.

———. *Upheavals of Thought: The Intelligence of Emotions.* Cambridge: Cambridge University Press, 2001.

Oliver, Kelly. *The Colonization of Psychic Space: A Psychoanalytic Social Theory of Oppression.* Minneapolis: University of Minnesota Press, 2004.

Pearlman, Wendy. *Occupied Voices: Stories of Everyday Life from the Second Intifada.* New York: Thunder's Mouth Press/Nation Books, 2003.

Puka, Bill. "Forgoing Forgiveness." In *Before Forgiving: Cautionary Views of Forgiveness in Psychotherapy,* ed. Sharon Lamb and Jeffrie G. Murphy, 136–53. Oxford: Oxford University Press, 2002.

Rancière, Jacques. *Disagreement: Politics and Philosophy.* Translated by Julie Rose. Minneapolis: University of Minnesota Press, 1999.

Remarque, Erich Maria. *All Quiet on the Western Front.* Translated by A. W. Wheen. New York: Ballantine Books, 1956.

Rill, Helena, Tamara Smidling, and Ana Bitoljanu, eds. *Twenty Pieces of Encouragement for Awakening and Change: Peacebuilding in the Region of the Former Yugoslavia.* Belgrade-Sarajevo: Centre for Nonviolent Action, 2007.

Rose, Jacqueline. *The Last Resistance.* London: Verso, 2007.

Rosen, David M. *Armies of the Young: Child Soldiers in War and Terrorism.* New Brunswick: Rutgers University Press, 2005.

———. "Child Soldiers, International Humanitarian Law, and the Globalization of Childhood." *American Anthropologist* 109, no. 2 (2007): 296–306.

Roth, Benita. *Separate Roads to Feminism: Black, Chicana, and White Feminist Movements in America's Second Wave.* Cambridge: Cambridge University Press, 2004.

Rothman, Jay, and Marie L. Olson. "From Interests to Identities: Towards a New Emphasis in Interactive Conflict Resolution." *Journal of Peace Research* 38, no. 3 (2001): 289–305.

Rounding, Virginia. "A Touch of Tolstoy in Russia's Vietnam." Review of *One Soldier's War,* by Arkady Babchenko, translated by Nick Allen. *Independent,* November 9, 2007. http://www.independent.co.uk/arts-entertainment/books/reviews/one-soldiers-war-in-chechnya-by-arkady-babchenko-trans-nick-allen-399565.html (accessed May 18, 2009).

Ruti, Mari. *A World of Fragile Things: Psychoanalysis and the Art of Living.* Albany: State University of New York Press, 2009.

Scherrer, Christian. *Ethno-Nationalismus als globales Phänomen: Zur Krise der Staaten in der Dritten Welt und der früheren UDSSR.* Duisburg, Germany: Gerhard-Mercator-Universität, 1994.

Schmelzle, Beatrix, and Martina Fischer, eds. *Peacebuilding at a Crossroads? Dilemmas and Paths for Another Generation.* Berghof Handbook Dialogue Series no. 7. Berlin: Berghof Research Center for Constructive Conflict Management, 2009. http://www.berghof-handbook.net/dialogue-series/no.-7-peacebuilding-at-a-crossroads (accessed February 10, 2011).

Schutte, Ofelia. *Cultural Identity and Social Liberation in Latin American Thought.* New York: State University of New York Press, 1993.

Sherman, Gabriel. "The Fog of Memoir: The Feud over the Truthfulness of Ishmael Beah's *A Long Way Gone.*" *Slate,* March 6, 2008. http://www.slate.com/id/2185928 (accessed March 28, 2010).

Sivan, Eyal. "Archive Images: Truth or Memory? The Case of Adolf Eichmann's Trial." In *Experiments with Truth: Documentaii_Platform2,* ed. Okwui Enwezor, Carlos Basualdo, Ute Meta Bauer, Susanne Ghez, Sarat Maharaj, Mark Nash, and Octavio Zaya, 277–88. Ostfildern-Ruit, Germany: Hatje Cantz, 2002.

Smyth, Marie Breen. *Truth, Recovery, and Justice After Conflict.* New York: Routledge, 2007.

Spivak, Gayatri Chakravorty. *The Postcolonial Critic: Interviews, Strategies, Dialogues.* Edited by Sarah Harasym. New York: Routledge, 1990.

Staub, Erwin. *The Psychology of Good and Evil: Why Children, Adults, and Groups Help and Harm Others*. Cambridge: Cambridge University Press, 2003.

Steinberger, Peter J. "Hannah Arendt on Judgment." *American Journal of Political Science* 34, no. 3 (1990): 803–21.

Stover, Eric, and Harvey M. Weinstein, eds. *My Neighbor, My Enemy: Justice and Community in the Aftermath of Mass Atrocity*. Cambridge: Cambridge University Press, 2004.

Suleri, Sara. "Woman Skin Deep: Feminism and the Postcolonial Condition." *Critical Inquiry* 18 (1992): 756–69.

Survey of War Affected Youth. "The Abduction and Return Experiences of Youth." SWAY Research Brief 1, April 2006. http://chrisblattman.com/documents/policy/sway/SWAY.RB1.pdf (accessed February 14, 2011).

Sykes, Charles. *A Nation of Victims: The Decay of the American Character*. New York: St. Martin's Press, 1992.

Taylor, Kathleen. *Cruelty: Human Evil and the Human Brain*. Oxford: Oxford University Press, 2009.

Teitel, Ruti G. "The Law and Politics of Contemporary Transitional Justice." *Cornell International Law Journal* 38 (2005). http://papers.ssrn.com/so13/papers.cfm?abstract_id=943069#%23 (accessed February 14, 2011).

———. *Transitional Justice*. Oxford: Oxford University Press, 2000.

Tochman, Wojciech. *Like Eating a Stone: Surviving the Past in Bosnia*. Translated by Antonia Lloyd-Jones. London: Portobello Books, 2009.

Tutu, Desmond. *No Future Without Forgiveness*. New York: Doubleday, 1999.

Twizere, Catherine. "Thinking About History: Adopting Critical Thinking Methods in Post-Conflict History Classrooms." Research paper, Institute on Globalization and the Human Condition, McMaster University, Hamilton, Ontario, 2010.

Unicef. "Adult Wars, Child Soldiers: Voices of Children Involved in Armed Conflict in the East Asia and Pacific Region," October 2002. http://www.worldcat.org/title/adult-wars-child-soldiers-voices-of-children-involved-in-armed-conflict-in-the-east-asia-and-pacific-region/oclc/51486381?pgload=backtoitem (accessed July 8, 2011).

———. "Cape Town Principles and Best Practices." Adopted at the Symposium on the Prevention of the Recruitment of Children into the Armed Forces and on Demobilization and Social Reintegration of Child Soldiers in Africa, Cape Town, April 27–30, 1997. http://www.unicef.org/emerg/index_childsoldiers.html (accessed May 21, 2010).

———. "Fact Sheet: Child Soldiers." http://www.unicef.org/emerg/index_childsoldiers.html (accessed May 21, 2010).

United Nations. "Human Rights in Palestine and Other Occupied Arab Territories: Report of the United Nations Fact Finding Mission on the Gaza Conflict." September 12, 2009. http://www2.ohchr.org/english/bodies/hrcouncil/specialsession/9/factfinding-mission.htm (accessed February 14, 2011).

———. Office for the Coordination of Humanitarian Affairs. "Afghanistan: Eight Thousand Children Under Arms Look for a Future." http://www.irinnews.org/InDepthMain.aspx?InDepthId=24&ReportId=66989&Country=Yes (accessed February 11, 2011).

———. Office of the Special Representative of the Secretary-General for Children and Armed Conflict. "The Machel Original Study, 1996: The Impact of Armed Conflict on Children." http://www.un.org/children/conflict/english/themachelstudy.html (accessed March 19, 2010).

Vetlesen, Arne Johan. *Evil and Human Agency: Understanding Collective Evildoing*. Cambridge: Cambridge University Press, 2005.

Visker, Rudi. "Is Ethics Fundamental? Questioning Levinas on Irresponsibility." *Continental Philosophy Review* 36, no. 3 (2003): 263–302.

Vukosavljević, Nenad. "One Injustice Cannot Be Made by Causing a New One." In *Twenty Pieces of Encouragement for Awakening and Change: Peacebuilding in the Region of the Former Yugoslavia*, ed. Helena Rill, Tamara Smidling, and Ana Bitoljanu. Belgrade-Sarajevo: Centre for Nonviolent Action, 2007.

Vuola, Elina. "Thinking Otherwise: Dussel, Liberation Theology, and Feminism." In *Thinking from the Underside of History: Enrique Dussel's Philosophy of Liberation*, ed. Linda Martín Alcoff and Eduardo Mendieta, 149–80. New York: Rowman & Littlefield, 2000.

Walker, Margaret Urban. *Moral Repair: Reconstructing Moral Relations After Wrongdoing*. Cambridge: Cambridge University Press, 2006.

Wallensteen, Peter, and Margareta Sollenberg. "Armed Conflict, 1989–99." *Journal of Peace Research* 37, no. 5 (2000): 635–46.

Wessells, Michael. *Child Soldiers: From Violence to Protection*. Cambridge: Harvard University Press, 2006.

Wimmer, Andreas. "Introduction: Facing Ethnic Conflicts." In *Facing Ethnic Conflict: Toward a New Realism*, ed. Andreas Wimmer, Richard J. Goldstone, and Donald L. Horowitz, 1–20. Toronto: Rowman & Littlefield, 2004.

Winslow, Philip C. *Victory for Us Is to See You Suffer: In the West Bank with the Palestinians and the Israelis*. Boston: Beacon Press, 2007.

Zertal, Idith. *Israel's Holocaust and the Politics of Nationhood*. Translated by Chaya Galai. New York: Cambridge University Press, 2005.

Zerubavel, Yael. *Recovered Roots: Collective Memory and the Making of Israeli National Tradition*. Chicago: University of Chicago Press, 1995.

———. "A Soft Focus on War: How Hollywood Hides the Horrors of War." *In These Times*, April 21, 2010. http://www.inthesetimes.com/article/5864/a_soft_focus_on_war/ (accessed June 2009).

Žižek, Slavoj. *Violence*. London: Picador, 2008.

INDEX